Footprint Handbook

Antigua, Montserrat, St K[illegible]

LIZZIE W[illegible]

This is
Antigua,
Montserrat,
St Kitts & Nevis

Antigua, Barbuda, Montserrat, St Kitts and Nevis are part of the Leeward Islands, a geographical grouping of small, mostly volcanic islands in the northeastern Caribbean. They share a chequered history of territorial struggles between European powers before becoming British colonies, with sugar plantations and slavery. Their geopolitical importance in the 18th and 19th centuries is still evident in the beautifully preserved fortifications, particularly at English Harbour and Nelson's Dockyard in Antigua and Brimstone Hill Fortress on St Kitts. Sailing vessels still fill the harbours of Antigua, but for more peaceful purposes. Regattas attract hundreds of yachts and their crews, who come ashore to party just like the sailors of old.

However, dependence on sugar is long gone and tourism is now king; most visitors, however, arrive by air in search of sun, sea and sand. Antigua and St Kitts both receive long-haul flights, with smaller planes fanning out from these hubs to connect with the other islands. This makes it easy to island hop and plan a two- or three-centre holiday. From Antigua it is easy to visit Barbuda and Montserrat, while St Kitts is paired with Nevis.

The coastline of Antigua curves into coves and graceful harbours with 365 soft white-sand beaches, among the most attractive in the West Indies. Its sister island, Barbuda, is blessed with a swathe of white sand stretching for 17 miles down its empty west coast – except where it is pink from crushed shells. St Kitts has powder-soft sandy beaches all round its hilly southeastern peninsula, while the west coast of Nevis is similarly endowed. Montserrat is different, however, boasting black sand on all but one of its beaches and for good reason: it is volcanic and the volcano is active. Yet, while beaches are not its main selling point, Montserrat does attract visitors to its waters, which are teeming with fish, coral and sponges; and on land, hikers and birdwatchers are rewarded by the island's bountiful flora and fauna in the hilly tropical forests.

Lizzie Williams

Best of Antigua, Montserrat, St Kitts & Nevis

top things to do and see

❶ Dickenson Bay, Antigua

Enjoy the holiday atmosphere on what is considered the premier beach of the island's 365 stretches of sand. There's something for every type of beachgoer: white sands, warm turquoise waters, resorts, beach bars, glass-bottomed boat tours and watersports. Page 33.

❷ Falmouth Harbour, Antigua

Admire the many superyachts and sailing schooners from Pigeon Beach or the Antigua Yacht Club Marina in this pretty horseshoe-shaped natural harbour; its bars and restaurants are always buzzing, especially during events like the Antigua Sailing Week Regatta. Page 39.

3

1

❸ Nelson's Dockyard National Park, Antigua

Explore this evocative historical district developed as a base for the British Navy and Horatio Nelson in the great age of sail; now completely restored, it is the only Georgian dockyard in the world and features a museum, hotels, restaurants and shops in the original buildings. Page 40.

❹ Shirley Heights, Antigua

Party at the top of this colonial observation post. The views extend out over English and Falmouth harbours and far across the Caribbean to Montserrat, and on Sunday there's a hugely popular barbecue with steelpan and reggae music that brings revellers from across the island. Page 43.

6

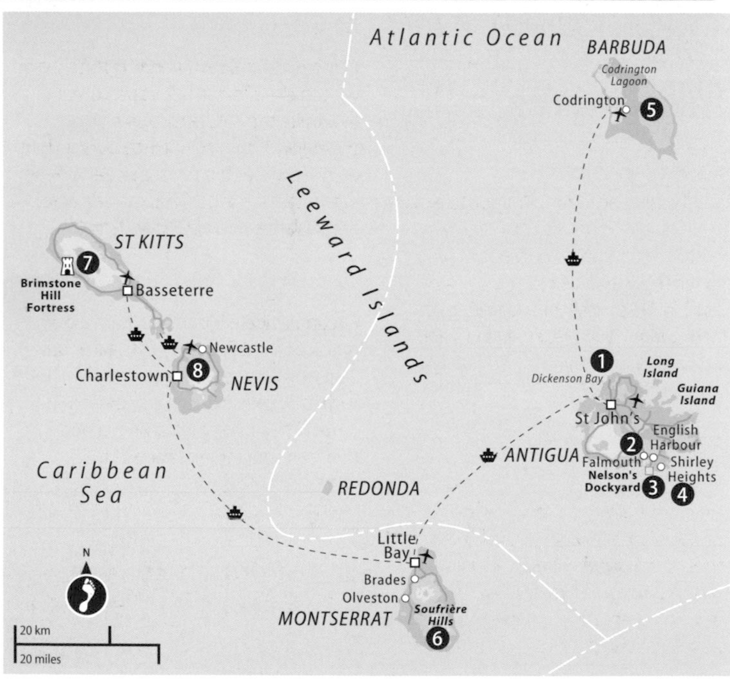
Atlantic Ocean
BARBUDA
Codrington Lagoon
Codrington
5
Leeward Islands
ST KITTS
7
Brimstone Hill Fortress
Basseterre
Newcastle
Charlestown
8
NEVIS
1
Long Island
Dickenson Bay
Guiana Island
St John's
English Harbour
2
ANTIGUA
Falmouth
Shirley Heights
Nelson's Dockyard
3
4
Caribbean Sea
REDONDA
Little Bay
Brades
Olveston
MONTSERRAT
Soufrière Hills
6
N
20 km
20 miles

❺ Barbuda

Take the ferry over from Antiqua to explore the white and pink sand, shell-strewn beaches, mangroves and lagoons of this relatively undeveloped little coral island. There's excellent snorkelling on the beautiful, well-preserved reefs and birdwatchers will enjoy the Frigate Bird Sanctuary. Page 47.

❻ Soufrière Hills Volcano, Montserrat

Witness the aftermath of this volcano's reawakening in 1995, when it left two-thirds of the island buried under volcanic ash and uninhabitable. The Montserrat Volcano Observatory's viewing balcony has spectacular views of the surrounding exclusion zone which is otherwise off-limits. Page 80.

❼ Brimstone Hill Fortress, St Kitts

Climb up to this commanding fortification with thick walls of black volcanic stone to admire the outstanding, well-preserved 17th- and 18th-century military architecture; at the top are endless views of the Caribbean and you can see up to six other islands on a clear day. Page 98.

❽ Nevis

Circumnavigate Mount Nevis on a day tour round the island by car, taxi or bus, stopping at pretty villages, old plantations with their great houses and sugar mill ruins, historic churches and perhaps the odd rum shop or two. Page 111.

View over the southeast peninsula of St Kitts across to Nevis

Route planner

putting it all together

This region of the Leeward Islands strings out prettily where the northeastern Caribbean Sea meets the western Atlantic Ocean. How you explore depends on where you arrive and whether you want a one-island holiday or a broader experience of this group of islands that lie in three dependencies: Antigua and its smaller sister island of Barbuda, the single island British Overseas Territory of Montserrat, and the two-island country of St Kitts and Nevis. Antigua is the easiest to reach for British holidaymakers seeking resorts, and it is one of the major yachting centres in the Caribbean. St Kitts is a bit more accessible from the US and is a major cruise ship destination on itineraries out of Miami. From both, it's possible to extend visits to the other islands on short flights or ferries, while some of the resorts on the smaller islands are stand-alone destinations.

To a certain degree budget plays a part on which ones of these enchanting islands you visit. Accommodation varies; from Antigua with its many large all-inclusive beach resorts and mid-range self-catering options, to Barbuda and Nevis, each with less than a dozen places to stay and mostly in the upper-bracket, with an appeal of exclusivity.

One to two weeks

lazy days, deserted beaches and historic harbours

Assuming you have arrived at Antigua's VC Bird International Airport, many holidaymakers are whisked to one of the all-inclusive resorts that ring the island. But Antigua is a good destination for independent travellers too, thanks to its good choice of accommodation, equally suitable for a one-night stay or a week. Even if you stay in a resort, the island is small enough to explore on excursions, and its famous 365 beaches offer a different view, snorkelling and picnicking, or partying with the locals at the characterful beach bars.

Few journeys take very long and include Antigua's little capital, St John's, with shopping and restaurants at the adjoining Redcliffe and Heritage Quays where the cruise ships dock. Easily the highlight of the island is English Harbour and its historic Nelson's Dockyard, which can be visited for the day, or there are plenty of places to stay around adjoining Falmouth Harbour, with its yacht marinas and good restaurants and nightlife.

With more time, Barbuda is reached from Antigua by a short flight or an enjoyable combined ferry and day tour, or you can mix it up a little and stay for a couple of nights to enjoy the solitude on what are some of the best beaches in this region.

Another trip only accessible from Antigua is Montserrat, dominated by its previously destructive Soufrière Hills volcano, and two-thirds of the island is still an exclusion zone. But the lava flows have created extraordinary landscapes, which are now the island's main attraction, and you can visit for the day or stay overnight at the friendly little guesthouses.

Two weeks or more

historic sugar plantations, commanding forts and quiet coves

With two weeks or more you'll have time to explore St Kitts and Nevis, a twin-island nation, both places dominated by volcanic peaks and just a couple of miles apart at their shortest crossing. Although St Kitts is a major destination for cruise ships, it has relatively few places to stay, but there are some charming and stately plantation inns and cheaper and livelier beach options. Nevis appeals to upmarket visitors for its fine accommodation, and peaceful and low-key atmosphere on an island that only has a 20-mile road ringing its perimeter. While the beaches may not be as pretty as Antigua, they feature black-grey sand due to the islands' volcanic character. Both St Kitts and Nevis are far less commercialized with a more local flavour, and still have some attractive bays for sunbathing and watersports. The edge that they have over flat and rather featureless Antigua is the scenery, and Mount Liamuiga on St Kitts and Nevis Peak on Nevis create mountainous and lush rainforest-covered interiors with hiking trails and outstanding views.

You can also explore the historic association of the old sugar industry, now reflected in crumbling sugar windmills and Great Houses. The historic forts too are interesting to visit; Brimstone Hill on St Kitts in particular has a fascinating history and commanding outlook across the Caribbean. The small and charming capitals of Basseterre on St Kitts and Charlestown on Nevis also contribute to learning about the great battles between the French and British in 17th and 18th centuries who both wanted control of these valuable territories. Both islands can be explored on highly entertaining day tours that encircle each perimeter, while time on the beaches with perhaps a view across to the other island make for a varied visit, or it's easy to flit across between the two by boat.

When to go

... and when not to

Climate

The climate in the Leeward Islands, like everywhere in the Caribbean, is tropical. The driest and least humid time of year is December-April, coinciding with the winter peak in tourism as visitors escape to the sun from cooler climates in North America and Europe. During this time temperatures are tempered by cooling trade winds and the climate is very pleasant without being unbearably hot. If it does rain, it is usually short bursts of tropical showers that are over in 10 minutes and which keep things green. At other times of the year the temperature rises only slightly, but greater humidity can make it feel hotter if you are away from the coast.

There are variations in rainfall depending on elevation. The volcanic, mountainous and forested islands attract more rain than the low-lying coral islands, so you can expect more frequent showers in mountainous Montserrat than you would on flat Barbuda. The very highest peaks – the Soufrière Hills on Montserrat, Mount Liamuiga on St Kitts, and Nevis Peak on Nevis – are often shrouded in cloud, but the coastlines are usually clear and sunny. The main rainy season runs from June to November, the peak of which is September and October, hurricane season. Although they do occur in the Leeward Islands in some years, you'd be very unlucky to experience an actual hurricane. (Antigua hasn't had one since 1999, for example.) During these months tropical storms are more likely than hurricanes and these can cause flooding and mudslides. This is low season, and the time of year that many hotels and resorts close.

Weather Antigua and Barbuda

January	February	March	April	May	June
27°C	27°C	27°C	28°C	28°C	29°C
23°C	22°C	23°C	23°C	25°C	26°C
30mm	20mm	30mm	30mm	60mm	70mm

July	August	September	October	November	December
30°C	30°C	30°C	29°C	28°C	27°C
26°C	26°C	26°C	25°C	24°C	23°C
80mm	80mm	90mm	110mm	90mm	50mm

Festivals

See also Festivals in Listings for individual islands and Public holidays, page 139.

Antigua

January-February **Antigua Yacht Club Round-the-Island**, usually the second Saturday in January, Falmouth Harbour, www.antiguayachtclub.com. The Antigua Yacht Club kicks off the sailing season with a round-the-island race. The **Superyacht Challenge Antigua**, late January or early February, English Harbour, www.superyachtchallengeantigua.com. Races of 12-30 miles for yachts in excess of 80 ft long. From January to the end of Sailing Week in May, Falmouth and English Harbours are so full of yachts, it's sometimes impossible to see the opposite shores of the bays.

April **Antigua Classic Yacht Regatta**, Falmouth Harbour, www.antiguaclassics.com. Usually held the second week of April, just before Sailing Week with four days of racing for traditional craft such as yawls, ketches, schooners and square-masted vessels, and the finale is a 20-mile race down the windward side of the island. Plus parades of classic boats, which look magnificent from shore, and there's plenty of evening action too.

April-May **Antigua Sailing Week**, last week of April/early May, Nelson's Dockyard, www.sailingweek.com. Following on from the Antigua Classic Yacht Regatta (see below), this event started in 1968 and now attracts more than 200 entries from over 30 countries and is one of the most prestigious sailing events in the Caribbean for the fastest and most powerful yachts. Formal racing over five days, followed by other events such as the Guadeloupe to Antigua race and Round-the-Island race, and plenty of partying and live music afterwards (there's even a 'Party Schedule' and bar/restaurant/hotel staff are left exhausted when it's all over). For spectators, the races are followed by many non-competing boats that tag along to see the action, and there are lookout points around the island; Fort Charlotte and Shirley Heights being prime spots.

July-August **Carnival**, last week in July and first week in August, takes place in the streets of St John's, and in the Antigua Recreation Ground, www.antiguacarnival.com. Held over the anniversary of emancipation from slavery, 10 days of music, dance and revelry, with street parades, jump-ups and formal evening shows such as calypso, steelpan, and Carnival Queen pageants. A festival village is set up where you can buy local food and plenty of rum. Carnival culminates in J'ouvert (meaning day break) on the first Monday in August; a massive street party when dancing goes on all night.

Late October-November **Antigua and Barbuda Independence Festival**, **Independence Day** (a public holiday) on 1 November. Ceremonial parades in both St John's on Antigua and Codrington on Barbuda with marching bands and fetes, along with a series of other formal celebrations over about 10 days toward the end of October.

Barbuda

May Caribana, Whitsun weekend, the seventh Sun after Easter, Codrington, Barbuda. The Barbudian carnival is the main event of the year on the island, with a weekend of calypso singing and Carnival Queen competitions, beach parties and horse racing, culminating in an early morning street party, J'ouvert, followed by the main costumed street parade on the Sunday.

Montserrat

July Calabash Festival, in the middle of the month, www.montserratcalabashfestival.com. A week-long festival named after the gourd from the calabash tree, traditionally used to make musical instruments, bowls and decorative household items. There are hikes, boat tours, cricket, a food fair at Little Bay, lectures, gospel concert and other entertainment.
December Montserrat Annual Festival, two weeks over Christmas until New Year's Day, see Facebook. Organized by the Montserrat Arts Council, there are beauty and talent shows, concerts, calypso competitions, jump-ups and masquerades and of course festivities and parties on New Year's Eve, and a costume parade on New Year's Day.

St Kitts

December Carnival, held over Christmas and New Year, www.stkittsneviscarnival.com. Also known as Sugar Mas, leading up to Christmas there are soca and calypso performances and competitions, Carnival Queen and Talented Teen pageants and the main events are the Boxing Day J'Ouvert street party and New Year's Day costume parade in Basseterre.

Nevis

July-August Culturama, end of July and finishing on the first Tuesday in August, www.culturamanevis.com. Nevis stages its Carnival in the summer with costumed parades, street bashes, a beauty contest and a calypso competition. Most of the action is centred on Charlestown, including an early morning Emancipation J'Ouvert jump-up on 1 August and a Last Lap Parade the following day.

What to do

from deep-water diving to sailing in a schooner

Diving and snorkelling

The reefs and small uninhabited islets around the islands provide good diving and snorkelling for all skill levels, from lazy drifts over coral gardens to challenging exploration of wrecks. Antigua has some shallow underwater shelfs with little or no current, good for snorkelling off the beach, and Cades Reef is popular for diving and snorkelling day trips by boat with perhaps a beach barbecue. There's only one dive school on Montserrat, which offers challenging diving at some of the 30 virtually undisturbed sites that are home to schools of reef fish and pelagics. St Kitts offers deep-water diving to wrecks, reefs, walls and caves and it's possible to get in several different types of dive on one visit, while the shallow shelf between the two islands offers snorkelling off the southeast beaches. Nevis lacks a ringing off-shore reef, but there are numerous dive sites offshore which are schooling grounds for big fish.

Golf

A round of golf in a warm sunny climate with gorgeous views of the Caribbean is a perfect way to spend a day on holiday, and all the islands with the exception of Montserrat have golf courses (although it once had one before the volcano covered it in ash). Antigua has **Cedar Valley Golf Club** and **Jolly Harbour Golf Club**, both attractive 18-hole courses with good facilities and packages for weekly visitors. On St Kitts is the prestigious **Royal St Kitts Golf Club**, a championship 18-hole course, which uniquely has greens overlooking the Caribbean and Atlantic, and there's also a fun nine-hole course on the island. Nevis has the **Four Seasons Golf Club**, a beautifully maintained, 18-hole, championship course with driving range, putting green and other facilities that make the upmarket **Four Seasons Resort Nevis** popular as a golfing destination for a week or more.

Hiking

Antigua and Barbuda are fairly flat and don't have mountainous cores flanked by rainforests like Montserrat, St Kitts and Nevis. Nevertheless walking is a good way of exploring, around Falmouth and English Harbours are some moderate hikes up to viewpoints to see the yachts in the bays, while on Barbuda trails lead off in all directions to quiet coves and beaches. The accessible part of Montserrat is so small, you can walk just about anywhere and there are established trails to remoter beaches and into the Central Hills which are good for birdwatching. St Kitts has more challenging trails including up to Dos d'Ane Pond on Verchild's Peak and the crater rim of Mount Liamuiga (the highest peak in all the Leeward Islands). On Nevis its peak of the same name is a steep and tough climb, but rewarding for fit hikers, and with one road around the entire island, you can just head off and see where you get to.

Sailing

Sailing is synonymous with the Caribbean and the constant trade winds and warm sun is a draw for both experienced and novice sailors. Antigua in particular is popular with the yachting fraternity and Falmouth and English Harbours draw thousands of vessels each year to their smart marinas, especially during exciting events like Antigua Sailing Week at the end of April; one of the premier sailing events in the world (see When to go, above). Watching the racing can be fun too, as are the lively after-parties. For those on holiday, there are some wonderful opportunities to enjoy the waters of these islands from the deck of a boat, whether it's under the full sail of a traditional schooner, or on a smart luxury catamaran. On both Antigua and St Kitts the options range from a sunset cruise or snorkelling excursion, full or half-day cruises around the islands with perhaps a barbecue lunch on a beach, to chartering a yacht with crew and simply going where you like.

Watersports

There are numerous options of playing in the gorgeous warm waters around these islands, from wind- and kitesurfing, hobie cats sailing and stand-up paddle boarding to jet-skiing, water-skiing and tubing. All-inclusive places and top luxury resorts include watersports in their packages, but there are also plenty of places to rent equipment for an hour or two. On Antigua, you can organize water toys on the popular beaches like Dickenson Bay, purchase a day pass to a resort with good watersports centres, or you can even go play on the D Boat, once an oil tanker, and now a water park and party boat. On St Kitts, watersports are on offer at the beach in Cockleshell Bay, you can rent snorkelling gear from the beach bars and go on guided kayaking tours. For swimming, remember it's always better in the Caribbean; some of the rough Atlantic waters can be dangerous because of strong currents and waves.

Improve your travel photography

Taking pictures is a highlight for many travellers, yet too often the results turn out to be disappointing. Steve Davey, author of Footprint's *Travel Photography*, sets out his top rules for coming home with pictures you can be proud of.

Before you go

Don't waste precious travelling time and do your research before you leave. Find out what festivals or events might be happening or which day the weekly market takes place, and search online image sites such as Flickr to see whether places are best shot at the beginning or end of the day, and what vantage points you should consider.

Get up early

The quality of the light will be better in the few hours after sunrise and again before sunset – especially in the tropics when the sun will be harsh and unforgiving in the middle of the day. Sometimes seeing the sunrise is a part of the whole travel experience: sleep in and you will miss more than just photographs.

Stop and think

Don't just click away without any thought. Pause for a few seconds before raising the camera and ask yourself what you are trying to show with your photograph. Think about what things you need to include in the frame to convey this meaning. Be prepared to move around your subject to get the best angle. Knowing the point of your picture is the first step to making sure that the person looking at the picture will know it too.

Compose your picture

Avoid simply dumping your subject in the centre of the frame every time you take a picture. If you compose with it to one side, then your picture can look more balanced. This will also allow you to show a significant background and make the picture more meaningful. A good rule of thumb is to place your subject or any significant detail a third of the way into the frame; facing into the frame not out of it.

This rule also works for landscapes. Compose with the horizon two-thirds of the way up the frame if the foreground is the most interesting part of the picture; one-third of the way up if the sky is more striking.

Don't get hung up with this so-called Rule of Thirds, though. Exaggerate it by pushing your subject out to the edge of the frame if it makes a more interesting picture; or if the sky is dull in a landscape, try cropping with the horizon near the very top of the frame.

Fill the frame

If you are going to focus on a detail or even a person's face in a close-up portrait, then be bold and make sure that you fill the frame. This is often a case of physically getting in close. You can use a telephoto setting on a zoom lens but this can lead to pictures looking quite flat; moving in close is a lot more fun!

Interact with people

If you want to shoot evocative portraits then it is vital to approach people and seek permission in some way, even if it is just by smiling at someone. Spend a little time with them and they are likely to relax and look less stiff and formal. Action portraits where people are doing something, or environmental portraits, where they are set against a significant background, are a good way to achieve relaxed portraits. Interacting is a good way to find out more about people and their lives, creating memories as well as photographs.

Focus carefully

Your camera can focus quicker than you, but it doesn't know which part of the picture you want to be in focus. If your camera is using the centre focus sensor then move the camera so it is over the subject and half press the button, then, holding it down, recompose the picture. This will lock the focus. Take the now correctly focused picture when you are ready.

Another technique for accurate focusing is to move the active sensor over your subject. Some cameras with touch-sensitive screens allow you to do this by simply clicking on the subject.

Leave light in the sky

Most good night photography is actually taken at dusk when there is some light and colour left in the sky; any lit portions of the picture will balance with the sky and any ambient lighting. There is only a very small window when this will happen, so get into position early, be prepared and keep shooting and reviewing the results. You can take pictures after this time, but avoid shots of tall towers in an inky black sky; crop in close on lit areas to fill the frame.

Bring it home safely

Digital images are inherently ephemeral: they can be deleted or corrupted in a heartbeat. The good news though is they can be copied just as easily. Wherever you travel, you should have a backup strategy. Cloud backups are popular, but make sure that you will have access to fast enough Wi-Fi. If you use RAW format, then you will need some sort of physical back-up. If you don't travel with a laptop or tablet, then you can buy a backup drive that will copy directly from memory cards.

Recently updated and available in both digital and print formats, Footprint's Travel Photography by Steve Davey covers everything you need to know about travelling with a camera, including simple post-processing. More information is available at www.footprinttravelguides.com

Where to stay

from plush resorts to plantation inns

Places to stay on the islands include large and small hotels and resorts, guesthouses, B&Bs, self-catering apartments or villas. High season is mid-December to mid-April, when rates are at their most expensive. There are often discounts of around 30% in low season, and the best deals can be found in the hurricane season. In terms of weather, this is roughly September to October, but for hotel rates, this 'down season' usually lasts through November until high season begins again in December. Rates can drop as low as 50% during these months, but this is also the worst time for rainy and windy weather and many hotels close altogether.

Good resources for hotels are on the websites of the tourist authorities; see Tourist information in listings of individual islands for details. Almost all places have websites to book direct, which gives the opportunity to ask questions and get further information from the proprietors/reservations teams, and the islands are well-represented on accommodation websites like **Expedia** ⓘ *www.expedia.com*, and **Booking.com** ⓘ *www.booking.com*.

Hotel rooms very from US$75 for a double/twin in the cheapest guesthouse to US$200-300 in a mid-range resort, to over US$800 per person per night in the top-end luxury retreats. Unless you're staying in all-inclusive resort, or have opted for a full meal package at a hotel, very few places include breakfast in room rates. A cost of breakfast (when available) can be the equivalent of US$5

Price codes

Where to stay

$$$$ over US$300

$$$ US$150-300

$$ US$75-150

$ under US$75

Price codes refer to a standard double/twin room in high season.

Restaurants

$$$ over US$30

$$ US$15-30

$ under US$15

Price codes refer to the cost of a two-course meal, excluding drinks or service charge.

for a simply local breakfast like saltfish and bake to US$20-30 for a full buffet. The best option for budget travellers – especially a group or family – is to book an apartment. Most have at least two double beds and/or pull out sofa beds, and costs can be brought down further by cooking. Eating in local cafeterias, drinking in rum shops and travelling on buses can also save money.

Tip...
On all the islands, a government hotel tax and service charge is applicable on accommodation, usually added to your bill at the time of a reservation or at the end of a stay. Antigua and Barbuda (22%); Montserrat (17-20%); St Kitts and Nevis (23%).

Quality of accommodation varies considerably across the budget range and some have been criticized for lack of maintenance and being in need of renovation. The tourist industry on some of these islands dates back to the 1960s, and so do some of the properties and you may find some of the resort-style places stuck in a time warp in terms of furnishings and decor. But there are also good modern and stylish properties, and the Caribbean is well-known as a retreat for the wealthy with some of the most luxurious resorts in the world. Cleanliness and standard of comfort is rarely an issue, and almost all rooms have air conditioning, cable TV and Wi-Fi (even at the budget end).

Antigua is particularly well served with good hotels and resorts. The greatest concentration of resort development is in the area to the west and north of St John's, in a clockwise direction to the airport, taking advantage of some of the best beaches. There are few options in St John's itself and little reason to stay there. A second cluster of hotels is around English Harbour and Falmouth Harbour in the southeast of the island. These are very pleasant with lovely views of the harbours and yachts at anchor but are more likely to be closed outside of the yachting season, roughly December to May. Antigua has more than a dozen all-inclusive resorts, most of which are not listed in this guide individually as they are similar in style and in terms of what they offer. Rates include accommodation, meals, drinks and some watersports (see box, page 56, for more information). In high season most are booked for a minimum of a week, often on a package with flights, but at quiet times they may accept bookings for a night or two and from walk-ins, and some also offer day passes to use the facilities. There are lots of self-catering apartments, cottages or family villas, but a common complaint is that sufficient provisions are not available locally and you have to go into St John's for shopping, requiring a taxi ride or car hire.

On Barbuda there are only three expensive and exclusive luxury resorts and just a few other options of either mid-range beach cottages or cheap guesthouses. However, it can be visited for the day from Antigua by ferry.

Montserrat also has only one hotel, and most of the limited accommodation is in guesthouses or with people who rent out rooms and apartments in their houses, or you can rent a villa through agencies.

St Kitts receives thousands of visitors, but most are day-trippers from cruise ships, so accommodation options are surprisingly few. But there are two big-name resorts – the **St Kitts Marriott Resort** and the **Park Hyatt St Kitts** – plus a fine plantation inn and a clutch of mid-range beach resorts, most with self-catering facilities.

Nevis again has few places to stay, but there's a good choice in the upmarket bracket with the 196-room **Four Seasons Resort Nevis**, and again a couple of stylish and tasteful hotels based around old English Great Houses. Mid-range places with a bit of character are either on the beach or on old sugar plantations.

Food & drink

from pepper-pot to black pineapples

Food

As you might expect of islands, there is a wide variety of seafood on offer, which is fresh and tasty and served in a multitude of ways. Locally caught fish varies according to the season, but you can find flying fish, tuna, bonito, mahi mahi, snapper and kingfish on the menu as well as lambi (conch), lobster, squid and octopus. Smoked herring and salt cod are locally called saltfish and is often eaten with a fried bake (a pan-fried bread), especially for breakfast. Because the islands are small, they don't support large herds of cattle, so beef is often imported from the USA, and there is no dairy industry, so cheese, yoghurt and milk are also usually imported. Goat, pork, chicken and some lamb are produced locally.

There is a riot of tropical fruit and vegetables and a visit to a local market will give you the opportunity to see unusual and often unidentifiable items. Don't miss the rich flavours of the soursop (chirimoya, guanábana), the guava, tamarind or the sapodilla (zapote). Breakfast buffets are usually groaning under the weight of pineapples, melons, oranges, grapefruits and mangoes, of which there are dozens of varieties, as well as papaya/pawpaw, carambola (star fruit) and sugar apple (custard apple or sweetsop). Caribbean oranges are often green when ripe, as there is no cold season to bring out the orange colour, and are meant for juicing not peeling. Portugals are like tangerines and easy to peel. Avocados are nearly always sold unripe, so wait several days before attempting to eat them. On Antigua, the native pineapple is called the Antigua black and is very sweet.

The breadfruit, a common staple, rich in carbohydrates and vitamins, is a large, round starchy fruit, usually eaten fried or boiled and it grows on huge trees with enormous leaves. Christophene is another local vegetable which can be prepared in many ways, but is delicious baked in a cheese sauce. Dasheen is a root vegetable with green leaves, rather like spinach, which are used to make the tasty and nutritious callaloo soup. Plantains are eaten boiled or fried as a savoury vegetable, while green bananas, known as figs, can be cooked before they are ripe enough to eat raw as a fruit.

The term 'provisions' on a menu refers to root or starchy vegetables such as dasheen, yams, sweet potatoes, tannia and pumpkins. The style of cooking is known as Creole and is a mixture of all the cultural influences of the islands' immigrants over the centuries, from starchy vegetables to sustain African slaves to gourmet sauces and garnishes dating from the days when the French governed the islands. The movement of people along the chain of Caribbean islands means that you can also find rotis (pancake-like parcel of curried chicken and veg) from Trinidad and spicy jerk meats from Jamaica.

Local dishes include pepper-pot (meat stew cooked on the bone with cassava and foungee, a kind of cornmeal dumpling), goat water (spicy goat stew), oildown (salt meat, breadfruit, dasheen and dumplings, cooked slowly in coconut milk), conch stew and the local staple, chicken and rice. Johnny cake is rather like a doughnut, usually savoury but can be made with grated coconut. Ducana is made from grated sweet potato and pumpkin, sugar and spices and boiled in a banana leaf.

Drink

For non-alcoholic drinks, there is a range of refreshing fruit juices, including orange, mango, pineapple, grapefruit, lime, guava and passionfruit. Sorrel is made from sepals of a plant from the hibiscus family, and tamarind is a bitter sweet drink made from the pods of the tamarind tree. **Ting**, the local grapefruit soft drink, is highly recommended with or without a tot of alcohol in it. Coconut water – the clear liquid inside young green coconuts – is often served fresh by using a machete to cut open the nut. Look for barrows and stalls piled high with coconuts and a knife-wielding vendor in markets, on the side of village streets and in car parks at the beaches.

Rum is excellent, and produced in distilleries in both Antigua and St Kitts. Rum punches and cocktails are popular at all the bars and range from mild fruity drinks to potent kicks; most local people have a strong tolerance for rum, and the uninitiated should take it easy. Beers include **Wadadli** lager, produced by the **Antigua Brewery**, and **Carib** and **Stag** lagers, brewed at the **Carib Brewery** on St Kitts, which also produces **Guinness** under licence. Wine (imported from Argentina, California and Europe) is generally not cheap but widely available in restaurants, supermarkets and hotel bars, and the boxed variety can often be seen on the shelf of a rum shop too.

ON THE ROAD

Limin'

A 'lime' is not just something to garnish a rum and Coke – it is also the expression for any (impromptu or pre-arranged) 'hanging out' session. In fact for hanging out to be considered 'liming', the activity cannot have a larger purpose than doing nothing while sharing food, drink, conversation and laughter with others – be it a family group enjoying a liming picnic on a beach at the weekend, or a group of friends sharing the after-work lime on a step outside a rum shop. Liming is an important part of the Caribbean culture, and everybody goes out of their way to make time for it. No visit to the islands would be complete without a 'lil lime'.

Eating out

For eating out, you can choose from gourmet eateries and coffee shops to local cafés and street stalls. If you are economizing, find a local place and choose the daily special, which will also give you a chance to try typical Caribbean food. Fast food is also available from international chains like KFC, but local versions of chicken and chips or burgers can be better.

There is a wide range of places to eat on Antigua offering most international cuisines such as Italian and Asian, and even if you're staying at an all-inclusive resort where meals are included, it's worth venturing out to try some of the better restaurants. Beach bars too are usually good places for food, especially seafood and barbecue grills.

On Barbuda, eating is limited to the resorts and a couple of beach bars, where you may have to talk to the owner or phone ahead if you want an evening meal. Several places on Montserrat do takeaway meals and there are lots of 'snackettes' where you can pick up a decent local lunch on the side of the road. The couple of upmarket restaurants on the island are very good, but reservations are required.

On St Kitts, Basseterre has a good choice of local food in small canteens, food stalls that set up along the waterfront street and the vendors market at the bus and ferry terminal. There are some good restaurants in North Frigate Bay, while along what is known as 'The Strip' in South Frigate Bay, beach bars offer snacks, light meals, and plenty of drinks. On the southeast peninsula, beach bars are also great places for food in lovely locations, and some, catering for cruise ship visitors, have comprehensive menus ranging from lobster to pizza.

On Nevis there are very few eating places in Charlestown, and the best upmarket restaurants on the island are in the hotels, where it is usually

Tip...

On all the islands, VAT is usually included in menu prices but a service charge of 10% is added to the bill; most menus stipulate what is and what is not included.

necessary to reserve a table. They offer exceptional cuisine as well as barbecues and entertainment. Some of the rum shops serve a daily meal and Pinney's Beach has beach bars too.

Opening hours listed for restaurants are liable to change at short notice, and many places close on Sundays and public holidays and sometimes another day of the week in low season. On Antigua, in the depths of low season, like hotels, they can close altogether. In the rural areas, smaller local places, kiosks and beach bars are often open daily, but more like when the vendor feels like it, especially where only one person does all the cooking – 'any day, any time'.

Restaurant prices vary and a higher cost for a meal does not always indicate good food. You could have a very expensive and awful meal just as easily as a cheap but very tasty one – and there's no way of telling what it's going to be. Street food snacks start at less than US$4, and portions of local stew, fried chicken, a simple burger or fish and fries will be roughly US$10-15. Beyond that menu prices steadily get higher to US$60 for a two- to three-course dinner with cocktails or rum in a smart restaurant, and even US$100 per head if you opt for lobster and fine wines.

Antigua
& Barbuda

Antigua

Antigua, covering about 108 square miles, is the largest of the Leeward Islands and one of the most popular. Its dependencies are Barbuda and uninhabited Redonda. There is nothing spectacular about its landscape, although the rolling hills and flowering trees are pretty. The coastline, however, curving into coves and graceful harbours with white-sand beaches fringed with palm trees, is among the most attractive in the West Indies.

English Harbour is particularly picturesque, with yachts filling a historic bay that has been a popular staging post for centuries. Nelson's Dockyard and ruined forts are overlooked by the old battery on Shirley Heights, now better known for the fun Sunday party with reggae and steelpan bands.

Direct, non-stop flights from Europe and North America together with the great beaches, watersports and safe swimming make Antigua ideal for introducing children to the Caribbean. Numerous holiday resorts cater for the all-inclusive family or honeymoon market, but Antigua also has a great choice of smaller, independent places to stay. It is also popular with the yachting crowd, with smart marinas, annual sailing events and good nightlife.

Some 30 miles north of Antigua, Barbuda is a tiny, remote, virtually flat coral island dotted with mangrove-lined lagoons and with some spectacular swathes of near-deserted beaches. Its few resorts are in the luxury bracket, though you can visit for the day on the ferry from Antigua.

Essential Antigua

Finding your feet

The new VC Bird International Airport is on the northeast coast of the island, about 4½ miles northeast of St John's. There's no public transport from the airport, but plenty of taxis at rates set by the government and taxi associations. Fares are US$11 to St John's, US$15 to Dickenson Bay, US$24 to Jolly Harbour, and US$30 to Falmouth Harbour and English Harbour.

Both cruise ships and the ferries from Barbuda and Montserrat arrive in St John's at docks that lead into the pedestrianized areas around Redcliffe Quay and Heritage Quay. There are four ports of entry for yachts in Antigua: Heritage Quay, St John's Deep Water Harbour, English Harbour and Jolly Harbour, each with customs and immigration facilities. See Transport, page 69.

Best restaurants

Cecilia's High Point Café, page 59
Jacqui O's Beach House, page 59
Le Bistro, page 59
Sheer Rocks, page 59
Cloggy's Café, page 60

Best beaches

Dickenson Bay, page 33
Jolly Beach, page 36
Darkwood Beach, page 37
Pigeon Beach, page 39
Half Moon Bay, page 46

Getting around

Buses (mostly minivans) go from both the West Bus Station and East Bus Station in St John's, but while there are services Monday-Saturday to the eastern and southern parts of the island, there are very few north of St John's and none to the airport. Frequency is variable, and drivers often abandon public routes in favour of more lucrative private hire. Renting a car is probably the best way to see the island's sights, and there are car hire companies in St John's, Jolly Harbour and Falmouth Harbour who will arrange delivery and drop off from hotels. Other options are renting a bike or scooter, or hiring a taxi for an island tour.

St John's

shopping on historic quays and the largest cruise ships afloat

Built around Antigua's largest natural harbour, St John's was formerly guarded by Fort Barrington and Fort James either side of the entrance to the bay. It has been the capital since colonization by the British in 1632, although few historical sights remain and the town is the busy, and somewhat tatty, commercial centre for the island. The harbour is a constant hive of activity with container ships, inter-island ferries and up to four cruise ships at a time. In season (October-April) several arrive each week from Miami and occupy every view of St John's.

Sights

Some of the historic buildings in St John's include the hilltop **St John's Anglican Cathedral** ⓘ *between Newgate and Long Sts, T268-461 0082, currently undergoing a major*

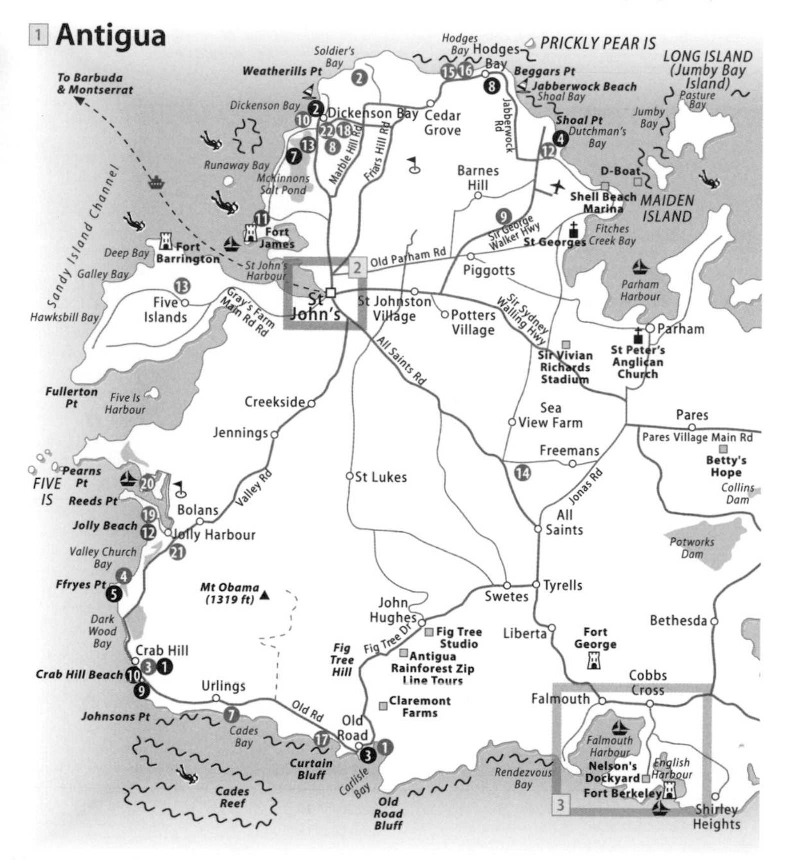

restoration; if it's open donations are requested, also known as the rather long-winded St John the Divine, the Cathedral Church of the Diocese of North Eastern Caribbean and Aruba. The cathedral is in its third incarnation, as earthquakes in 1683 and in 1745 destroyed the previous wooden structures, It was then built again in 1843 of stone. Its twin towers can be seen from all over St John's and by cruise ship passengers coming into port. It has a wonderfully cool interior lined with pitch pine timber.

The **Antigua Recreation Ground** a couple of blocks east of the cathedral contains what was the main cricket pitch, used for Test matches, but this was replaced by a new ground for the 2007 Cricket World Cup, the **Sir Vivian Richards Stadium** off Sir Sydney Walling Highway.

There are some run-down parts of the town but the cruise ship docks area has been developed for tourism, where boutiques, duty-free shops and restaurants compete for custom. Most activity takes place around the two pedestrianized quay developments. **Redcliff Quay** ⓘ *www.historicredcliffequay.com,* is a picturesque area that is one of the oldest parts of the town, dating back to the 17th and 18th centuries when it was a busy waterfront dock and a trading centre for slaves, rum and sugar. Today it features a seaside

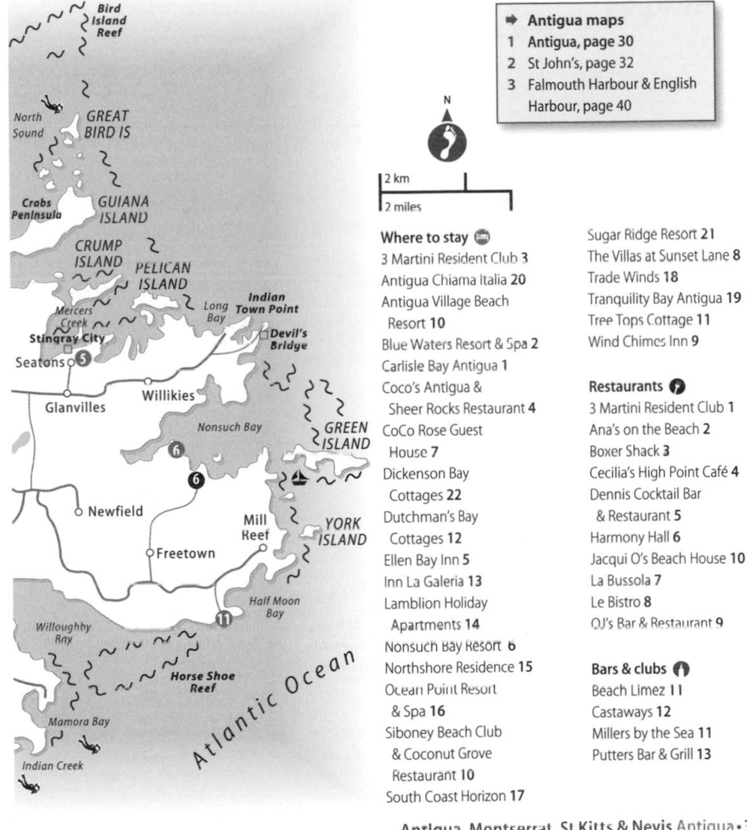

promenade, and the restored historical buildings are home to boutiques, souvenir shops, bars and cafés; **Heritage Quay** ⓘ *www.heritagequayantigua.com,* is a modern duty-free shopping complex with a casino strategically placed to catch cruise ship visitors. When a cruise ship is in dock many passengers come ashore and it becomes very crowded, but otherwise it's fairly quiet and you may even be able to negotiate discounts in the shops when ships are not in, which the proprietors call 'dry days'. The Vendor's Mall between the two quays sells souvenirs and women here offer (overpriced) hair-braiding.

The **Museum of Antigua and Barbuda** ⓘ *Long St, T268-462 4930, www.antiguamuseums.net, Mon-Fri 0830-1630, Sat 1000-1400, free (donations requested)*, at the former courthouse is worth a visit, both to see the exhibitions of anthropology of Antigua, pre-Columbian and colonial archaeology, and for the courthouse building itself, believed to be the oldest building in town, dating from 1750. Cricket fans will be pleased to see Viv Richards' cricket bat, with which he scored the fastest century, among the more recent exhibits. There's an interesting gift shop with locally made crafts and books on Antiguan history and local cookbooks.

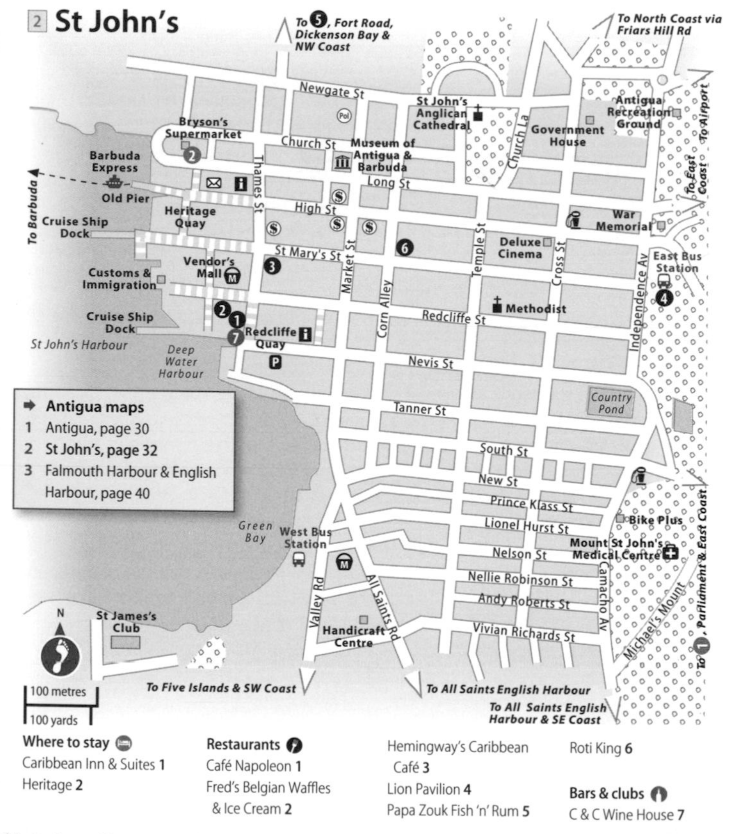

Antigua maps
1 Antigua, page 30
2 St John's, page 32
3 Falmouth Harbour & English Harbour, page 40

Where to stay
Caribbean Inn & Suites **1**
Heritage **2**

Restaurants
Café Napoleon **1**
Fred's Belgian Waffles & Ice Cream **2**
Hemingway's Caribbean Café **3**
Lion Pavilion **4**
Papa Zouk Fish 'n' Rum **5**
Roti King **6**

Bars & clubs
C & C Wine House **7**

The northwest and north

holiday fun on bone-white sands and in brilliantly blue seas

Although there are resorts ringing the entire island, the northwest is one of the more popular areas for a sun, sea and sand holiday with long stretches of beach, warm and shallow water, and plenty of places to stay, restaurants, bars and nightlife, as well as watersports and easy access to the Cedar Valley Golf Course. Windsurfing and kitesurfing are good off the windier north coast, while there is snorkelling and diving at the reefs and small uninhabited islets.

North of St John's

At the north side of the entrance to St John's Harbour are the ruins of **Fort James**, from where you can get a good view of St John's. There was originally a fort on this site dating from 1675, but most now dates from 1749. In the second half of the 18th century there were 36 guns and barracks for 75 soldiers. In the 19th century a gun was fired at sunrise, sunset and to salute visiting warships. The ruins are sorely neglected and in dire need of attention and preservation, and there is not much of historical interest to see, except the 1805 cannon, but the views are lovely. To get there, head north out of St John's, turn west to the sea on Fort Road, then follow the road parallel to the shore to the end.

There is a lovely beach here and the area is popular with Antiguans at weekends when they come to lime (see box, page 23), eat at the beach bars, **BeachLimerZ** and **Millers By The Sea** (see page 62), play beach cricket or volleyball and listen to live music, and cruise ship passengers are brought here as it is so close to the port. Sun loungers and umbrellas can be hired, but at times the sea can be rough and then turns milky in appearance with lots of weed, and is not good for swimming.

Dickenson Bay and Runaway Bay

Due north and a short taxi ride away from St John's, **Dickenson Bay** and **Runaway Bay** are adjacent long stretches of white sand, separated by a small promontory. Just inland is McKinnons Salt Pond, which was once a mangrove-lined lagoon but because of development along the shore is now cut off from the sea (except for a small culvert that allows a limited exchange of water). The majority of the mangroves have died, although small stands of skeleton mangroves remain on the southern and western edges, and it's still good for birdwatching. Egrets, herons, whistling ducks and other waterfowl can be seen, and brown pelicans and laughing gulls are sometimes attracted by the semi-saline water.

Dickenson Bay is wall-to-wall, low-rise hotels, the largest of which is the monster all-inclusive adults-only 373-room **Sandals Grande Antigua Resort & Spa** (www.sandals.com), which has recently added a multi-storey block that dominates the back of the beach. Day passes are available (which are overpriced unless you eat and drink a lot); costing US$100 1000-1800, US$100 1800-0200, and US$200 all-day 1000-0200. Nevertheless, while Dickenson Bay is not the most secluded beach on Antigua, it is appealing, well looked after and has watersports, bars and restaurants, and a lively atmosphere. The sea is crystal clear and calm, and perfect for children, with roped off areas to ensure safety from motor craft. Given that it's west-facing, it's also a great spot to watch the sun go down.

Tip...

Sun loungers and umbrellas are available to rent at Dickenson Bay, and all the bars and resorts have free Wi-Fi that has coverage along most of the beach.

BACKGROUND

Antigua and Barbuda

Antigua and Barbuda were settled first by the Arawaks, and then the Caribs, but the islands were abandoned around the 16th century due to the shortage of fresh water. Christopher Columbus sighted Antigua in 1493 during his second Caribbean voyage, and named it after a church in Seville, Santa María de la Antigua. After unsuccessful attempts at colonization by the Spanish and French, Antigua was colonized by Sir Thomas Warner in 1632 and formally became a British colony in 1667.

In 1674, Sir Christopher Codrington, an enterprising man, came to Antigua to find out if the island would support the sort of large-scale sugar cultivation that already flourished elsewhere in the Caribbean. His efforts proved to be successful, and by the mid-18th century the island was dotted with more than 150 cane-processing windmills, each the focal point of a sizeable plantation. Today, almost 100 of these picturesque stone towers remain; most are in ruins but some have been restored as part of hotels, and at Betty's Hope (see page 44), Codrington's original sugar estate that he established in 1674, visitors can see a fully restored sugar mill. In 1680 Charles II granted Barbuda to the Codrington family (who held it until 1860), who used it to grow food and keep slaves to service their fields on Antigua. After the official abolition of the slave trade in 1807, the Codringtons established a 'slave-farm' on Barbuda, where children were bred to supply the highly profitable plantations until slaves were emancipated in 1834.

As the only Caribbean island under British rule to possess a good harbour, Antigua was used by the Royal Navy from 1725 until 1889, and had control over the major sailing routes to and from the region's rich island colonies in the British West Indies. Horatio Nelson arrived in 1784 at the head of the Squadron of the Leeward Islands to

The adjacent **Runaway Bay Beach** to the south has also got soft white sand and clear water, but after years of hurricane erosion, there are barely enough palms left for shade, and fewer facilities. There are no large resorts here and it is almost entirely backed by McKinnons Salt Pond, making it is much quieter, except at weekends and on public holidays when it is popular for liming (see box, page 23) and family picnics, or when a cruise ship shore excursion offloads for a few hours. Swimming is good and it's a great spot for a long walk from Dickenson Bay, although the beach is not always kept litter-free. There are just a couple of small beach bars, catering for locals rather than the tourist market, the best of which is **Mystic** (T268-723 4723, daily 0900-1800), which offers changing rooms, outdoor showers, sun loungers and umbrellas, and Wi-Fi for a small fee.

North coast

From Dickenson Bay, Anchorage Road turns inland and then joins the north coast at Hodges Bay. Before it gets there, turn-offs go to Soldier's Bay, located just to the northeast of Dickenson Bay around Weatherills Point, and where the excellent **Blue Waters Resort & Spa** is located. There's good snorkelling at the shallow 1-mile-long coral reef offshore. The couple of resorts at Hodges Bay only share a narrow stretch of beach but are quiet and secluded. If you visit the Sottovento Beach Club at the **Ocean Point Resort & Spa**, notice the restored sugar mill in the reception.

develop the naval facilities at English Harbour and to enforce stringent commercial shipping laws. The first of these two tasks resulted in construction of Nelson's Dockyard; the second resulted in a rather hostile attitude toward the young captain. These acts prohibited trade with the newly formed United States of America, and most of the merchants in Antigua depended upon American trade, so many of them despised Nelson. He spent almost all of his time in the cramped quarters of his ship, declaring the island to be a 'vile place' and a 'dreadful hole'. While Nelson was stationed on Antigua, he frequently visited the island of Nevis, where he met and married a young widow, Fanny Nisbet.

After Britain abolished slavery in the empire in 1834, the prosperity of the sugar industry began to wane significantly. In 1918 sugar cane workers on the remaining estates went on strike and rioted as a response to a slash in wages, and this was the first movement towards a strong labour movement. This peaked in the 1940s, under the leadership of Dr Vere Cornwall Bird who had formed the country's first trade union in 1939. Later he became leader of the Antigua Labour Party (ALP) which provided the impetus for independence. Under the West Indies Act 1967, Antigua and Barbuda became an associated state with internal self-government, an associated state of the Commonwealth, and in 1981 it achieved full independence. In 1993, on the retirement of Vere Bird, his son Lester Bird became prime minister.

Although Antigua and Barbuda has experienced three changes of government since independence, today the ALP is currently again in power under the leadership of Prime Minister Gaston Browne. Only a tiny amount of sugar is harvested each year today, and is mostly used for the production of ethanol; the modern-day industry has suffered from the unwillingness of people to work in the sugar cane fields. Because of the lack of agriculture, Antigua imports roughly 25% of its food; tourism and its related service industries is by far the biggest mainstay of the economy.

Offshore from Beggars Point, **Prickly Pear Island** ⓘ *T268-460 9978, www.pricklypearisland.com, Tue, Thu and Sat 1000-1500 or other days by arrangement, US$95, children (4-11) US$60, under 4s free,* is an islet 1 mile or a five-minute boat ride off the north coast, which is popular for day trips (usually organized through the resorts) for a barbecue seafood lunch and snorkelling.

From Hodges Bay, the road bends around the northern tip of the island and becomes Jabberwock Road and goes past the sprawling campus of the American University Of Antigua, (opened in 2010, a private medical college affiliated to medical boards in the US), and then on to Dutchman's Bay. Windsurfing and kitesurfing are good in this area, and **Jabberwock Beach** is the most popular spot for both, where conditions are excellent with cross-onshore winds averaging 12-18 knots, a long sandy beach and shallow water. **Dutchman's Bay** is also popular for windsurfing and has a quiet reef-protected beach, although seaweed can be a problem here. **Cecilia's High Point Café**, where there are sun loungers on the beach and free Wi-Fi, is a popular place to come for the day for those on an evening flight, as the airport is only a five-minute drive south of here.

Tip...

If you're into windsurfing or kitesurfing, both **Windsurf Antigua**, www.windsurfantigua.net, and **Kitesurf Antigua**, www.kitesurfantigua.com, have kiosks on Jabberwock Beach; also see What to do, page 66.

The southwest

Antigua's best coral reef, a forested drive and a popular harbour

The hilly southwest corner of Antigua south of St John's has a beautiful series of bays on the Caribbean, where the beaches are generally less developed than those further north, although there is still a number of resorts, and beach bars cater for locals at weekends, day visitors and those coming ashore from yachts. On the small Five Islands peninsula are good views back to St John's, especially if you want to see the massive cruise ships in the harbour. Further south you pass the marina and large development at Jolly Harbour, before reaching quieter beaches such as Valley Church, Dark Wood or Crab Hill, and then one of Antigua's best reefs at Cades Bay on the road to Old Road round the southwest coast.

West of St John's

There are several attractive beaches on the Five Islands peninsula which lies about 3 miles west of St John's and is reached by Gray's Farm Main Road. The peninsula and the village of the same name are called after five rocks in the sea further south. On a promontory on the northern side called Goat Hill overlooking Deep Bay, which marks the southern entrance to St John's Harbour, are the ruins of **Fort Barrington**. It was erected by Governor Burt, who gave up active duty in 1780 suffering from psychiatric disorders; a stone he placed in one of the walls at the fort describes him grandly as 'Imperator and Gubernator' of the Carib Islands. The previous fortifications saw the most action in Antigua's history, with the French and English battling for possession in the 17th century. Today the fort is mostly in ruins and overgrown, but it is a good walk up the hill and you get a wonderful view of St John's Harbour on one side and Deep Bay on the other. It's a bit of a scramble in places so wear trainers or proper shoes.

Deep Bay has an arched beach and the calm water is good for swimming. A wreck lies in the middle of the bay, the *Andes*, a barque from Trinidad that sank in 1905 at a depth of only 35 ft; its mast pokes out of the water at times and you can snorkel around it easily. If you go through Five Islands village you come to **Galley Bay**, a secluded and unspoilt hotel beach for the all-inclusive Galley Bay Resort & Spa which is also popular with locals and joggers at sunset.

The four **Hawksbill beaches** at the end of the peninsula are crescent-shaped and very scenic. Hotel guests of the all-inclusive Hawksbill by Rex Resorts tend to use the second beach, leaving the other three empty. Take drinks to the furthest one (clothes optional, secluded and pleasant) as there are no facilities and you may have the place to yourself.

Jolly Harbour

On the coast close to Bolans, south of Five Islands Harbour and 7 miles south of St John's on Valley Road, is the extensive purpose-built village and development of Jolly Harbour (www.jollyharbourantigua.com). It has shops including a branch of Epicurean Fine Foods, an ATM, a pharmacy, restaurants and bars, holiday villas and a golf course. In the sheltered bay are moorings for the Jolly Harbour Marina; some homeowners can dock right in front of their villas and there are customs and immigrations facilities for visiting yachts. The Jolly Harbour Golf Club has an 18-hole championship course (see page 65).

Beyond Reeds Point is the mile-long **Jolly Beach** which is home to the vast all-inclusive family-oriented Jolly Beach Resort & Spa (www.jollybeachresort.com), popular with British holidaymakers. Casual visitors can rent sun loungers and umbrellas. The resort also offers day passes: 1030-1800 includes breakfast, lunch, house drinks and (non-motorized) watersports, US$75, children (3-11) US$45, under twos free; 1800-2400 includes dinner, entertainment and drinks; US$70/42: and all-day 1030-2400, US$97/59.

Valley Road to Old Road

South of Jolly Harbour, Valley Road passes **Valley Church Bay**, with a palm-lined beach and fishing boats dotting the picturesque bay. Chairs/umbrellas are available for rent. Despite the calmness and beautiful colour, the water is not very clear for snorkelling, but it's shallow with gently sloping sands. **Coco's Hotel Antigua** is here, one of the island's prettiest resorts with cottages climbing up the hillside, and the **Nest Beach Bar & Restaurant** (T268-562 7958, daily 0900-1800) with toilets, changing rooms and showers. The **Sheer Rocks** restaurant, at Cocos Hotel Antigua, is another option for a lazy day where lunchtime diners can use the day beds and plunge pool.

Tip...

To get to Jolly Harbour and the beaches further south, take minibus No 22, which runs from West Bus Station in St John's down Valley Road to Old Road.

Darkwood Beach has beautiful white sand and is comparatively empty as there is no hotel here. Looking out across the turquoise sea you get a good view of Montserrat. Again, there's a beach bar, **Darkwood Beach Bar** (T268-462 8240, daily 0900-1800), serving cold beer and food, and it has decent toilets, showers, changing facilities and parking. It also rents out loungers, umbrellas and snorkels to explore the small reef; in high season massages are also available.

Valley Road continues through the village of **Crab Hill** (about 11 miles south of St John's), where Crab Hill Beach is also known as Turner's Beach after **Turner's Beach Bar** (T268-462 9133, daily 1000-2200), which has a covered terrace and loungers/umbrellas on the sand and is especially popular with locals on a Sunday afternoon. **Jacqui O's Beach House** (see page 59) and **OJ's Bar & Restaurant** (see page 60) are other options. On exceptionally clear days Montserrat can be seen.

From Crab Hill, the road goes past Johnsons Point and the fishing village of Urlings, and then turns eastwards as Old Road along the southern coast of the island and Cades Bay, where offshore the 2½-mile **Cades Reef** is popular with snorkellers and divers. Boat trips by catamaran from Jolly Harbour come down here for a day of snorkelling and a barbecue lunch on the beach. There are also glass-bottomed boats from the resorts, **Antigua Scuba School** is based in Urlings and other dive operators do trips to Cades. Marine life on the reef includes spiny lobsters, conch, parrotfish, moray eels, eagle rays and barracuda, and nurse sharks are sometimes found sheltering under the coral overhangs.

Fig Tree Drive

The village of Old Road is overlooked by Mount Obama (formerly Boggy Peak), which lies to its northwest, and here **Curtain Bluff Resort** and **Carlisle Bay Antigua** are the dominant resorts on the central southern coast. It is also where the road turns inland and becomes Fig Tree Drive, a steep, winding road, through mountainous rainforest towards All Saints and Liberta.

If travelling by bicycle make sure you go *down* Fig Tree Drive heading towards Old Road; the hill is very steep. It is greener and more scenic here than most of the island, but the rainforest is scanty and incomparable with islands like Dominica. It does, however, give you a good idea of what Antigua must have looked like before the land was cleared for sugar and you can see banana plants, mango, soursop and breadfruit trees. There are

ON THE ROAD

Mount Obama

Formerly known as the (oddly named) **Boggy Peak**, the highest point on Antigua (1319 ft) was renamed Mount Obama on August 4 in 2009; the 48th birthday of US President Barack Obama. It has vaguely historical importance as during the 17th and 18th centuries, it served as a refuge for escaped African slaves ('maroons'), but today the summit is fenced off and crowned by a very noticeable cluster of telecommunications antennas. It can be climbed from its southern side, but it is advised not to drive up here as the ascent is on a very steep and straight single-lane concrete maintenance track; tough even for a sturdy 4WD.

At Cades Bay you can be dropped off by minibus on the main road just over half a mile east of Urlings where the Mount Obama Road starts off as a dirt track and goes for about a mile before it starts to climb up the hill. It takes about 45 minutes to one hour to the top and is not overly strenuous, although you are advised not to wander around alone. Unfortunately the gate to the communications compound is locked, but you can follow the trail around the fence for the wonderful views over to Guadeloupe, St Kitts, Nevis and Montserrat.

no figs; the name comes from the local name for the green banana, which is green fig. To the east of the road are the pineapple fields of **Claremont Farms** (www.claremontfarms.com) which grows the Antigua black; a particularly sweet and small species that is very dark green (almost black), hence its name. Claremont Valley was the first area settled and cultivated by the British in the late 1600s. The largest freshwater pond on the island was situated directly south of this valley (now long gone) but it would have made the area a central focal point for earlier Amerindian occupation as well, and later for the first colonial settlements. This pond was a very important source of water during dry periods for the garrisons at Nelson's Dockyard, who would have carried the water several miles by ox cart over the hills to the east.

Antigua Rainforest Zip Line Tours ⓘ *Fig Tree Drive, Wallings, T268-562 6363, www.antiguarainforest.com, Mon-Sat tours at 0900, 1000 and 1100, in high season extra tours at 1200 and 1400 and opens Sun on request, US$60-89, under 13s US$45-55, depending on how many you do,* is a series of zip lines and aerial walkways strung up to 300 ft above the gorge in Wallings Forest, a popular activity for cruise passengers and families with teenagers. There's a café and gift shop where you can buy photos of your excursion. **Fig Tree Studio Art Gallery** ⓘ *Fig Tree Drive, John Hughes village, T268-460 1234, www.figtreestudioart.com, Mon-Sat 0930-1730 Nov-Jun,* is an interesting place to stop, showcasing the work of Sallie Harker (www.sallieharker.com) and lots of local and regional art and crafts.

Tip...

Along Fig Tree Drive there are roadside booths where you can try whatever fruit is in season (including the Antigua black pineapple); all amazingly sweet, fresh and tasty.

a yachting mecca, good nightlife and a colonial naval stronghold

The southeast is the area of most historical interest, with the old naval dockyard in English Harbour which had major strategic importance in the 17th and 18th centuries. It lies just to the east of Falmouth Harbour, a magnet for yachts from all over the world and many world-class yacht races are held here.

Yachtsmen and women need entertainment and there are several good hotels, lots of restaurants, bars and nightlife in both Falmouth Harbour and English Harbour, which are also the best places to arrange a wide range of watersports. Former military buildings dot the hillsides up to the top of Shirley Heights, from where you get a spectacular view of the coastline, popular with visitors on Sunday for a barbecue, steelpan bands and reggae.

Falmouth Harbour

You can come from the interior of the island via **Liberta**, the third largest town in Antigua whose name is derived from it being a place of freed or liberated slaves. This brings you to the northern shore of Falmouth Harbour and the village of the same name. From here Dockyard Drive winds its way around this picturesque naturally sheltered horseshoe-shaped bay, which is full of yachts at several marinas, while luxurious villas are dotted around the gentle hills. Some of the most prestigious yachts in the world come here during the winter season, especially for events such as the **International Yacht Show** in December, and the **Antigua Classic Regatta** and **Antigua Sailing Week** in April (see Festivals, page 12). The **Falmouth Harbour Marina** ⓘ *www.antigua-marina.com*, has berths big enough to accommodate superyachts up to 330 ft in length, while on the south side the **Antigua Yacht Club Marina** ⓘ *www.aycmarina.com*, has an attractive wooden jetty over the water with shops catering to yachties selling sailing gear and swimwear, a supermarket, and cafés offering excellent coffees and cocktails (at **Seabreeze Café/ Gelateria**, try the delicious homemade Italian *gelato*). It's a pleasant place to come for a drink and watch the comings and goings of the yacht crowd, and any would-be crew can have a look at the vast noticeboard here. Bars and restaurants line Dockyard Drive, especially around the junction where it heads south the short distance to English Harbour.

Follow the road past the Antigua Yacht Club Marina over a small hill to **Pigeon Beach**, a five- to 10-minute walk, which is a lovely stretch of sand with good views into Falmouth Harbour and a favourite spot for the local community as well as visitors. West-facing, it's perfect for a sundowner at either the delightful beach bar at the north end, **Bumpkins Beach Bar** (T268-562 2522, Monday-Wednesday 1100-1800, Thursday-Sunday 1100-2200), which is famous for its banana piña coladas, strong rum punch and jerk chicken on the large wooden veranda, or at the good restaurant at the other end, **Catherine's Café Plage**, see page 60.

For a good view of Falmouth Harbour, and English Harbour beyond, hike to the top of 700-ft-high **Monk's Hill** and the remains of **Fort George**, an important and large defence post built in the 1680s. The perimeter of the massive fortifications exceeded over a mile, but the low remains of the walls are now overgrown. The views are tremendous and you get views of

Tip...

Bus No 17 from the West Bus Station in St John's will get you down to Falmouth and English harbours; the furthest point on this bus route is the petrol station on Dockyard Drive at the junction with English Harbour.

much of the island along the hike. Although the track is very steep at times, and the acacia thorns are rife; wear good shoes. It starts at Cobbs Cross junction, and follows the eastern side of the primary school fence and then and keep walking up towards the mobile phone antennas on top of Monk's Hill and you will get to the fort. The distance is about 2 miles from the junction.

English Harbour and Nelson's Dockyard

T268-481 5028, www.nationalparksantigua.com. Between 0800-1800 the entrance fee to the restored dockyard, and all other sites such as Shirley Heights and Dow's Hill, is US$8, under

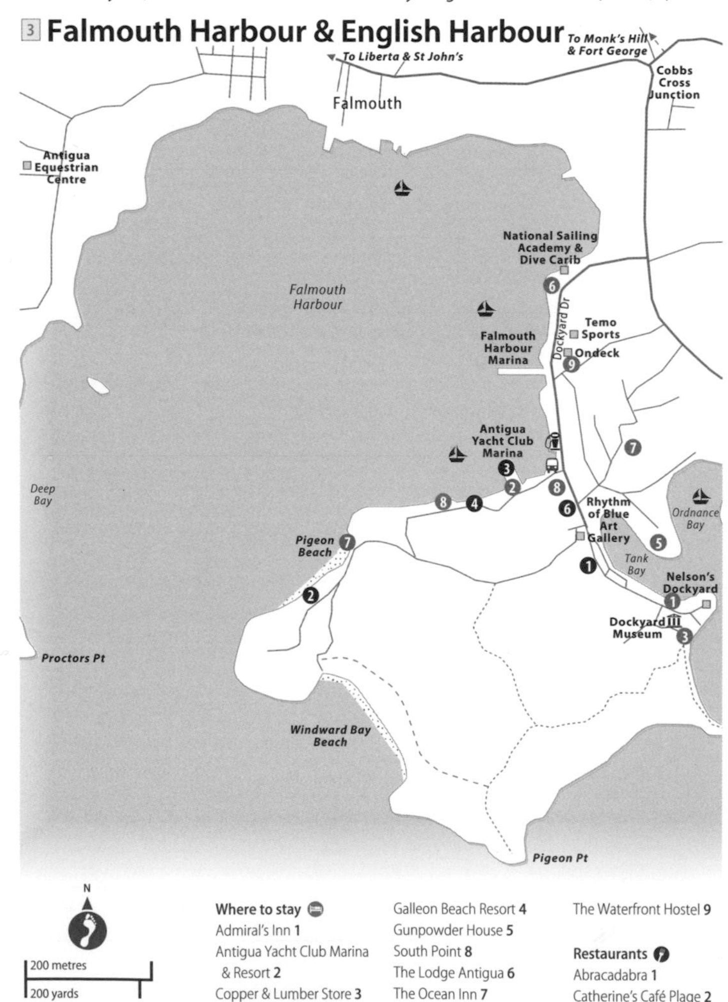

12s free, but there is no charge if you are staying at the hotels, visiting the restaurants in the evening, or have a yacht moored in the marina (for which there is a fee in any case). Guided tours are available on request.

On the eastern side of Falmouth Harbour is **English Harbour** (a five-minute walk along Dockyard Drive from the Antigua Yacht Club Marina junction), which is another attractive yachting centre and takes its name from the deep-water sheltered bay in which the Royal Navy established its base of operations for the area during the 18th century. Now fully restored, Nelson's Dockyard is the only existing Georgian Naval Dockyard in the world, and the major sites around its shores and hillsides are part of the 15 square miles of the **Nelson's Dockyard National Park**. It includes the marina, once a mooring for battleships, now yachts; restored buildings in the historic naval dockyard, some of them now restaurants, cafés, hotels and shops; the Dockyard Museum, where Nelson's telescope and tea caddy are on display; Dow's Hill, where visitors can watch a 15-minute presentation on the history of the island at the Interpretation Centre; and the old observation point and signal station at Shirley Heights. See also box, page 42.

The main entrance and information centre is at the end of Dockyard Drive, from where you first walk through a covered vendor's market selling souvenirs (there are toilets and a Bank of Antigua ATM here), and then the route goes though the **Pillars Restaurants** of the Admiral's Inn hotel. This Georgian brick building dating from 1788 was once a store room for pitch, turpentine and lead, while upstairs were the offices for Royal Navy engineers. Here look out for its boat and mast yard, slipway and boathouse pillars, although still standing they suffered earthquake damage in the 19th century. From the hotel, paths fan out attractively throughout the other old

➜ **Antigua maps**
1 Antigua, page 30
2 St John's, page 32
3 **Falmouth Harbour & English Harbour, page 40**

Cloggy's Café **3**
Club Sushi **4**
Shirley Heights Lookout **5**
Trappas Restaurant & Bar **6**

Bars & clubs
Bumpkins Beach Bar **7**
Life on the Corner **8**

Tip...
From in front of the Copper & Lumber Store Hotel, you can catch water taxis over to the splendid Galleon Beach on Freeman's Bay (US$3.70) or negotiate to do a little harbour tour by water.

BACKGROUND

English Harbour

In the early 18th century, the British Royal Navy recognized the strategic importance of English Harbour in protecting ships from hurricanes and for monitoring French naval activity; its position on the south side of the island meant it was well positioned to observe the French island of Guadeloupe. By 1723 it was in regular use and officers petitioned for the building of maintenance facilities, as it was the only harbour in the Eastern Caribbean large and sheltered enough for safe repairs prior to the return voyage across the Atlantic to Britain, particularly for battle-damaged vessels.

In 1728 the first dockyard, St Helena, was built on the east side of the harbour and had a capstan house (where ships were careened, or were turned on their sides, for cleaning, caulking, or repairs), a stone storehouse for supplies, and three wooden sheds for careening gear. Operations soon outgrew the small dockyard and the western side of the harbour was developed from the 1740s, when slave labourers from the plantations in the vicinity were sent to work on the dockyard.

Most of the buildings seen today were constructed during a building programme between 1785 and 1794; these include the Engineer's Offices, Pitch and Tar Store, Copper and Lumber Store, Capstan House, Saw Pit Shed and Blacksmith's Shop. This construction overlapped with Horatio Nelson's tenure in the dockyard from 1784 to 1787. He served as captain of HMS Boreas, and was sent to Antigua at the head of the Squadron of the Leeward Islands to develop the naval facilities at English Harbour and to enforce British shipping laws in the colonies.

The Sail Loft was built in 1797, the Pay Master's Office around 1806, the Officers' Quarters building in 1821, and the Clerk's House and Admiral's House in 1855. However, after peace was established among the islands after about 1815, and with the growing use of steamships, the dockyard's importance declined, and in 1889 the Royal Navy officially closed it. Restoration began in 1951 and a decade later it was opened to the public and renamed Nelson's Dockyard in honour of the years he spent in Antigua.

buildings of the dockyard and on to the waterfront area with the jetties and berths of the yacht marina.

The **Dockyard Museum**, located in the former Admiral's House (1855), has exhibits on the history of the dockyard and a bust of Nelson above the entrance. Also here is a good gift shop. Behind it is an old stone kitchen, which still serves as the small **Dockyard Bakery** selling bread and pastries. The **Copper and Lumber Store** (1789) was built to store the lumber and sheets of copper required for repairing and maintaining the wooden sailing ships of the time, and sailors from ships being repaired sometimes permitted to sleep upstairs. Its walls are 3 ft thick and built entirely of yellow bricks imported from Britain as ship ballast. It is now a hotel (see page 54), pub and restaurant (see page 60). Other buildings to look out for are the Officers' Quarters building (1821), now an art gallery, and the Pay Master's Office (1806), now a supermarket and liquor store catering to yachties.

A footpath leads from the dinghy dock in the marina around the bay to **Fort Berkeley** at the harbour mouth. It is well worth the walk for the wonderful views; it only takes about 10-15 minutes including some wooden steps over the hilly parts. Constructed in 1704, long

to explore. However, in 2016 the 108-acre oceanfront property was bought by a resort company so may well be developed soon. For now a snack bar serves cold drinks and ice cream, but has irregular opening hours, while vendors ply their wares in the car park.

Barbuda

laid-back island with bone-white and pink beaches and frigate birds

Lying 27 miles to the north of Antigua, and one of the two island dependencies, Barbuda covers 68 square miles of mostly flat coral limestone and lagoons, where the near-deserted beaches are an outstanding feature, and the Frigate Bird Sanctuary offers close-up encounters with these unusual birds. With a population of only around 1800, it's a quiet place with few paved roads and one main village, where life is slow and simple and the people friendly. Barbuda's charm lies in this easy-going way of life and its isolated beauty, and there are some wonderful barefoot luxury places to stay, as well as a couple of cheaper simple guesthouses. It's also close enough to Antigua to visit for the day.

Most residents live in the only village on the island, **Codrington**, which stands on the edge of the large lagoon of the same name and has an estimated population of around 1800. It is named after the Codrington family who leased Barbuda for 185 years from 1685 until 1870, and used it to supply their sugar estates on Antigua with food and slaves. They built a castle which dominated the town, but it was badly damaged by an earthquake in 1843 and little now remains.

After emancipation, all property belonged to the Codringtons and the freed slaves were trapped with no jobs, land or laws. After many years and court cases, Antiguan law was applied to the island, but while Barbudans may own their own houses today, all other land is generally held by the government.

The village is strung along the eastern side of Codrington Lagoon, which takes up much of the west of the island; its access to the sea is via Cuffy Creek at the northern tip. The water is shallow, and much of the shore of the northern half is marshland. It's an easy

Essential Barbuda

Finding your feet

The airport is a short walk to the centre of Codrington. Barbuda's ferry dock is called River Wharf Landing and is on the south side of the island; taxis meet the ferry and it's a 15-minute drive to Codrington. See Transport page 70.

Getting around

The island is very small so is easily explored on foot, or there are taxis, with drivers doubling up as informative guides. Car hire is available but sometimes difficult; the cost of spare parts and supply of fuel make it an expensive business for Barbudans to maintain.

Tip...
Barbuda has one bank, the Antigua Commercial Bank near the airport. It has an ATM, but is not to be relied on; bring cash from Antigua as few places in Barbuda have card machines so payments in guesthouses, bars, shops or for taxis are in East Caribbean dollars cash.

and pleasant place to wander around, and if you're lucky you'll enjoy some time chatting to the Codrington residents. Codrington has a tiny airport, a bank, fuel station, **Digicel** phone shop, bakery, small grocery shops and vendors selling fruit and vegetables, street food and coconut water, and a few rum shops. Cattle, horses and donkeys often wander about in the village and sheep and goats can be seen trotting off to their pens at sunset. There are occasional small horse races and on Sundays, starting about 1400 at the grassy low-key racetrack on the edge of the village.

Frigate Bird Sanctuary

Water taxis are organized from the jetty in Codrington any time of day but mornings are best for bird activity and it's not permitted to go after 1800, US$50 per boat of 4 people, and US$12 per additional person. Alternatively, you can visit as part of the Barbuda Express day trip, or one of the hotels on the island can organize an trip.

A 15-minute boat ride goes across to the impressive Frigate Bird Sanctuary in the mangroves towards the north end of the **Codrington Lagoon**, where thousands of birds mate and breed roughly between September and January. The sanctuary is well worth a visit to see these extraordinary birds (see box, opposite) and the colony is a contentious place indeed, where birds argue over landing rights, perch ownership and who owns each twig.

It is believed to be the largest breeding colony in the world, larger even than that of the Galápagos, and locals will tell you that there are some 2500-5000 birds. Visitors are taken to only one or two spots to view the birds, and ropes keep the boats from getting too close. The rest of the birds are left alone but you get near enough for photos of the male birds puffing out their red chests and flapping their wings. The lagoon is also home to other birds including brown pelicans, warblers, snipes, ibis, herons and kingfishers, and brown boobies nest alongside the frigates.

Barbuda

Where to stay
Barbuda Belle 3
Barbuda Cottages 6
Bus Stop Guest House 5
Coco Point Lodge 2
Lighthouse Bay Resort 1
North Beach 4
Palm Tree Guesthouse 7

Restaurants
ArtCafé 1
It's a Bit Fishy 1
Outback 2
Uncle Roddy's Beach Bar & Grill 3

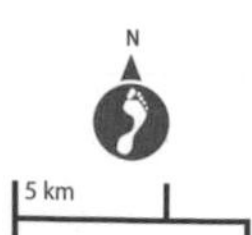

Around the island

Much of the island is covered in impenetrable bush with only one main paved road (in various states of disrepair) going from the River Wharf Landing in the south (an area of the island generally referred to as River), to Two Foot Bay in the northeast. But there are dirt roads and tracks fanning out to most of the beaches. Not far from River Wharf Landing are the ruins of **Martello Tower and Fort**, a popular spot for island weddings. This 32-ft-tall tower and fort were built by the British in the early

ON THE ROAD

Frigate birds

With a wing span of 8 ft and the ability to fly up to 22 mph, sometimes at heights of 2000 ft, frigate birds (*Fregata magnificens*) are indeed magnificent when seen soaring high in the air, using the thermals to suspend themselves. They cannot, however, walk or swim, having very short legs and small feet despite a weight averaging about 3 lbs, so they need to take off from a high vantage point. They've picked up a trick or two, including piracy, which has earned them the nickname of the man-o'-war bird. Because they can't swim, or have waterproof feathers, their fishing technique relies on finding fish or squid close to the surface which they can just skim off. But failing that they have developed a method of hassling other seabirds, encouraging them to regurgitate whatever they have just caught, and in an amazing display of aerobatics, the frigate birds manage to catch the food before it hits the water and get themselves a free meal.

Their breeding season is roughly September-January, although even later you can still see males displaying their bright red pouches, blowing them up like balloons to attract a mate. It is the male who chooses a nest site, and when he is sure he has found a long-term partner, he builds a precarious nest of twigs in the mangroves alongside all the other males. The female lays a single egg, which the male incubates and initially cares for once it is hatched. The chick is born white and fluffy and sits on the twiggy nest, suspended above the water, for eight to 10 months until it is fully fledged. It takes a lot longer to be fully proficient at flying and feeding itself, and it will be about six years before they start breeding themselves.

1800s and once had three guns to guard the main anchorage on the southwestern side of Barbuda. It was also used as a lookout for incoming ships, and information of their arrival was then signalled onward to Codrington to the north. The name 'Martello' is derived from a tower at Cape Mortella in Corsica that the British had difficulty in taking in 1794.

As an island composed of limestone, Barbuda has many caves, and the easiest to get to is the series of caves around **Two Foot Bay**. Used for shelter since the days of the Amerindians, they run along the sea cliffs and you might see crabs, huge iguanas and tropicbirds. The entrance to **Indian Cave** is close to a roofless stone ruin near the shore, which was probably a house associated with the phosphate mining operation undertaken at Gun Shop Cliff in the 1890s. Inland and about a 45-minute walk from Codrington (local people can show you the route), **Darby Cave** is not a true cavern but a vertical-sided sink hole; the cliffs are about 70 ft high and the hole is about 350 ft in diameter. It contains lush ferns and tall trees, the commonest of which is the palmetto palm. From the overhang there is an intermittent dripping of water, which in parts has created stalagmites of calcium.

Beaches

The beaches on the Atlantic side of the island are wild and dotted with driftwood and shells, while the Caribbean on the western side is perfect for swimming and snorkelling. The beaches are fabulous, and are possibly the most magnificent in the whole Caribbean. The longest beach is a gently curving swathe of dazzling white sand stretching for 14 miles down the west side along **Low Bay**. Also known as Palm Beach (although there

ON THE ROAD

Redonda

Uninhabited Redonda is Antigua's second dependency and lies 35 miles to the southwest between Montserrat and Nevis. A rocky volcanic islet, it is about half a mile square. It rises extremely steeply from sea level in wall-like cliffs, and is 971 ft tall at its highest point.

Columbus sighted the island on 12 November 1493 and named it after a church in Cadiz called Santa María la Redonda. He did not land, however, and so did not formally claim the island. Neither did anyone else until 1865 when Matthew Dowdy Shiell, an Irish sea trader from Montserrat, celebrated the birth of a long-awaited son by leading an expedition of friends to Redonda and claiming it as his kingdom. In 1872, the island was annexed by Britain and came under the jurisdiction of the colony of Antigua, despite protests from the Shiells. The title of king, however, was never disputed, and in 1880 MD Shiell 'abdicated' in favour of his son, Matthew Phipps Shiell, who became King Felipe of Redonda.

On his death in 1947, he appointed as his successor to the throne his friend John Gawsworth, the poet, who became Juan, the third King of Redonda. His reign was notable for his idea of an 'intellectual aristocracy' of the realm of Redonda and he conferred titles on his literary friends, including Victor Gollancz, the publisher, JB Priestley, Dorothy L Sayers and Lawrence Durrell. This eccentric pastime hit a crisis when declining fortunes and increasing time spent in the pub sparked a rash of new titles to all and sundry, and a number of abdications in different pubs. The title of 'King' died along with Gawsworth in 1970 although technically the title still survives today and numerous characters have claimed it since in a half-serious fashion.

The island was never inhabited, thanks to the steepness of the surface, the lack of a safe place to land a boat, and no freshwater source. However, it attracts a huge a number of seabirds and was an important source of guano collection from the 1860s to start of the First World War, when many thousands of tons of phosphates were shipped from Redonda to Britain. Today the lizards and seabirds live an undisturbed life, although scientists from the Montserrat Volcano Observatory visit the island by helicopter periodically, as they use it as an observation point from which to take measurements of the Soufrière Hills active volcano on Montserrat.

are few palms left, thanks to hurricane damage) it is located along the west coast of the Codrington Lagoon and so most if it is only accessible by boat. But it's a great place to sunbathe, swim, and snorkel; ask your boatman to drop you near one of the groves of casuarina trees for shade and pick you up at an agreed time later in the day. It's possible to stroll along for miles without seeing another soul, but there are no facilities. You can't rely on the few beach bars being open, so it's important to take plenty of water and food.

The 8-mile-long beach that stretches from **Palmetto Point** to **Cocoa Point** in a series of slightly indented coves along the southwest coast goes under a variety of names but collectively is called **Pink Sand Beach** as it's made up of crushed tiny pink shells and broken coral. There tends to be a good breeze. There are a couple of beach bars near the Martello Tower; **Pink Sand Beach Bar** and **River Beach Bar** (open 'any day, any time') which rent out sun loungers and umbrellas, while **Uncle Roddy's Beach Bar & Grill** (see page 61) is further southwest at Spanish Well Point.

Tourist information

Antigua *map page 32.*
There is no tourist information desk at the new VC Bird International Airport (although there are plans to open one). The head office for the **Antigua & Barbuda Tourism Authority** is at ACB Financial Centre, High St, St John's, T268-562 7600 www.antigua-barbuda.org, Mon-Fri 0830-1630. They also run a kiosk in Redcliffe Quay; opening days are not consistent, but it's always open 0900-1700 when cruise ships are in.

The best online guides are **Antigua Nice** (www.antiguanice.com) and **Antigua & Barbuda Buzz** (www.visitantiguabarbuda.com). Many hotels have brochures and maps to pick up.

Barbuda *map page 48.*

Artcafé
See page 61. Mon-Sat 1100-2100.
This café has good local information. Or see the websites of **Antigua & Barbuda Buzz** (www.visitantiguabarbuda.com) and the **Antigua & Barbuda Tourism Authority** (www.antigua-barbuda.org). Best of all is **Barbudful** (www.barbudaful.net), a community website for all things related to the island and Barbudans.

Where to stay

Unless otherwise stated, all hotel rooms have a/c, TV and Wi-Fi. Hotel sale tax (12%) and service (10%) is charged by all accommodation options, usually as a single charge of 22%. Check if this has been included in quoted rates.

St John's *map page 32.*

$$ Caribbean Inn & Suites
Pyform St, T268-562 0210, caribbeaninn@hotmail.com.
Perched on the top of Radio Range Hill on the western outskirts of St John's. The top floor communal balcony has incredible views of the southern side of the island, and across town to the cruise ships. 10 singles or doubles with kitchenettes, the larger ones have living rooms. Slightly outdated furniture, but clean and and well-priced.

$$ Heritage Hotel
Long St, T268-462 1247, heritagehotel@candw.ag.
Close to Heritage Quay, large local conference-style hotel with 46 old-fashioned and tired rooms (the bathroom fixtures most certainly need replacing), some with kitchenettes, but also helpful staff and a surprisingly good and generous buffet breakfast is included. The best choice in town (although there's little reason).

The northwest and north *map page 30.*

$$$$ Blue Waters Resort & Spa
Soldier's Bay, T268-462 0290, www.bluewaters.net.
One of the most upmarket resorts on the island, with lush tropical gardens and huge mature trees on a 17-acre plot lining the very pretty bay. Offers 74 large colonial-style rooms, suites, cottages and villas with patios or balconies, and cool, clean decor. Rates are B&B or all-inclusive. There's a pool, watersports, gym, spa and tennis.

$$$$ The Villas at Sunset Lane
Sunset Lane, McKinnons, T268-562 7791, www.villasatsunsetlane.com.
An all-inclusive option, but small and charming and a very popular adults-only coral pink hotel on a hillside overlooking Dickenson Bay, with 10 elegant individually decorated rooms and villas with kitchens. Owned and run by chef Jackie who is outstandingly hospitable and produces delectable Caribbean-European fusion cuisine. Pool, gym, pleasant gardens with fruit trees and veg which end up on your plate, and a few mins' walk to the beach.

$$$$-$$$ Siboney Beach Club

Marina Bay Rd, Dickenson Bay, T268-462 0806, www.siboneybeachclub.com.

Antigua hotelier and proprietor Tony Johnson (now in his 90s) has made this one of the best small, independent places to stay and has 12 comfortable suites in a 3-storey block just back from the beach behind **Coconut Grove** restaurant (see page 59). Decor is slightly dated but each place has a bedroom, sitting room with sofa bed, kitchenette, and balcony/patio overlooking the lovely gardens with pool. Seek out Julius Caesar, the gardener who has been here for more than 30 years, as he feeds the yellow-breasted chats sugar water.

$$$ Dutchman's Bay Cottages

Dutchman's Bay Dr, Dutchman's Bay, T268-764 7333, www.dutchmansbay.com.

Very chic, quiet and relaxing, these 7 newly-built Caribbean-style whitewashed 1- and 2-bedroom cottages are directly on the beach, and have neat kitchens, no a/c but ceiling fans, shutters and a porch with hammock. Handy for the airport and owner David Fuller is a personable host. A short walk from excellent **Cecilia's High Point Café** (see page 59).

$$$ Ocean Point Resort & Spa

Hodges Bay Main Rd, Hodges Bay, T268-562 8330, www.oceanpointantigua.com. Closed Sep-Oct.

This classy resort has good hands-on Italian management, 68 smart rooms with colourful decor, balcony/terrace, and there's a vast pool and small spa area right on the sand. Rates are either B&B or inclusive of Mediterranean-style meals and some drinks at the property's super-stylish **Sottovento Beach Club** with its luxurious furnishings (open to all for lunch and dinner, or day passes are US$79, with live music at least 2 evenings a week). No under-16s.

$$$ Trade Winds Hotel

J Hadeed St, Dickenson Bay, T268-462 1223, www.twhantigua.com.

Modest hotel up on a hillside (a steep 10-min walk from the beach) offering 50 spacious rooms with sofa beds for children and a balcony/patio, in gardens shaded by bougainvillea. Not all have views, which are superb, so try and get one of the loft rooms. Small pool, shuttle service to beach, restaurant and terrace bar.

$$$-$$ Antigua Village Beach Resort

Marina Bay Rd, Dickenson Bay, T268-462 2930, www.antiguavillage.net.

This timeshare resort has around 100 self-catering units from good-value studios to 3-bedroom villas; each is individually owned and decorated and some are in better condition than others. Right on the beach, good pool, pretty gardens, close to restaurants and supermarkets; the only downside is that it suffers from noise of **Sandals Grande Antigua Resort & Spa** next door.

$$$-$$ The Northshore Residence

Hodges Bay Main Rd, Hodges Bay, T268-725 2467, www.northshoreantigua.com.

Old-fashioned hacienda-style blocks built in the 1980s, but each of the 30 well-equipped, self-catering apartments are spacious with balcony/terrace and sofa-beds and are well-priced and it's presently being refurbished. No pool but small beach, good coffee, cocktails, breakfasts and lunches, and you can eat dinner at **Sottovento Beach Club** next door or get taxis to restaurants. Rents out bikes.

$$ Dickenson Bay Cottages

Trade Winds Dr, Dickenson Bay, T268-462 4940, www.dickensonbaycottages.com.

A 7-min walk from Dickenson Bay Beach, this is a relaxed complex in gardens with a pool and ocean views. It has 14 airy 1- and 2-bedroom cottages with kitchens and living areas, pull-out sofas (US$35 per each additional person up to 4), balconies or terraces and some have loft-style bedrooms. A little kitschy with cane furniture and tropical-style fabrics, but good value and comfortable.

The southwest *map page 30.*

$$$$ Carlisle Bay Antigua

Old Rd, T268-484 0000, www.carlisle-bay.com. Tucked away on its own south coast beach in a protected pretty bay with a view of Montserrat, the 82 huge suites here all have sea views, dark wooden furniture and clean minimalist lines, patios or balconies. Breakfast and afternoon tea is included in rates, and there are 4 restaurants and bars, a cinema, library, 9 floodlit tennis courts, pool, spa, gym, a yoga pavilion, and watersports. Part of The Leading Hotels of the World group.

$$$$ Cocos Hotel Antigua

Valley Rd, Valley Church Bay, T268-460 2626, www.cocoshotel.com.
One of the more romantic all-inclusive options with 30 wooden cottages with gingerbread fretwork in a lovely location built on a bluff and arranged like a little village. Each has a gorgeous balcony, outdoor shower and hammock to enjoy the pleasant breezes and a view of Jolly Beach and Five Islands. Multi-tiered and well-regarded restaurant, **Sheer Rocks** (see page 59), pool and friendly understated service.

$$$$ Sugar Ridge Resort

Tottenham Park, off Valley Rd, T268-562 7700, www.sugarridgeantigua.com.
This refined resort is about 1 mile south of Jolly Harbour and Bolands, and has 60 airy, contemporary, and well-equipped rooms in blocks of 4, dotted around the hillside with balconies; some have plunge pools and extra high ceilings. Restaurant with a piano and bar, the lively **Sugar Club** is a chic terrace eatery serving sushi and tapas, spa, 2 pools, free beach shuttle and complimentary bikes.

$$$ Tranquility Bay Antigua

Jolly Harbour, T268-562 5183, www.tranquilitybayantigua.com.
An all 'suite' resort – but really 75 1- and 2-bedroom apartments (can be joined to make 3-bedroom) with well-equipped kitchens and balconies. Good value for a family or group, in gardens next to the beach with a lively beach bar and large pool. You can self-cater or walk to restaurants, or there's the option of an all-inclusive option whereby you get a (pricey) day pass to eat at the 5 restaurants at the **Jolly Beach Resort & Spa** next door.

$$ 3 Martini Resident Club

Valley Rd, Crab Hill, T268-460 9306, www.3martiniresidentclub.com.
Nothing to do with the drink, this budget place has 6 rooms, 3 on each floor, spacious with balconies, fans, kettle and fridge. From the 2nd floor Montserrat is visible most days and the sunsets are spectacular. Peaceful, across the road and uphill from the beach. There's a restaurant and bar for simple meals or you can walk to **Jacqui O's Beach House** (see page 59). The bus stop is nearby.

$$ CoCo Rose Guest House

Urlings, T268-562 6104, www.cocoroseguesthouse.com.
On the beautiful wild beach at Cades Bay, this delightful guesthouse is well manged by Rose and her team. The 10 spotless rooms are simple and spacious with ceiling fans, neat kitchenettes, most have balconies and breakfast is included in the rates. It's a 10-min drive south of Jolly Harbour for the supermarket and restaurants and you can also catch buses on the main road.

$$-$ Antigua Chiama Italia

Jolly Harbour, T268-783 3395, www.antiguachiamaitalia.it.
The Italian owners of this villa on the seafront street on the north side of Jolly Harbour rent out 3 rooms with shared kitchen, washing machine and a communal seating area/ veranda with TV and sea views. Like sharing a large flat, ideal for a group of friends or family, although it's a bit of walk (about 30 mins) around the bay and past the golf course to the Jolly Harbour complex for supermarket and restaurants.

$$-$ South Coast Horizon
Old Rd, T268-562 4074, www.southcoasthorizons.com.
This group of 12 timber-clad, self-catering studios and bungalows with verandas have a peaceful cottagey feel, and are set in neat gardens with a lovely little swimming pool. Extra beds for children, US$30 per night. On the bus route, about a 20-min walk to Cades Bay Beach and can organize boat trips out to Cades Reef for snorkelling.

$ Inn La Galleria
Five Islands village, T268-460 6060, www.innlagalleria.com.
On a hilltop and quite a climb up the steep driveway, this basic B&B has 12 rooms from a windowless single to a double studio, with worn fixtures and fittings. Mosquitos are a problem. However, owner Gregory is helpful, it's a 10-min bus ride from St John's, and the redeeming highlight is the spectacular view from the rooftop terrace/breakfast room across to Deep Bay and Fort Barrington.

The southeast *map page 40.*

$$$$ South Point
Falmouth Harbour, T268-562 9600, www.southpointantigua.com.
A recently opened super-stylish (and expensive) group of 23 1- and 2-bedroom apartments, luxurious contemporary furnishings, designer kitchens (groceries can be delivered), stunning pool overlooking a small strip of beach, upstairs cocktail lounge with chilled music, gourmet restaurant on deck suspended over the water with stainless steel open kitchen, sushi bar and moorings for dinghies (open to all, 0700-2230). SUPs and kayaks available and by the time you read this the spa and gym will be open.

$$$$-$$$ Admiral's Inn & Gunpowder House
Nelson's Dockyard, English Harbour, T268-460 1027, www.admiralsantigua.com.
This Georgian brick building dating from 1788 was once a store room for pitch, turpentine and lead, while upstairs were the offices for Royal Navy engineers. It features hand-hewn beams, wrought-iron chandeliers and a bar which was an old work bench scarred by the names of ships that once docked here. New suites have been added in the converted Gunpowder House on the point opposite, where there's also an infinity pool. Excellent location, good food in the **Pillars Restaurant** overlooking the water, and dinghy service to the beach in the outer harbour and across to Gunpowder House.

$$$$-$$$ Galleon Beach Resort
English Harbour, T268-562 7814, www.galleon-beach-antigua.com. Closed 1 May-1 Nov.
On the beach at Freemans Bay, 31 comfortable self-catering cottages and villas in different styles with an additional sofa bed and veranda. Quality and price vary from a simple 1-bed unit from US$175 to a 4-bed villa at US$1000; good weekly rates. Spacious grounds, glorious views, **Roxy's Beach Bar & Grill**, ferry (0900-1700) and later water taxis to restaurants at Nelson's Dockyard.

$$$ Antigua Yacht Club Marina & Resort
Falmouth Harbour, T268-460 6910, www.aycmarina.com.
The 30 studio apartments with kitchens and 19 hotel rooms are on the hillside above the Antigua Yacht Club Marina and are popular with sailors and those wanting to experience the yachting scene. Modern and well-equipped, most have balconies and fantastic views over Falmouth Harbour, there's a spa and **Cloggy's Café** is opposite in the marina building (see page 60). No pool but a 10-min walk or free shuttle by golf cart to Pigeon Beach.

$$$ Copper & Lumber Store Hotel
Also see page 42, Nelson's Dockyard, English Harbour, T268-460 1058, www.copperandlumberhotel.com.
A former 18th-century storehouse for shipbuilding materials built in 1789 for the Royal Navy, this delightful Georgian-style

hotel has 14 studios and suites, each named after one of Lord Nelson's ships, well-restored features and decorative touches include sash windows, period furnishings, wood-beamed ceilings, and exposed stone and brick. There's a polished restaurant with terrace and a traditional British pub popular with the yacht crowd (see page 60).

$$ The Ocean Inn

Turn uphill off Dockyard Dr between Falmouth and English Harbours, T268-463 7950, www.theoceaninn.com.

On a hillside with a spectacular and breezy view of the yachts and old buildings and a small pool. A rather haphazard appearance of rooms, having been built below the main house when the owner felt like it, but are adequate and well-priced, 2 of the cheaper rooms in the main house share a bathroom. Breakfast is included, honesty bar, friendly owner, and a 5-min walk down the hill to restaurants and bars.

$$-$ The Lodge Antigua

Dockyard Dr, Falmouth Harbour, T268-562 8060, www.thelodgeantigua.com.

In the grounds of the National Sailing Academy; sailing courses, kayaking and stand-up paddle-boarding can be arranged. There are 5 budget rooms with shared bathrooms, and 2 self-contained apartments with kitchenettes, a garden, barbecue, terrace with views, and the **Academy Café** offers all meals and has a lively bar. Minimum 2-night stay.

$ The Waterfront Hostel

Dockyard Dr, Falmouth Harbour, T268-460 6575, www.caribbean-hostels.com. Closed 30 Apr-1 Jul.

Popular with yacht crews from all over the world, this great hostel offers 10 clean, comfortable rooms sleeping up to 3; US$45/65/85 for 1/2/3 people, and a 5-bed dorm room with bunks; US$25 per person, each with a shower and sink and the toilets are down the hall. The highlight is the long open lounge/bar/restaurant at the front on the main street which is a fantastic place to socialize. Reserve (and pay a deposit) well in advance in high season.

The east and northeast *map page 30.*

$$$$ Nonsuch Bay Resort

Nonsuch Bay, T268-562 8000, www.nonsuchbayresort.com.

In a secluded part of the east side of Antigua, 62 spacious, comfortable and well-equipped apartments, villas and cottages in a contemporary style with vaulted ceilings and tiled roofs on a hillside, all with sea views and kitchens. The beach is man-made and there is sea grass on the seabed, but there are 3 swimming pools and a sailing and kiteboarding school suitable for all ages and abilities. Though the restaurant is excellent, other dining options are limited due to the resort's remote location and Harmony Hall and Half Moon Bay are a taxi ride away.

$$ Ellen Bay Inn

Seatons, T268-561 6826, www.ellenbayinn.com.

A small, family-run village inn in the northeast and a short drive to the nearest beaches with 6 rooms, simple but comfortable, good views from upstairs, restaurant downstairs for all meals (order dinner by 1600). Also runs **Ellen Bay Cottages** in Seatons village; 5 self-catering units with 1 or 2 bedrooms (www.ellenbaycottages.com). Taxis, car and bicycle hire can be arranged.

$$ Wind Chimes Inn

Sir George Walter Hwy, Carlisle, T268-728 2917, www.windchimesinnantigua.com.

Unremarkable but well-run airport hotel opposite the runway (plane-spotters will love the views from the balconies), convenient if you have a delayed flight, aircraft noise during the day but no flights at night. The 7 rooms are non-seasonal at US$95 B&B, a cold breakfast is delivered to the door, there are tea and coffee facilities and fridge in reception for cold beers and soft drinks.

ON THE ROAD

All-inclusive options on Antigua

There are numerous all-inclusive resorts around the coast of Antigua, most of which sit on beautiful beaches and have one or more swimming pools and (non-motorized) watersports. Most packages provide three meals a day, an afternoon snack, appetizers at cocktail hour, and non-alcoholic and house drinks. Breakfast and lunch are normally buffets, while the evening meal might be a themed buffet, barbecue, or a set menu with three or four choices; the larger resorts have up to several restaurants and bars.

They vary in price considerably; at the cheaper end of the scale they might be sprawling properties which might feature blocky-style rooms and mediocre meals, and at the top end, intimate luxury hideaways with stylish interiors and gourmet food. However, unless you eat and drink a lot, their value is not always any greater than paying for meals as you go, some of them can be rather soulless places where you will only mix with guests of one nationality (depending on where the resort is marketed), many of whom may not even leave the property for their entire holiday, the food may start to look and taste similar after a few days, and any extras (boat trips, spa treatments, airport transfers and the like) will be at a very high price.

If all-inclusive does appeal Antigua offers more choice than many other Caribbean islands, and they vary in level of luxury, character and style. Examples include:

Curtain Bluff Resort, Old Road, www.curtainbluff.com.
Galley Bay Resort & Spa, Five Islands, www.galleybayresort.com.
Grand Pineapple Beach Antigua, Long Bay, www.grandpineapple.com.
Halcyon Cove by Rex Resorts, Dickenson Bay, www.rexresorts.com.
Hawksbill by Rex Resorts, Five Islands, www.rexresorts.com.
Hermitage Bay Antigua, Five Islands, www.hermitagebay.com.
Jolly Beach Resort & Spa, Jolly Beach, www.jollybeachresort.com.
Jumby Bay, A Rosewood Resort, Long Island, www.rosewood hotels.com.
Sandals Grande Antigua Resort & Spa, Dickenson Bay, www.sandals.com.
St James's Club, Five Islands, www.stjamesclubantigua.com.
The Verandah Resort & Spa, Long Bay, www.verandahresort andspa.com.

$$-$ Lamblion Holiday Apartments
Freemans Village Main Rd, T268-764 2642, www.lamblionapt.com.
This bright blue block in pretty flowering gardens has 11 simply furnished but neat studios, 1- and 2-bedroom units. Geographically right in the centre of the island, so a 15-min drive to beaches and restaurants, or a short walk to bus stop, run by charismatic husband and wife team Lionel and Lorilyn who will pick up from the airport and take you to get groceries.

Barbuda *map page 48.*
A new lease is presently being negotiated by a consortium that includes actor Robert De Niro and Australian tycoon James Packer to redevelop the site of the former **K Club** in the south of the island; a once-exclusive resort favoured by celebrities (including Princess Diana) which has been closed since 2004. Several private homes offer accommodation, although these change if a long-term rental is taken. See www. barbudaful.net for further options.

$$$$ Barbuda Belle
Cedar Tree Point, T268-783 4779, www.barbudabelle.com. Closed 1 Sep-1 Nov.
The newest property on the island which opened in 2015 in a stunning isolated beach location on Low Bay among the mangroves, and is accessed by boat across Codrington Lagoon. The 7 spacious wooden bungalows are elevated above the sand and have 4-poster beds with the a/c in them allowing you to sleep with all the windows open, one has 2 bedrooms/bathrooms, French gourmet cuisine in the open-sided restaurant/bar, watersports include kayaking, snorkelling and sunset boat rides.

$$$$ Barbuda Cottages
Spanish Well Point, T268-720 3050, www.barbudacottages.com. Closed 1 Aug-1 Nov.
On a glorious stretch of the Pink Sand Beach next to **Uncle Roddy's Bar,** these 2 solar-powered rental self-catering properties (one with 3 bedrooms/2 bathrooms; another 1-bed cottage) are built on stilts in the sand in an idyllic position and are very homely and comfortable with a veranda for sunset watching. Tours, activities and car hire can be arranged by owner, Kelcina Burton-George.

$$$$ Coco Point Lodge
In the far south, T268-462 3816, www.cocopoint.com. Closed 1 May-3 Dec.
A hideaway since the 1960s and the ultimate in exclusivity, set on a stunning white-sand beach in Coco Bay, it occupies 164 acres of the peninsula at the tip of Barbuda. There are 34 rooms either in the main building with shady verandas or cottages of different sizes with high ceilings, living room, bar and a beachfront patio. Service is attentive and caring, rates are all-inclusive and include transfers to its private airstrip from Antigua by 6-seater plane, all food and drinks, and watersports.

$$$$ Lighthouse Bay Resort
Low Bay, T1-877-766 6718 toll-free, www.lighthousebayresort.com.
Sandwiched on the thinnest ribbon of land between the Low Bay beach on the Caribbean and the Codrington Lagoon, this small resort with just 9 sumptuous villas surrounding the swimming pool has a tranquil and beautiful location, accessible only by helicopter or by boat. Comfortable with all modern amenities, tennis, some spa services, beach bar, watersports and horse riding, the food is of gourmet standard, and service is excellent.

$$$$ North Beach
Goat Island, T268-721 3317, www.barbudanorthbeach.com.
The 4 comfortable whitewashed cottages on stilts make up this isolated hideaway on the northern tip of the island accessible only by boat. Owner Reuben James keeps it low key and rustic (no Wi-Fi or TV), and it will appeal to those who want to escape modern life and do nothing except explore the beautiful beach and reef. Food is good, staff very accommodating and snorkelling gear and kayaks are available. Rates include meals and soft drinks but not alcoholic beverages; 3-night minimum stay.

$$-$ Bus Stop Guest House
Codrington, T268-721 2796, lyntonthomas@ymail.com.
Lynton Thomas's guest house is located near the centre of Codrington village, close to (as the name suggests) the bus stop. There are 3 doubles with private bathroom and reliable hot water, and the little bar serves tasty fried chicken, burgers and ice cream, and breakfast and other meals to order; on Sat afternoons he grills fish and lobster. Thomas (as he's known) is very friendly and offers taxi tours of the island.

$ Palm Tree Guesthouse
Codrington, T268-722 5496.
Cerene Deazle runs this basic but comfortable guesthouse about 15 mins' walk from Codrington village centre, set in pretty gardens and the porch is good

for relaxing. All 8 rooms are spacious and clean and have private bathroom, fridge, kettle and 2 connect to make a family unit. Meals available from **Cerene's** bakery and restaurant in the village.

Restaurants

VAT on restaurant bills is 15%, but this is nearly always included in menu prices, but 10% service charge is usually added to the bill.

St John's *map page 32.*

$$ Papa Zouk Fish 'n' Rum
Hilda Davis Dr, off Dickenson Bay St, T268-464 0795. Mon-Sat 1900-2130, bar later.
Unprepossessing place in a rustic house in a leafy side street on the outskirts of St John's, known for its specialities of bouillabaisse, a meal in itself, paella Creole, fresh fish and seafood, although chicken and meat is also available and vegetarian food on request. Congenial host, Bert Kirchner, considers this a rum shop with food, and there's a huge selection of rum.

$$-$ Café Napoleon
Redcliffe Quay, T268-562 1802, www.historicredcliffequay.com. Mon-Thu and Sat 0830-1630, Fri 0830-2200, closed Aug.
In the middle of Redcliffe Quay with pavement tables, a good spot for casual breakfast and lunch, from fry-ups and filled croissants to wraps and grilled fish, and drinks include frozen rum and coffee cocktails and milkshakes. Popular with islanders as well as visitors

$$-$ Hemingway's Caribbean Café
St Mary's St, T268-462 2763, www.hemingwayantigua.com. Mon-Sat 0930-2200.
This green-and-white painted breezy restaurant is upstairs in a typical wooden West Indian house, built in 1829, with views on to Heritage and Redcliffe quays. Breakfasts, burgers, sandwiches, salads, fresh seafood, extensive range of island dishes, desserts and cocktails including their Antigua black pineapple daiquiri.

$ Fred's Belgian Waffles & Ice Cream
Redcliffe Quay, T268-460 7025. Mon-Sat 1000-2200, Sun 1500-2100.
Another of several eateries in Redcliff Quay, and considered one of the best ice cream bars on the island. Lots of rich and creamy flavours, as well as sorbets, waffles, frozen drinks and coffee. There's a cute little terrace to watch the cruise ships.

$ Lion Pavilion
East Bus Station, off Independence Av, T268-771 4803, see Facebook. Mon-Sat 0900-1700.
This family-run brightly painted wooden eatery serves healthy and colourful vegetarian and vegan food to takeaway or eat in on the shaded deck. Lots of variety, menu changes daily depending on what is fresh and available, but might include veggie lasagne, pizza or roti, black bean burgers, fried cassava balls or chickpea curry. Great juices and desserts too such as sweet potato pudding.

$ Roti King
Corner St Mary's St and Corn Alley, T268-462 2328. Mon-Thu 0930-2400, Fri-Sat 0930-0200.
Good friendly place to come for a filling lunch with really good roti (beef, chicken, shrimp, pork or veggie) with rice, salad and homemade juices, popular with school children and office workers. Limited seating at lunch but you can get a takeaway.

The northwest and north *map page 30.*

$$$ La Bussola
Rush Night Club Rd, Runaway Bay, T268-462 8433, www.labussolarestaurant.net. Daily except Tue 1830-2300.
Fine Italian dining in a lovely beachfront garden, with a shaded gazebo and comfortable loungers. Pricey, but the concise menu offers specialities like lobster thermidor served with saffron sauce, pan-fried jumbo shrimps, meat and vegetarian choices, and tiramisu for dessert.

$$$ Le Bistro

Hodges Bay, T268-462 3881, www.antigualebistro.com. Tue-Sun 1830-2230. Reservations required.

One of the best restaurants on the island with elegant interiors, romantic ambience, polished and personalized service and excellent French food prepared by head chef Patrick Gauducheau. The menu includes duck, lamb and lobster, vegetarian options and melt-in-the-mouth pastries, with an excellent wine list of French vintages and champagne.

$$$-$$ Ana's On The Beach

Dickenson Bay, T268-562 8562, www.anas.ag. Daily 1100 2300, closed 1 Sep-15 Oct.

In a great location, right on Dickenson Bay beach, adjacent to **Antigua Village Beach Resort**, very stylish with day beds that have curtains and cushions, an elegant wooden deck, and all-white decor. Wines, cocktails and coffees and a Mediterranean menu of seafood, grills and vegetarian options and plates of 'Anapasti' to snack on at sunset.

$$$-$$ Cecilia's High Point Café

Dutchman's Bay, T268-562 7070, www.highpointantigua.com. Mon, Thu 1200-2100, Fri-Sun 1200-1600, closed Tue and Wed and late Jun to late Oct.

Traditional-style wooden house with tables on the veranda, sun loungers on the beach and free Wi-Fi. This is a great place to come for the day, shower off the sand and have a long, leisurely lunch or romantic dinner. Many come here before catching their flight home as it is only 5 mins from the airport. Daily specials always include fresh fish, home-made pasta and delicious desserts. Reservations recommended.

$$ Coconut Grove

In front of Siboney Beach Club, Dickenson Bay, T268-462 1538, www.coconutgroveantigua.com. Daily 0700-2300.

On the beach with a typically Caribbean feel, very popular with resort guests from Dickenson Bay for its lively atmosphere and busy bar with good rum punches and cocktails. The menu includes seafood, steak and chicken or lighter meals such as club sandwiches or burgers; all pretty standard (with plenty of chips) but good enough for a beach lunch.

The southwest *map page 30.*

$$$ Sheer Rocks

Cocos Hotel Antigua, Valley Rd, Valley Church Bay, T268-464 5283, www.sheer-rocks.com. Tapas daily from 1200-sunset, à la carte dinner Mon-Sat 1800-2100.

The tiered pavilions here with day beds and a plunge pool are perched on rocks in a sunset-facing setting with waves splashing below, ideal for a leisurely lunch or romantic evening meal. Very high standard of Mediterranean and Cajun cuisine and the large plates of tapas at lunch are ideal to share. Reservations required.

$$$-$$ Jacqui O's Beach House

Crab Hill, T268-562 2218, see Facebook. Tue-Sun 1000-2000, lunch 1230-1630, closed late-Aug to late-Oct.

Excellent setting on the beach with a chilled Caribbean vibe and seating in the restaurant, at the bar or picnic tables on the sand. Bar snacks and platters to share and more sophisticated main dishes like fish bouillabaisse or whole red snapper plus a good wine and cocktail list. Luxurious beach sofas to relax on after your meal.

$$ Boxer Shack

Old Rd, T268-723 5143, see Facebook. Wed-Sat 1100-2200, Sun 1100-1800, closed early May to mid-Sep.

Located right between Carlisle Bay and Curtain Bluff resorts, with stunning views over the Caribbean, this offers good seafood, salads, steaks and curries, and a Sun lunchtime roast; booking advised. They also have a good selection of aged rums and wines. Car park and moorings for yachts, and access to the beach with sun loungers.

$$-$ Dennis Cocktail Bar & Restaurant
Ffryes Point, off Valley Rd, near Cocos Hotel Antigua, T268-462 6740, www.dennis antigua.com. Nov-Mar daily, Apr-Oct Tue-Sun 1030-2100.
In a pretty spot on a low headland between Ffryes and Jolly beaches, and owned by Dennis Thomas who is the chief cook serving up a mix of local fare and international dishes; try his saltfish, curried goat and Johnny cakes, plus there's lobster, garlic shrimp, catch of the day, and grilled chicken and pork chops. He also hosts a regular pig roast on Sun afternoons. The 3 breezy wooden decks are great sunset vantage points.

$$-$ OJ's Bar & Restaurant
Crab Hill, T268-460 0184, see Facebook. Daily 1000-2200.
Charming husband and wife team Oliver and Angie have built up an established following for their well-priced simple food including a tasty lobster salad, grilled red snapper, garlic shrimps, home-made burgers and sandwiches. Shady terrace right on the beach decorated with driftwood and shells, and a live band on Sun afternoon in high season.

The southeast *map page 40.*

$$$-$$ Abracadabra
Dockyard Dr, English Harbour, T268-460 2701, www.theabracadabra.com. Daily 1000-1500 and 1800-0100, closed mid-Jun to mid-Nov.
Firmly established Italian restaurant and bar close to the entrance of Nelson's Dockyard, has a café menu for late breakfasts and lunch, then a more sophisticated menu for dinner until 2300 with home-made pasta, seafood and steak, and serves pizzas until 0100. Pumping with the yacht crowd in high season when there's usually outside dancing on a white-sand dance floor under illuminated palm trees.

$$$-$$ Catherine's Café Plage
Pigeon Point Beach, Falmouth Harbour, T268-460 5050, www.catherinescafe.com. Wed-Mon 1200-1900 for lunch and tapas until sunset, Wed and Fri 1200-2200 for dinner too, closed 1 Jun-12 Nov.
In a beautiful setting in a plantation-style house right on the water overlooking the harbour, this offers an inventive menu of predominantly French bistro-style dishes, tapas and seafood. There's live jazz on Wed evening and an additional gourmet set dinner menu on Fri.

$$$-$ Copper & Lumber Store Hotel
Nelson's Dockyard, T268-460 1058, www.copperandlumberhotel.com. Daily 1200-2200, no lunch Fri.
With great historical character, the more formal **Wardroom** restaurant is in a charming dining room opening out to a courtyard filled with bougainvillea, while light meals are served in the **Mainbrace Pub** with a shaded patio overlooking the yachts in English Harbour. A good choice of international cuisine mixed with Caribbean staples. Seafood Fri from 1900 is a popular event; make a reservation.

$$ Cloggy's Café
At the Antigua Yacht Club Marina, Falmouth Harbour, T268-460 6910, www.aycmarina. com. Tue-Sat 1200-1630, Wed-Sat 1830-2130, bar 1200-late, closed Jul-Aug.
Located on upper floor decks and popular with the sailing fraternity for its convenient location and hearty food. Stunning views over the yachts in Falmouth Harbour and always lively and fun. Happy hour 1630-1800.

$$ Club Sushi
Next to and run by the Antigua Yacht Club Marina, Falmouth Harbour, T268-562 8512, see Facebook. Daily 1100-2200.
Great view of the yachts in the basin below from the upper deck, freshly made sushi with tempura ice cream for dessert, plus a steak and grill menu including surf and turf and catch of the day. Quiz night Wed at 1900.

$$ Trappas Restaurant & Bar

Dockyard Drive, English Harbour, T268-562 3534, see Facebook. Mon-Sat 1600-2300, bar later, closed Mon in summer.

On the way to Nelson's Dockyard, lively spot with street side terrace and great food in big portions at good prices (main meals are US$19 plus tax), from sautéed mussels to Cajun grouper.

The east and northeast *map page 30.*

$$$ Harmony Hall

Brown's Bay Mill, Nonsuch Bay, T268-460 4120, www.harmonyhallantigua.com. Tue-Sun 1200-1530, Wed-Sat 1930-2200, closed early May to 3rd week in Nov.

Old plantation house and sugar mill dating back to 1843 and now a restaurant, art gallery and hotel, reached via long dirt road or by boat to their dock. It's worth it though for a long relaxed lunch on the patio overlooking Nonsuch Bay and Green Island. Excellent (and expensive) gourmet Italian, with creative antipasti, home-made pasta, lobster, tuna, pork belly, and some gooey desserts. The 6 rooms here (**$$$**) are in 2 separate villas, and the pool, beach and complimentary boat trips to Green Island are offered to diners and hotel guests. Reservations essential.

Barbuda *map page 48.*

Eating out is limited to just a handful of places outside the resorts. Always phone in advance or call earlier in the day if you want an evening meal as most places open only on demand and they will need to get enough food in for your visit. Transport can sometimes be arranged at the same time. In Codrington look out for street food from vendors including bread pudding, meatballs, fried chicken and fish, patties and Johnny cakes.

$$$-$$ Outback

Low Bay, T268-721 3280/721 1972.

Simply furnished informal beach bar and grill restaurant in a wonderful location on Palm Beach and only accessible by boat across the lagoon, popular for lunch on people on day tours or you can arrange lunch or dinner any time, usually lobster, fish or chicken with rice, salad, garlic bread and plantains. Book in advance and allow time relax on the beach with a cocktail after dining or owner brothers Jala and Calvin can take you by boat to the Frigate Bird Sanctuary. Reservations only.

$$$-$$ Uncle Roddy's Beach Bar & Grill

Spanish Well Point, next to Barbuda Cottages, T268-785 3268.

Advance bookings required to make sure that Roddy is there and cooking. Laid-back, island style, in a green and white wooden building on the beach and delicious food including lobster and barbecue chicken, served with rice and peas, and washed down with rum punch or cold beer. Roddy is full of stories and will pick you up if you wish.

$$$-$ ArtCafé

Two Foot Bay Rd, Codrington, T268-460 0434, see Facebook. Mon-Sat 1100-2100.

Owner, author and artist Claire Frank runs this café, gift shop and art gallery. There are teas, juices, coffee and cake, and a lunchtime dish of the day at lunchtime, as well as excellent pre-booked suppers like fresh fish, lobster, venison, local lamb and pork, and vegetarian options. Friendly and informative hosts. Crafts for sale, including Claire's silk paintings and hand painted T-shirts.

$$-$ It's a Bit Fishy

River Rd, Codrington, T268-772 3525, www.itsabitfishy.com. Tue-Sat from 1700, reservations required.

With tables and sofas in a reed hut or on the sand, this beach bar and grill is run by Arthur and Rosalind and serves fish, lobster, conch, burgers, some vegetarian pasta dishes and cocktails, but you must phone ahead during the week. Fri-Sat get quite lively when there is often karaoke sessions in the evening. Arthur can organize fishing trips.

Bars and clubs

Antigua

Many restaurants and beach bars are venues for evening drinking, some of which have live music in high season. The website of **Antigua Nice** (www.antiguanice.com) has daily listings of what's on.

BeachLimerZ

Fort James Beach, T268-562 8574, www.beachlimerz.com. Daily 1100-late.

Attractive wooden beach bar, popular with Antiguans as well as visitors, great cocktails and other drinks, good and reasonably priced food, Sat local soups when you can try goat water, bull foot or pigtail soup, Sun barbecue from 1300, happy hour Mon-Fri 1700-1900.

C & C Wine House

Redcliff Quay, St John's, T268-460 7025, www.ccwinehouse.com. Mon 1000-1700, Tue-Sat 1000-2300.

Named after owners Cutie and Claudine, this wine bar and bistro serves finger food, soups, salads and pastas in a historic building, with South African wines. It's very popular with the local professional crowd and shoppers as well as tourists. Thu is lasagne night, and there's karaoke on Sat.

Castaways

South Beach, Jolly Harbour, T268-562 4446. Daily 0800-2400.

With free sun loungers, volleyball and showers, this rustic beach bar is popular with Jolly Harbour residents and **Jolly Beach Resort & Spa** guests. It serves steak and fish (though a tad overpriced). Mon is Caribbean Night with a live band and specials like pepperpot and jerk pork, and Fri is a barbecue with a bonfire, DJ and dancing. Plus there's a children's playground and kiddies menu. Happy hour 1630-1830.

Life on the Corner

Corner Dockyard Dr and road to Antigua Yacht Club Marina, Falmouth Harbour, T268-562 8073, see Facebook. Tue-Sat 1700-0100.

In the heart of things in Falmouth Harbour, there's always a good atmosphere in this eclectic bar, with sofas to kick back on with a cocktail. The music volume increases around 2200 for dancing, and there's a good selection of burgers, kebabs and nachos (1800-2130). If the harbour's full of yachts, there are regular Sun roasts and party nights (including dress-up) when it's simply humming. Happy hour 1700-1900.

Millers by the Sea

Fort James Beach, T268-462 9414, see Facebook. Daily 0900-2300.

Beach bar with changing rooms and showers, serving breakfast, lunch and dinner. There's not a tremendous choice and dishes can take a long time, but there's often seafood including snapper, lobster and shrimps. On Sun there's a buffet of grilled lamb, chicken and fish (1130-1630). Background music is usually reggae, and sometimes has live bands with dancing on the sand. Happy hour Mon-Fri 1700-1900.

Putters Bar and Grill

Marina Bay Rd, Dickenson Bay, T268-463 4653. Mon-Sat 1700-0200.

At the back of the beach at Dickenson Bay, this casual open-air bar is popular with resort guests who can bring their children thanks to the mini crazy golf course and jungle gym, plus pinball and pool tables for teenagers. Nightly specials vary from hot dogs and burgers to T-bone steaks and shrimps, at reasonable prices. There's also football on TV, and quiz and bingo nights. Happy hour 1800-1900.

Entertainment

Antigua
Casinos

Grand Bay Casino, *Dickenson Bay, T268-481 7700, www.thegrandbaycasino.com.* A huge glitzy property at the back of **Sandals**, which opened in early 2016. Slot machines, table games and bar. Irregular opening times and inexperienced management and staff.

ON THE ROAD

Shirley Heights Sunday Party

The biggest event on the island for more than 30 years is held at the Shirley Heights Lookout bar and restaurant (T268-728 0636, www.shirleyheightslookout.com), which has a phenomenal view overlooking both English Harbour and Falmouth Harbour, dotted with yachts, and faces due west for the sunset.

On Sunday an excellent foot-tapping steelpan band plays 1600-1900, followed by an equally good reggae band 1900-2200; it's very loud, very busy, very infectious, and everyone gets up to dance on the outdoor paved area in front of the historical battery. It's touristy; buses bring guests from resorts around the island, it's heaving during big yachting events, and is drunken and rowdy after the rum punch has flowed for a while. But it's also one of Antigua's must-dos and tremendous fun for both visitors and locals, who usually come up later to see the reggae band as it attracts some of the best performers in the Caribbean.

Entry is US$7.40, and food is a barbecue, from US$9 per plate, with a choice of burgers (meat, vegetarian or fish), jerk chicken or saucy ribs. To get there independently, you'll have to get a taxi up to Shirley Heights; about US$11 from Falmouth Harbour. Plenty of taxis wait at the top to take people down (though you may have to locate the drivers on the dancefloor).

King's Casino, *Heritage Quay, St John's, T268-462 1727, www.kingscasino.com. Mon-Sat 1000-0200, Sun 1800-0200.* Popular with cruise ship passengers with table games, 250 slots and a lounge/bar area with live entertainment on Fri and Sat nights.

Cinemas

Caribbean Cinemas, *Antigua Megaplex 8, Friars Hill Rd, T268-562 4000, www.caribbeancinemas.com.* Next to the big branch of **Epicurean Fine Foods**, this complex has 8 screens showing movies daily 1400-2100.

Deluxe Cinema, *corner High and Cross streets, St John's, T268-462 3664, www.deluxecinemas.com.* 3 screens showing the latest releases daily at 2030.

Festivals

Antigua

Jun Antigua & Barbuda Sport Fishing Club Tournament, usually the 1st weekend, Nelson's Dockyard, www.antiguabarbudasportsfishing.com. Deep-sea fishing over 3 days including the Marlin Classic, culminating in an awards ceremony and party. All the fish is also for sale from stalls.

Shopping

Antigua

Redcliffe Quay (www.historicredcliffequay.com) and Heritage Quay (www.heritagequayantigua.com) in St John's have numerous shops for the cruise ship market selling tacky arts and crafts, souvenirs and duty-free items. Opening hours vary, but they'll all be open any day when a ship is in port.

Art and crafts

Fig Tree Studio Art Gallery, *Fig Tree Drive, John Hughes village, T268-460 1234, www.figtreestudioart.com. Nov-Jun Mon-Sat 0930-1730.* The studio and gallery of sculptor Sallie Harker (www.sallieharker.com) showcasing lots of local and regional art and crafts.

Harmony Hall, *Brown's Bay Mill, near Freetown, T268-460 4120, www.harmonyhallantigua.com. Nov-Apr daily 1000-1800.* An art gallery and gift shop, exhibiting and

ON THE ROAD

Spirited

One of Antigua's live bands on the circuit is Spirited, a party band playing everything from soca, calypso, reggae, R&B and other popular styles. They include rhythm guitarist (Sir) Richie Richardson and bass guitarist Curtly Ambrose, better known to the world as famous ex-West Indies cricketers. They often play during Antigua Sailing Week (see Festivals, page 12), cricket events, for private parties and at some of the resorts; regular venues include the Shirley Heights Sunday Party, the Sottovento Beach Club in Hodges Bay and the King's Casino in St John's. T268-726 5098, or see Facebook for gig information.

selling paintings, sculpture and crafts from leading Caribbean artists, plus a line of locally made natural body care products like oils and soaps, popular for a lunch stop (see Restaurants, above) while touring by car or yacht.

Rhythm of Blue Art Gallery, *Dockyard Dr, English Harbour, T268-562 2230, www.rhythmofblue.com. Mid-Nov to mid-May, Mon-Sat 1000-1800, by appointment only in summer.* The gallery and studio of Antigua-born Nancy Nicholson who specializes in ceramics and also sells artwork and hand-crafted jewellery from other local artists. Most pieces and the shop have an ocean-inspired theme.

Sarah Fuller's Pottery Shop, *Redcliffe Quay, St John's, T268-462 5503, www.sarahfullerpottery.com. Mon-Fri 0930-1600.* Lovely pottery and interesting designs by Sarah Fuller, hand crafted using local clay while some of the glazes use ash from Montserrat's volcano. You can visit the studio on the beach, 2 miles north of the airport. It's well signposted, and they will make anything to order. Her work is also exhibited at Harmony Hall and some hotel gift shops.

Food

Epicurean Fine Foods, *Friar's Hill Rd, next to Caribbean Cinemas, T268-484 5400. Daily 0700-2300; Jolly Harbour Marina near the main entrance, T268-481 5480, daily 0700-2100, www.epicureanantigua.com.* Antigua's largest and most extensive supermarket, with pharmacies, deli and bakery, hot food to go, beer, wine, and liquor, yacht provisioning, and also have ATMs.

First Choice Supermarket, *Anchorage Rd, T268-463 3663. Mon-Sat 0800-1900, Sun 0800-1300.* Stocks a good variety of goods, including fresh fish, meat, bread, booze and fruit and vegetables, and is the nearest large supermarket to Dickenson Bay.

St John's Market, *Valley Rd, opposite West Street Bus Station. Mon-Sat 0530-1500.* Also known as Heritage Market, this large covered complex is busiest on Sat mornings when local villagers come in to sell their fruit and vegetables and additional stalls spring up on the streets outside. Look out for breadfruit, mangoes, soursops, sugar apples, pineapples, dasheen and tamarind; if you don't recognize them, just ask the friendly vendors.

Barbuda

For arts and crafts visit the **Artcafé** (see page 61). There are several small shops in Codrington that sell a range of things from hardware to food and drink. But supplies often sell out and are more expensive than Antigua, given that most things have to be imported on the ferry or on small weekly cargo boats.

Lil Lincs Plus, *on the main street in Codrington, T268-460 0080. Mon-Sat 0800-1700, Sun 0900-1300.* Has most groceries including cold drinks, fresh fruit and vegetables, frozen meat, butter, milk, cheese and yoghurt, and you can top up your phone here too.

What to do

Antigua

Cricket

Cricket is the national sport and Antigua has produced many famous cricketers, including captains of the West Indies team Sir Viv Richards and Sir Richie Richardson, and fast bowlers Sir Andy Roberts and Sir Curtly Ambrose.

Sir Vivian Richards Cricket Stadium, *Sydney Walling Hwy, between St John's and the airport.* This was built for the Cricket World Cup in 2007, and was named after Viv Richards, the 'Master Blaster', who ranks among the greatest cricketers of all time with an international career spanning from 1974 to 1991. In the Test against England in 2015, the north and south ends were renamed after Sir Curtly Ambrose and Sir Andy Roberts. It is a multi-purpose stadium, but used principally for cricket with a practice pitch, training infrastructure, a media centre and underground tunnels for the players to use. Matches are helped along by lots of music and entertainment. For fixtures, contact the **West Indies Cricket Board**, T268-460 5462, www.windiescricket.com.

Diving

The southern and eastern coasts of Antigua are surrounded by shelfs, providing excellent conditions for shallow diving and snorkelling. There is little or no current in most places, and visibility ranges from 50 to 140 ft. Popular sites are Cades Reef, which runs for 2½ miles along the leeward side of the island, and the wreck of the *Andes*, a 3-masted merchant ship that sank in 1905 and now rests at less than 30 ft in (ironically) Deep Bay. Many dive shops are at the resorts. Expect to pay US$70-95 for a single dive, US$110 for a 2-tank dive, US$135 for PADI Discover Scuba Diving and US$550 for a PADI Open Water course. Discounts are available for several dives over 3-5 days.

Antigua Scuba School, *Urlings, T268-785 8436, www.antiguascubaschool.com.*

Dive Carib, *National Sailing Academy, Dockyard Dr, Falmouth Harbour, T268-732 3475, www.divecarib.com.*

Dockyard Divers, *Nelson's Dockyard, English Harbour, T268-729 3040, www.dockyard-divers.com.*

Indigo Divers, *Jolly Harbour Marina, T268-562 3483, www.indigo-divers.com.*

Jolly Dive, *on the beach in front of Jolly Beach Resort & Spa, T268-462 8305, www.jollydive.com.*

Fishing

Deep-sea game fishing charters can be arranged for marlin, sailfish, wahoo, tuna, mahi mahi and barracuda for about US$450 for 4 hrs, US$680 for 6 hrs and US$800 for 8 hrs, plus a tip, for a maximum of 6 people; good for beginners or experienced fishermen.

Antigua Fly Fishing & Light Tackle Charters, *Cades Bay, T268-560 4354, www.antigua-flyfishing.com.* This outfit specializes in saltwater fly fishing for jacks, tarpons and bonefish by wading or small inflatable boats; from US$250 for 2 anglers for 4 hrs.

Antigua Sport Fishing Charters, *T268-464 7112, Jolly Harbour, www.fishingantigua.com.*

Nightwing Charters, *Jolly Harbour, T268-464 4665, www.fishantigua.com.*

Overdraft, *English Harbour, T268-720 4954, www.antiguafishing.com.*

Golf

Cedar Valley Golf Club, *off Friars Hill Rd, near St John's, T268-462 0161, www.cedarvalleygolf.ag.* An 18-hole, par-70 championship course which sometimes gets dried out but has pleasant coastal views. There is a driving range and pros are available. Green fees are US$60 for 18 holes, weekly rates available and clubs and carts can be rented, and there's a good restaurant/bar (0800-2000). The Antigua Open is played here in Nov.

Jolly Harbour Golf Club, *T268-462 7771, www.jollyharbourantigua.com/golf.* A par-71 championship course in a parkland setting with sea and beach views and 7 lakes designed by Karl Litton.

Green fees US$57.50 for 18 holes and weekly rates, clubhouse, pro-shop, cart and club rental, tuition, restaurant.

Hiking

Hiking can be a good way of exploring the island and given there are no steep hills, it's not especially challenging; always take plenty of water, snacks, a phone and wear sturdy shoes. In the Nelson's Dockyard National Park there are trails of up to 2 miles in the hills, past fortifications and with fantastic views; see page 40. These and several hiking routes around the island are described on the website of **Antigua Outdoors**; www.antiguaoutdoors.com.

5AM Hike, *contact Oral Evenson, T268-732 0059, see Facebook for where to meet*. Every Sat at 0500 they hike 3-4 miles exploring the island. There can be up to 70 walkers as this is popular with Antiguans. It's free of charge although donations to a good cause are sometimes requested.

Antigua Hash House Harriers, *T268-724 1359, see Facebook for where to meet*. Arranges 2-hr hikes/runs off the beaten track every other Sat at 1530, free of charge, after which they set up a barbecue. Food and drinks are for sale or BYO.

Environmental Awareness Group (EAG), *office upstairs at the Museum of Antigua and Barbuda in St John's, T268-462 6236, www.eagantigua.org. Mon-Fri 0900-1600*. Offers monthly excursions or field trips, usually the 3rd Sat of the month, which could be birdwatching at McKinnons Salt Pond at Dickenson Bay, a hike to Fort Barrington overlooking St John's Harbour, or a trip out to Prickly Pear Island. A donation of about US$9.25 is expected.

Footsteps Rainforest Hiking Tours, *Fig Tree Drive, T268-460 1234, www.hikingantigua.com*. Dassa Spencer leads walks starting from **Fig Tree Studio Art Gallery** to Wallings Dam, through the rainforest and up Signal Hill, Tue, Thu 0900, 2 hrs, US$45, under 16s US$25, moderate fitness required, water provided. Other walks can be custom designed, depending on what you want to do.

Horse riding

Antigua Equestrian Centre, *Springhill Riding Club, near the village on the western side of Falmouth Harbour, T268-460 7787, www.antiguaequestrian.com*. Offers some wonderful trail rides through the hills with scenic views, or treks to the beach at Rendezvous Bay with the opportunity to swim with your horse. All rides go with a maximum of 4 riders and leave the stables Mon-Sat 0830; US$65 for 1-hr ride suitable for novices, US$125 for 2 hrs for those who are able to canter.

Kite- and windsurfing

Both of these are on Jabberwock Beach, and are open daily 0900-1700 if it's windy.

Kitesurf Antigua, *T268-720 5483, www.kitesurfantigua.com*. IKO-approved school offering equipment rentals from US$30 for 1 hr to US$70 per day, 4-hr kitesurfing lessons for beginners from US$220, to a 2- to 3-day 'kite clinic' which will take you to IKO Level 2 from US$500.

Windsurf Antigua, *T268-461 9463, www.windsurfantigua.net*. Rentals from US$30 for 1 hr to US$80 per day, instruction for beginners, US$60 for 2 hrs, intermediate and advanced windsurfers US$60 per hr.

Sailing and boating

There are a number of options from a sunset cruise or snorkelling excursions, to full or half-day cruises around the island or chartering a yacht.

Adventure Antigua, *T268-726 6355, www.adventureantigua.com*. Boat trips including 'The Xtreme Circumnav' all the way around the island by speedboat with lunch and drinks and 5 stops: Stingray City, lunch on Green Island, Nelson's Dockyard, snorkelling off Fort Charlotte, and relaxing at Rendezvous Bay; US$170, or a classic yacht tour on a 40-ft wooden Carriacou sloop with snorkelling on Cades Reef and a lunch stop at Carlisle Bay; US$170.

Antigua Reef Riders, *Jolly Harbour Marina, T268-728 5239, www.antiguareefriders.com*. Tours by inflatable boats with outboard motors from Jolly Harbour down the southwest coast to Cades Reef for snorkelling. An exhilarating trip with time to play making figures of eights and other tricks at speeds up to 30 mph; 3 hrs, US$70 per person if 2 in the boat, US$100 if 1 person.

Caribbean Yacht Charters, *Falmouth Harbour, T268-464 7662, www.antiguayachtcharters.com*. Crewed sailing holidays on monohulls, catamarans or classic wooden sailing yachts; charters are usually on a 7-night, all-inclusive basis, but you could go across to Barbuda for a weekend.

Catamaran Sailing Antigua, *www.catamaransailingantigua.com*. On the Cool Cat catamaran, charters for full and half day cruises around the island, 3- to 4-hr lunch or sunset cruises, or across to Barbuda; takes up to 10 so can be well priced for a large group with food and drink.

Creole Cruises, *Jolly Harbour Marina, T268-460 5130, www.creolecruisesantigua.com*. The Lobster Lunch Cruise by motorboat starts in Jolly Harbour and then picks up at most of the resorts along the west and north coasts and sets down on Great Bird Island for a barbecue and snorkelling; US$130, children (2-9) US$100, under 2s free.

Ondeck, *T268-562 6696, Dockyard Dr, Falmouth Harbour, www.ondecksailing.com*. Half-day crewed yacht charters from US$450, full day US$850, and can organize charters for 2 or more days to take you across to Montserrat or further afield.

Tropical Adventures, *T268-480 1225, www.tropicalad.com*. A number of options from a 2½-hr sunset sail with drinks from Dickenson Bay for US$85, to a 6-hr circumnavigation of the island with lunch for US$130. Discounts under 12s.

Wadadli Cats, *T268-462 4792, www.wadadlicats.com*. 3 routes offered: around the island (US$110); to Cades Reef (US$95); and to Bird Island (US$110). Guests are picked up from their hotels in the northwest before sailing down to Cades Reef for snorkelling, lunch, then a stop on Turner's Beach before being dropped off again at their starting point. The trip to Bird Island also has snorkelling and swimming and the circumnavigation trip stops at Green Island for lunch.

Stand-up paddle boarding (SUP)

The beautiful calm waters are perfect for this sport and many resorts have boards for their all-inclusive guests. Prices vary but rentals are around USC$30 per hr or US$50 for 3 hrs.

SUP Antigua, *at Antigua Village Beach Resort, Dickenson Bay, T268-724 8150, www.standuppaddleantigua.com. Daily 0900-1800*. Can also organize lessons and rent out waterproof cameras.

Salty Dogs Rentals, *Jolly Harbour Marina, T268-562 8444, www.saltydogsrentals.com. Daily 0900-1700*. Rents out boards with life jackets and delivers to some of the resorts around Jolly Harbour and on the south coast.

Turtle's Surf Shop, Antigua Yacht Club Marina, *Falmouth Harbour, T268-783 3592, www.turtles-surf-shop.com. Daily 1000-1900*. SUP-ping around the yachts and marinas is a great experience and will get you up close to the superyachts for a nosey.

Tennis

Many large resorts have courts. **Carlisle Bay Antigua** (T268-484 0000, www.carlisle-bay.com), and **Curtain Bluff Resort** (www.curtainbluff.com), both in Old Rd, have large tennis centres with pro-shops offering lessons and clinics.

Temo Sports, *Falmouth Harbour, near Falmouth Harbour Marina, T268-463 6376. Mon-Fri 0700-2200, Sat 0700 1600 in season, reduced hours in summer*. A tennis/squash club open to the public with floodlit tennis courts, glass-backed squash courts, equipment rental, and a round-robin tennis tournament every Fri 1730-2030. There's also a bar with pool table, darts and TVs to watch sports, and **Bar-B's Café** is open for

ON THE ROAD

Tours to Montserrat

Some tour operators in Antigua can package together scheduled FlyMontserrat flights (or the ferry if it's running) in a day tour of Montserrat, where a taxi is organized to take you to sites such as Montserrat Volcano Observatory, including lunch and an island tour. It costs US$295 per person, with a minimum of four people. Do not forget your passport.

Carib World Travel, St John's, Antigua, T268-480 2999, www.carib-world.com.
Jenny Montserrat Tours, St John's, Antigua, T268-722 8188/9092, www.jennymontserrattours.com.
Montserrat Jolly Up Tours, Jolly Harbour, Antigua, T268-785 1443, www.montserratjollyuptours.com.

breakfast (including full English) and lunch Mon-Sat 0700-1500.

Tour operators

Many taxi drivers can take you around the island for the day visiting such places as Shirley Heights and Nelson's Dockyard, Devil's Bridge, Betty's Hope and Fig Tree Drive, with perhaps a lunch stop somewhere and time on the beach; official rates per hr per car (1-4 people) are US$24. See also Bike and scooter hire under Transport, below.

Antigua Buggys, *off Valley Rd near Jolly Harbour opposite Sugar Ridge Resort, T268-789 9686, www.antiguabuggys.com.* 4- to 5-hr guided tours in mokes; drivers must be over 25 and have a local driver's permit; US$149 per person inclusive of lunch and soft drinks. Children over 7 can come along.

Caribbean Helicopters, *VC Bird International Airport, T268-460 5900, www.caribbeanhelicopters.com.* Offers a number of flights including a half-island tour, 20 mins, US$145 per person; full-island tour, 30 mins, US$185 per person; a charter to Montserrat for a bird's-eye view of the Soufrière Hills Volcano and the charred remains of Plymouth, 50 mins, US$1615 for up to 6 people; and a return trip to Barbuda with lunch and time on the beach, US$1315 for up to 6.

Salty Dogs Rentals, *Jolly Harbour Marina, T268-562 8444, www.saltydogsrentals.com.* Organizes 3-hr guided tours by scooter or moke for US$95.

Tropical Adventures, *T268-480 1225, www.tropicalad.com.* 6-hr island tours on a variety of itineraries taking in the sights and beaches by comfortable a/c SUVs or open-sided Land Rovers, US$100-115, half price for children under 12, and there's the option of adding in some kayaking in the mangroves or a 1-hr cruise by catamaran off Turner's Beach.

Watersports

A wide range of watersports is available from all the resorts. However, Dickenson Bay is the only beach with public hire of watersports equipment, but some resorts will hire to the public, especially out of season, and a few offer day passes.

Tony's Water Sports & Bar, *Dickenson Bay, T268-462 6326, www.tonyswatersports.com. Daily 1000-1800, bar (much) later.* Jet skiing, wakeboarding, water skiing, parasailing, tubing, banana boats, hobie cats and more, all based at a lively beach bar with great music, rum punch and ice cream.

Transport

Antigua

Air

Named after Dr Vere Cornwall Bird, the 1st prime minister of Antigua and Barbuda (1981-1994), the new **VC Bird International Airport** (T268-484 2300, www.vcbia.com), opened in 2015 next to the old facility. See Finding your feet, page 29, for details of transport from the airport.

It has a good choice of duty free shops and restaurants and there are ATMs and a bureau de change (Mon-Fri 0900-1900, Sat-Sun 1200-1900). It's the airline hub for the region with flights from the UK, USA and other destinations in the Caribbean. See page 129 for details.

There are flights with **FlyMontserrat** between Antigua and Barbuda, see below. **Caribbean Helicopters** (VC Bird International Airport, T268-460 5900, www.caribbeanhelicopters.com) offers flights to St Kitts, Nevis and several other islands, and organizes charter transport over to the resorts on Barbuda, 18 mins. Departures are from the airport or their helipad at Fort Rd in St John's. See also Tour operators, above.

Bike and scooter hire

Cycling on Antigua is a good option to get to the beaches; the island is fairly flat and traffic light outside of St John's. The mostly residential interior however, may not appeal to adventurous mountain bikers. For scooters and other smaller vehicles, drivers need to be over 18 and, like car hire, will need a local driver's permit.

Bike Plus, Independence Dr, St John's, T268-462 2453, see Facebook. Mon-Sat 0800-1700. This big bike and sports store offers mountain or road bike hire at US$18.50 per day (1 free day if you hire for a week), and provides a map and directions to all the beaches.

Cheke's Scooter & Car Rental, English Harbour, T268-562 4646, www.chekesrentals.com. Scooters, 50-150cc, from US$65 per day or US$400 per week, and quad bikes, US$100 per day, and will deliver to accommodation and cruise ships.

Paradise Boat Sales Rentals and Charters, Jolly Harbour Marina, T268-460 7125, www.paradiseboats.com. Rents boats but also mountain bikes, US$23 per day, discounts for more than 2 days, 10% discount for more than 2 bikes, child seats available.

Salty Dogs Rentals, Jolly Harbour Marina, T268-562 8444, Redcliffe Quay, St John's, T268-783 5366, www.saltydogsrentals.com. Rents scooters, 50cc from US$45 per day, 125cc US$55, and colourful open-top mini-mokes from US$65 per day. Discounts for weekly rentals.

Bus

Buses are mostly 15-seater privately owned minivans with their route numbers posted in the front windows, although there is the occasional larger vehicle serving the more popular routes such as between St John's and Falmouth Harbour. They go from the 2 bus terminals in St John's: West Bus Station near the junction with Market St and Valley Rd, and East Bus Station on Independence Av. Very few vehicles go north to the tourist area around Dickenson Bay and none go to the airport. There are marked bus stops along the roadsides but the buses will stop anywhere. Fares are US$0.90-1.50.

They are scheduled to run from St John's Mon-Sat 0530 to 1800 and frequency can be variable; drivers often abandon their routes if there are not many passengers around and will become taxis at any opportunity. The most useful routes for visitors are from West Bus Station: No 61 to the Five Islands peninsula, No 17 to Falmouth and English Harbours via All Saints, and No 22 to Old Road via the turn-off to Jolly Harbour, Darkwood Beach and Turner's Beach. From East Bus Station No 31 goes to Parham and No 33 to Willikies.

Car hire

Drivers must be over 25 and a local driver's permit, US$20 valid for 3 months, must be purchased on presentation of a foreign (not international) licence; the car hire companies will arrange this.

A list of hire companies can be found on the websites of the **Antigua & Barbuda Tourism Authority** (www.antigua-barbuda.org) and **Antigua Nice** (www.antiguanice.com). Rates are from US$40-50 per day depending on the size of the car, US$300-400 per week. Basic hire generally only includes statutory third party insurance; it is advised to take out the optional collision damage waiver premium at US$12-15 per day as even the smallest accident can be very expensive. All companies will arrange pick-up/drop-off at VC Bird International Airport, and given that the airport is fairly new, some companies are likely to open up desks there. See page 133 for further details about hiring a car and driving.

Taxi

Taxis are either regular cars or minivans that become taxis if you are paying for single use. They are plentiful but are expensive and non-negotiable rates are set by the government and taxi associations; rates are US$6 for a short drop even within 1 mile, US$11 for a 4- to 5-mile journey (eg from the airport to St John's), rising to US$30 across the island (such as from the airport to Old Road or Falmouth Harbour). If you want to hire one for an hour or 2, standard fixed rates are US$24 per hr. Taxis gather at the airport and a taxi rank on St Mary St in St John's (near Redcliffe Quay and Heritage Quay). Otherwise any hotel/restaurant can phone one, or if you find one you like get the driver's card/phone number.

Barbuda

Air

Coco Point Lodge, in the far south, organize flights for guests to their own airstrip, while **Caribbean Helicopters** can also land there and at the helipad at Lighthouse Bay Resort. **FlyMontserrat** (VC Bird International Airport, T268-562 7605; Barbuda, T268-732 9141; www.flymontserrat.com) operates the only scheduled flight (20 mins), which depart daily from Antigua at 0800 and 1600, returning from Barbuda at 0830 and 1630. Fares are approximately US$65 one way. You must reconfirm within 24 hrs as the flights can be cancelled or times altered. The planes are very small; sometimes just 7-seaters, so luggage space is restricted and everything (including you) will be weighed. The 20-min flight is quite wonderful; from Antigua first you pass over Maiden Island and Long Island, and on the approach to Barbuda, you can see the southernmost point and the beach along the west coast, before crossing over the lagoon to the airport in Codrington. You can also charter a plane with **FlyMontserrat**, or with **ABM Air Montserrat**, (Antigua, T268-562 7183/8033; Barbuda T268-562 8089; www.montserrat-flights.com), or a helicopter with **Caribbean Helicopters** (see under Antigua Transport, above); work out the costs, because sometimes chartering can be cost effective if there are 5 or more people with a lot of luggage.

Boat

The **Barbuda Express** catamaran ferry (T268-560 7989, www.barbudaexpress.com) is often preferred by Barbudans because of the greater capacity to carry shopping and luggage and the large number of seats (56). It takes 90 mins and departs from St John's Tue-Sat at 0900, and returns from Barbuda

Tip...

The **Barbuda Express** ferry offers a day tour to Barbuda Tue-Sat – you depart St John's in Antigua at 0900 and are back at around 1730. It includes a taxi tour around the island to see Codrington and other sites, a boat trip out to the Frigate Bird Sanctuary, and a barbecue lunch on the beach with time for swimming and snorkelling. Costs are US$169, children (3-12) US$100, under twos free; without the bird sanctuary US$139/100.

at 1600, Sun 1200, returning at 1600. There are no ferries on Mon and the ferry times on Sun do not allow for a day trip. Round trip fares are US$81.50, one-way US$44, children (7-12 years) US$74/37, (3-6 years) US$44/22, (under 2 years) US$15/7.50.

You can also go on a day tour organized by **Barbuda Express** (see Tip box). The crossing can be a bit rough but the friendly staff on board will give you a travel sickness tablet, and if the weather is too bad it will be cancelled.

Car hire

There are not many cars available as spare parts are difficult to get hold of. A taxi tour may be more productive as your driver will also be an informative guide. It's possible to hire jeeps from **C and J Rent a Car**, T268-725 4970/734 2509. Rates are either a short day price to fit in with the flights, US$46, or per day/24-hrs, US$61. Like Antigua, you need a temporary driver's permit (US$20). There is only 1 fuel station on the island; **G & B Service Station**, near the airport, T268-722 7472, Mon-Fri 0700-1700, Sat 0700-1300, closed Sun. Sometimes fuel runs out (it has to be shipped across from Antigua) so fill up while you can.

Taxi

Taxi rates are set by the **Barbuda Council**, all drivers should have a price list and hourly rates are US$24.

Montserrat

Montserrat

Montserrat lies 34 miles southwest of Antigua and is like nowhere else. The Irish-influenced 'Emerald Isle' is totally unspoiled by tourism but its volcano has put it on the map, having wiped out the southern part of the island. Montserrat covers 40 square miles and is mountainous, with three ranges of hills: Silver Hills, Centre Hills, and Soufrière Hills. The estimated 3000-ft-high Soufrière Hills Volcano has been erupting since 1995. The south of the island, which like the rest of the island used to be all lush green, is now grey with ash and the former capital, Plymouth, is a modern Pompeii. Its eruption resulted in the emigration of over half the population of 12,000 and those that remained relocated to the northern 'safe' zone, protected by the Centre Hills, where they rebuilt their lives.

Montserrat was off-limits to tourism for a few years, and two-thirds of the island is still an exclusion zone, but now the still-active volcano is the island's biggest visitor attraction. Here you can enjoy views of volcanic moonscapes, deserted black-sand beaches, a network of challenging mountain trails, waters teeming with fish, coral and sponges, and some of the friendliest people in the region.

Essential Montserrat

Finding your feet

John A Osborne Airport is in the north of the island at Gerald's. Ferries from St John's in Antigua arrive at the ferry jetty at Little Bay. However, at the time of writing, the ferry was not in operation; see Note, page 86. Taxis gather at both the airport and the ferry jetty to meet incoming flights and ferries. Yachts must clear in and out at customs and immigration facilities in the port at Little Bay (Monday-Friday 0800-1600; after-hours port security can contact officers and there's an on overtime charge). See Transport, page 86.

Best sightseeing

Little Bay Beach, see below
National Museum of Montserrat, page 77
Montserrat National Trust Botanical Garden, page 79
Centre Hills, page 79
Montserrat Volcano Observatory, page 80

Getting around

The island only has about 16 miles of surfaced roads, and the two main routes go down to just beyond Jack Boy Hill on the east coast, and the village of Fleming on the west coast. Buses (minivans) have no schedules but run up and down the main roads during daylight hours; just stick your hand out when you see one. Car hire is available.

Around the island

a huge grumbling volcano, eerie ash-covered landscapes and pretty hill walking

The southern two thirds of the island are off-limits and subject to an exclusion order following the eruption of the volcano and the evacuation of the population. It is illegal to enter as it is dangerous. The boundary runs from the coast north of Plymouth in a north-easterly direction between the Centre Hills and Soufrière Hills to the east coast just north of the old airport. The smouldering volcano that looms over every aspect of life on Montserrat is the main attraction, but other draws include hiking and birdwatching, snorkelling and diving, and the wonderfully unhurried pace of life on the island.

Little Bay and Brades

On the northwest end of the island, Little Bay is now the main port of entry due to the destruction of the former capital Plymouth by volcanic activity of Soufrière Hills since 1995. Little Bay has the ferry jetty, the market and an appealing beach, which is a great spot to watch boats, and its consistently calm waters are good for swimming and snorkelling. It's a popular place to unwind at the several beach bars here, some in a newly built thatched complex known as Marine Village, with toilets, changing rooms and showers for beach-goers.

About a mile south of Little Bay is another beach along Carr's Bay. On the way, on the hillside, are the **National Museum of Montserrat**, the **Montserrat Cultural Centre**, and the **Montserrat Sports Complex**, used for cricket, basketball and netball tournaments. Looking out to sea from Carr's Bay, you can see Redonda (see box, page 50) and, beyond that, Nevis. There is a small, ruined fort here with several cannons pointing out to deter invaders. Also here is a replica of the War Memorial and Clock Tower that were destroyed in Plymouth. The rocks here are home to iguanas, which you can sometimes see

Montserrat
North West Bluff
To Antigua
Thatch Valley
Hell's Gate
Silver Hill (1322 ft)
Pinnacle Rock
Rendezvous Bay
National Museum of Montserrat
Yellow Hole
Little Bay
Montserrat Cultural centre
Drummond's
Marguerita Bay
Carr's Bay
Davy Hill
Gerald's
Sweeneys
Lookout
Blake's Estate
Soldier Ghaut Bay
Brades
Collins River
St John's
Judy Piece
Caribbean Sea
Cudjoe Head
Statue Rock
Baker Hill
St Peter's
Bunkum Bay
Fogarthy Hill
Oriole Walkway Trail
Bottomless Ghaut
Jack Boy Hill
Lawyer's Mountain
Katy Hill
Trant's Bay
Woodlands Bay
Woodlands
Lawyer's River
Runaway Ghaut
Montserrat National Trust Botanical Garden
Trant's
Farm Bay
Lime Kiln Bay
Olveston
Nantes River
Centre Hills
Farm River
Farm
Spanish Point
Spanish Point
Old Towne
Salem
Waterwork Estate
Frith
Monserrat Volcano Observatory
Farrell's Estate
Harris
Bethel
Old Road Bay
Windy Hill
Iles Bay
Belham River
Paradise River
Tuitt's
Molyneux
Garibaldi Hill
Cork Hill
Dyer's
Streatham
Fox's Bay
Bransby Point
St George's Hill
Long Ground
Montserrat Springs
Tar River Estate
Gages
Soufrière Hills
Ghaut Mefraimie
Gages Estate
Chances Peak (3000-3300 ft)
Plymouth
Wapping
Roche's Bluff
Sugar Bay
Kinsale
Spring Estate
Galway's Soufrière
Roche's Estate
Fairfield
South Soufrière Hills
Landing Bay
White River
St Patrick's
Germans Bay
Morris
N
Shooters Hill
Triangle Rock
500 metres
500 yards
Old Ford Point
Shoe Rock
Guadeloupe Passage
Where to stay
Erindell 2
Essence Guesthouse 4
Gingerbread Hill 3
Grand View B&B 6
Hot Rock Youth Hostel 7
Miles Away Villa Resort 9
Olveston House 11
Tropical Mansion Suites 10
Turtle Bay Apartments 2
Restaurants
Hilltop Coffee House & Family Centre 1
JavaLava Art Café 2
Pont's Beach View 3
Sips & Bites 4
Soco Cabana 5
The Attic 7
The People's Place 1
Time Out 8
Tina's 9
Watermelon Cottage 6
Ziggy's 10

sunbathing. There are plans to build a marina for visiting yachts, many of which come over from Antigua, particularly after Antigua **Sailing Week** in April (see Festivals, page 12), and a cruise ship terminal on the Carr's Bay waterfront area.

Government administrative offices are at **Brades**, the de facto capital of the island since 1998, although even after more than 20 years since the main eruption it's very much a work in progress. However, the pace of development doesn't need to be very hurried given that the island population is only about 5000.

Brades has several small shops, a post office, library and pharmacy and the only two banks on the island, both with ATMs: the **Royal Bank of Canada** and the **Bank Of Montserrat**.

In 2012, the **Montserrat National Trust** moved its headquarters and collection to a new building in Little Bay from its previous site in Olveston where it had been since 1940, and it is now called the **National Museum of Montserrat** ⓘ *Robert W Griffith Dr, T664-491 3086, www.montserratnationaltrust.ms, Tue and Fri 0830-1230, Sat 0930-1230, other times on request, US$1.85, children under 12 free.* The previous national museum was in a historic sugar mill in Plymouth, but was evacuated when events escalated in 1996 and is now covered in ash. However, at the time the Trust, assisted by several organizations including the Museum Association of the Caribbean, salvaged many items and for a while they were on display at the old Trust headquarters in Olveston. This new museum was officially opened by UK royals the Earl and Duchess of Wessex in 2012.

The museum documents the island's history and culture from the pre-Columbian times to present. It's small but includes many aspects of the island, such as colonial lime and sugar production, dioramas and photographs of the volcano and Plymouth, St Patrick's Day costumes, the history of Sir George Martin's AIR Studios, cricket, and flora and fauna of the island. The gift shop is excellent and sells T-shirts, arts and crafts, jewellery and a map of the hiking trails on the island. The lovely Montserrat National Trust Botanical Garden and another gift shop are still in Olveston (see below).

A prominent landmark in Little Bay, at the roundabout on Davy Hill, the **Montserrat Cultural Centre** ⓘ *Robert W Griffith Dr, T664-491 4242, www.themontserratcultural centre.ms*, was built in 2006, and was the brainchild of the former Beatles' producer-composer, the late Sir George Martin, who was instrumental in fundraising for its construction. In 2009, Sir George and broadcaster Sir Trevor Mcdonald helped to install a 'Wall of Fame' in the centre, made up of the handprints cast in bronze of the famous musicians who recorded at **Sir George's AIR Studios** on Montserrat (see box, page 78) in the 1980s, including Sir Paul McCartney and Sir Elton John. The cultural centre has an auditorium seating 500, and is the venue for local concerts, festivals, films and even legislative meetings and weddings. There's also an outdoor stage for open-air performances.

The north

There are a number of beaches on Montserrat including Carr's Bay, Little Bay, Woodlands, Bunkum Bay and Old Road Bay, but because of the volcano, most are light grey to dark grey sand. The island's only white coral beach is at **Rendezvous Bay** to the north of Little Bay, tucked in a cove under a forested cliff. There is no road access and it is a stiff one-hour hike along the steep, mountainous, 1.3-mile Rendezvous Nature Trail, which starts behind the concrete block company in Little Bay and climbs over a saddle, with a lovely view south into Little Bay, before descending into Rendezvous Valley and the beach. Take food, water and a hat; it is very hot and there is no shade on the beach. Avoid the poisonous manchineel trees and look out for the spiny sea urchins among the rocks at the north end.

ON THE ROAD

AIR Studios Montserrat

To many, Sir George Martin (1926-2016) is simply remembered as the 'fifth Beatle', but he was also responsible for building a musical outpost to record some of the biggest selling music of the 1980s. In 1977, he fell in love with Montserrat and decided to build the ultimate get-away-from-it-all recording studio. He had founded the Associated Independent Recording (AIR) studios in London in 1969, and in 1979 opened AIR Studios Montserrat, which offered all the technical facilities of its London predecessor, but with the advantages of an exotic location.

For a decade, AIR Studios Montserrat played host to classic recording sessions by a who's who of rock, including Dire Straits, The Police, Sir Paul McCartney, Sir Elton John, Duran Duran, Michael Jackson, Stevie Wonder, Ultravox, The Rolling Stones, Lou Reed, Black Sabbath and Eric Clapton. In total, 76 albums were recorded here including a couple of the best-selling rock albums of all time; The Police's *Synchronicity* and Dire Straits' *Brothers in Arms*.

The studio's glittering story came to an abrupt end when it was forced to close in 1989 because of Hurricane Hugo, but Martin maintained ties with Montserrat throughout his life until his death at the age of 90 in 2016. Most significantly, he was raising funds for short-term relief for the islanders after the volcano's eruption.

The most publicized events included the star-studded *Music for Montserrat* concert at the Royal Albert Hall in London in 1997, which featured performances from many artists who had previously recorded on the island. In 2001 500 limited edition signed lithographs of the score for the Beatles song *Yesterday* were released, complete with mistakes and tea-stains, raising US$1.4 million.

It is, however, a delightful and beautiful spot, unblemished by human interference. The waves can be a little rough at times, but snorkelling is good on the reef offshore, which is quite shallow and calm. The coral is healthy and abundant and you can often see stingrays and turtles as well as lots of reef fish. Fruit bats roost in Bat Cave, which you can swim in to. You can also take a boat to Rendezvous Bay, or walk there and arrange for a boat to come and pick you up.

There is another, longer hiking route to Rendezvous Bay which starts at Drummonds, north of the airport; it's about 2½ miles but is challenging so allow three hours. At the end of the paved road, follow the dirt road north until you get to a junction of three tracks. Turn left, northwest through dry forest and open grassland until it drops down to Rendezvous Bay. Take a swim to cool off before heading over the saddle back to Little Bay. Drummonds is also the starting point to hike up **Silver Hill** (1322 ft), an extinct volcano, at the top of which is a communications mast and a great view to Antigua.

The west coast

The road south from Brades continues inland via Cudjoe Head, meeting the coast again at tiny **Bunkum Bay**. There are volcanic black sand beaches here, which means the sand may be a silvery grey or dark golden brown colour, and a bit further south at **Woodlands Bay**, where there is a covered picnic area with tables, outside showers and toilets.

Montserrat has many deep ravines or ghauts – pronounced guts – that carry rainwater from the hills down to the sea. The most famous is **Runaway Ghaut**, located on the western side of the road just after Woodlands. The signposted short Runaway Ghaut Trail takes you to the stream (or river in the rainy season) through a lush riparian patch of forest, where there are fruit trees attracting a number of birds. There is a saying that 'if you drink the waters from this burn, to Montserrat you will return.' Runaway Ghaut got its name because it was the escape route for the French when they were driven off the island in 1712 and the ravine on the other side of the road is called Frenchman's Creek.

On the main road in Olveston (Salem Road) is the **Montserrat National Trust Botanical Garden** ⓣ *1664-491 3086, www.montserratnationaltrust.ms, Mon-Fri 0830-1630, Sat on request 1000-1300, US$1.85*, which was established in 2005 with the help of Kew Royal Botanic Gardens in the UK. The grounds have a wonderful selection of herbs and plants, and it is dedicated to conserving indigenous species which include the heliconia, Montserrat's beautiful national flower popularly known as lobster-claw or false bird-of-paradise, as well as two endemics to Montserrat, the *Epidendrum Montserratense*, an endangered orchid, and pribby, a flowering shrub. There are pleasant paths, an orchid house and medicinal garden and a gift shop.

The Belham Valley bridge, which connected the north to the south and the golf course, is now buried under volcanic debris. You can walk in the valley, but only when the weather is dry. An interesting beach to visit is the one at **Old Road Bay**, below the old Vue Pointe Hotel, which has been impacted by volcanic mudflows, creating strange patterns. The beach is now much bigger than it was and the original pier is now firmly on dry land. Be careful in rainy weather as mud can flow very quickly down the valley behind the beach. **Fox's Bay** is a deserted beach in a zone which at the height of the volcanic crisis was a no-go area and is now part of the Day Time Entry Zone. The beach is a delight. From the northern end of **Barton Bay**, below the abandoned Montserrat Springs Hotel in Richmond Hill, you can walk round to Fox's Bay at low tide. Take the road down to the old hotel beach bar.

Centre Hills

The loss of two thirds of the island after the volcanic eruptions has left natural vegetation confined mostly to the Centre Hills, thus also the last viable habitat for Montserrat's endemic and threatened wildlife. Montserrat doesn't have many wild animals, although it has agoutis, bats and lizards, including iguanas which can grow to over 4 ft in length (they used to take the balls on the golf course, mistaking them for eggs), and tree frogs contribute to the island's 'night-music'. Covered in tropical rainforest, these hills are also home to most of Montserrat's 34 species of land birds and large numbers of migrant songbirds including the endangered Montserrat oriole (*Icterus oberi*), the national bird. Other species include the forest thrush, bridled quail dove, mangrove cuckoo, trembler and purple-throated carib.

The 1.3-mile **Oriole Walkway Trail** is the most popular and straightforward hike into the Centre Hills and takes around 1½ hours. The trail meanders through thick foliage with occasional glimpses of the blue Caribbean, then climbs up Lawyers Mountain to a clearing at the top (1278 ft), with fabulous views of the island. You can start the signposted trail from behind the **Hilltop Café** on Fogarty Hill or on the main road in Woodlands, although a refreshing drink at the café at the end may be appreciated. Wear long sleeves and trousers and put on plenty of mosquito repellent.

Tip...

Pick up a trail map and booklet at either the tourist office in Little Bay or at the Montserrat National Trust gift shops. It details hiking trails on the island, eight of which are in the Centre Hills.

BACKGROUND

Volcanic violence

In July 1995 the lives of Montserratians were turned upside down when the 'dormant' volcano erupted, and residents of Plymouth and villages in the south were evacuated to the north as lava, rocks and ash belched from the Soufrière Hills. Activity increased in 1997; during March and April pyroclastic flows reached 2 miles down the south side of the volcano. The former tourist attractions of the Great Alps Waterfall and Galways Soufrière were covered, there was a partial collapse of Galways Wall and lava flowed down the Tar River Valley.

In May the lava dome was growing at 800 gallons per second, and in June a huge explosion occurred when a sudden pyroclastic flow of hot rock, gas and ash poured down the volcano at 200 mph. It engulfed 19 people, destroyed seven villages and some 200 homes. The flow, which resulted from a partial collapse of the lava dome, came to within 50 yards of the sea, close to the airport runway, which had to be closed. The eruption sent an ash cloud 6 miles into the air. In August another bout of activity destroyed Plymouth, which caught fire under a shower of red hot lava. It now looks like a lunar landscape, completely covered by grey ash. In December 1997 there was a huge dome collapse which created a 600-yard amphitheatre around Galways Soufrière and destroyed several deserted communities. The White River delta was increased to about 1 mile and the water level rose by about 3 ft. During 1998-1999 dome collapses continued, with ash clouds at times up to 8 miles high.

In 2000 and in 2003 the lava dome collapsed again, and in late 2006, streaks of red from the pyroclastic flows became visible. On 8 January 2007 an evacuation order was issued for areas in the Lower Belham Valley. In July 2008, an eruption began without any precursory activity and the pyroclastic flow reached Plymouth, and a small part of the eastern side of the lava dome collapsed. Several large explosions were registered, with the largest ash column was estimated at being 7½ miles high. On 5 February 2010, an explosion propelled flows down several sides of the mountain, and on 11 February 2010, another partial collapse of the lava dome sent large ash clouds over sections of nearby islands including Guadeloupe and Antigua. Since then activity has been relatively quiet although the volcano is still only slumbering.

Soufrière Hills Volcano

The Soufrière Hills Volcano is named for the French word *soufrière*, meaning 'sulphur outlet' and is a complex stratovolcano. It erupted in the 17th century, around 1630, and although non-eruptive seismic events occurred in the 1890s, 1930s and 1960s, after some 365 years of being fairly quiet, Soufrière Hills came back to life in 1995 and erupted pyroclastic flows over much of Montserrat and started to build a new lava dome. The volcano is topped by Chances Peak. Its height is always changing due to movement of this lava dome but it's estimated to be a restless 3000-3300 ft tall.

The volcano is best viewed from the **Montserrat Volcano Observatory (MVO)** ⓘ *Hope Dr, Flemmings, follow signs up from the main road in Salem, T664-491 5647, www.montserratvolcanoobservatory.info, visitor centre Mon-Thu 1000-1630, observation platform always open, US$3.70 per person*, which was established rapidly after the first phreatic eruption on 18 July 1995. The observatory is staffed by scientists, and its role is to monitor volcanic activity. If the volcano is dangerously active visitors are excluded. A fascinating 20-minute film is screened (at 15 minutes past the hour every hour 1015-1515) about the eruption and its impact, which shows great footage of Plymouth before, during and after. There are also a few exhibits of volcanic artefacts and displays explaining the techniques used in monitoring seismic activity, but it is the film that is the main event so try and time a visit to see it. From the observation platform you can see the volcano, Plymouth and the abandoned AIR Studios, destroyed by Hurricane Hugo in 1989.

Tip...
If you can afford it, the most dramatic view of Soufrière Hills Volcano and the charred remains of Plymouth is on the 50-minute sightseeing trip from Antigua with **Caribbean Helicopters** (US$1615 for up to six people, T268-460 5900, www.caribbeanhelicopters.com).

Spectacular views of the volcano and its damage can also be viewed in safety from the **Jack Boy Hill** picnic spot in the east. Where Blakes Road reaches the east coast, a turn-off goes into the hills and leads to this viewpoint overlooking the old airport and villages now covered by pyroclastic flows, close to the start of the Exclusion Zone. From here you can see the grey, ash-covered flanks of Chances Peak, in stark contrast with the Centre Hills, which are still green, forested and fertile. This viewing spot is popular at night time as you get excellent views of the glowing dome. There is a viewing platform with telescope, barbecue pit and grill, toilets and a short trail.

Listings Montserrat *map page 76*

Tourist information

Montserrat Tourism Division
Little Bay, T664 491 4700, www.visitmontserrat.com. Mon-Fri 0830-1630.
The visitor centre run by the government tourist board. Staff can advise on Montserrat's attractions, accommodation and transport, have maps to give out and can phone taxis.

Where to stay

There is only 1 hotel and a clutch of guesthouses and B&Bs on the island. All of them are reasonably priced, but those wanting something a little more private and upmarket may prefer to rent an apartment or villa.

Montserrat Villas (www.montserratvillas.com), **Montserrat Enterprises** (www.montserratenterprises.com) and **Tradewinds** (www.tradewindsmontserrat.com) are local agents. Government hotel tax is 10% (guesthouses, B&Bs and villas 7%), and there's a 10% service charge. Check if these have been included in quoted rates. Also on Montserrat, some places charge an extra US$10 per day for use of the a/c. Unless otherwise stated, all rooms have a/c, TV and Wi-Fi.

$$$ Miles Away Villa Resort
Mayfield Estate Dr, Olveston, T664-491 7362, www.milesawayvillaresort.com.
An upmarket guesthouse (rather than what the name suggests), the 6 rooms here are in a modern property with plenty of balconies and terraces in lovely grounds on a hillside with good ocean views, 4 have kitchenettes while the 2 cheapest/smallest rooms have kettles. Continental breakfast included and dinner on request, swimming pool and a short trail down to the Nantes River.

$$$-$$ Tropical Mansion Suites
404 Sweeney's Rd, Sweeneys, T664-491 8767, www.tropicalmansion.com.

A 2-storey 16-room hotel with views over Little Bay and the sunset from some rooms, a small pool and a tennis court. It's a little plainly furnished, but has friendly staff and good service. There's reasonable food in the restaurant/bar and it's popular with holidaymakers, government and business visitors.

$$ Olveston House

Olveston, T664-491 5210, www.olvestonhouse.com.

This iconic guesthouse is on the estate owned by the late George Martin of **AIR Studios Montserrat** fame (see box, page 78). During the 1980s, Paul McCartney, Sting, Elton John and Eric Clapton among other famous recording artists stayed here. It's a charming and hospitable place in 5 acres of attractive grounds, with 6 spacious rooms in the lovely house with wraparound porch, and there's an excellent restaurant and bar (see Restaurants, below) pool and tennis court.

$$-$ Erindell

Gros Michel Dr, Woodlands, T664-491 3655, www.erindellvilla.com.

Run by amicable Shirley and Lou who can share lots of information about the island and pick you up from elsewhere, 2 pleasant rooms with a swimming pool alongside the family home, with no a/c but fans, fridge, microwave and toaster. All meals available and a welcome pack includes snacks, fruit and drinks. A 1-min walk to the bus on the main road, and a 15-min walk to Woodlands Beach.

$$-$ Essence Guesthouse

Bluff Dr, Old Towne, T664-491 5411, www.essencemontserrat.com.

On a hillside with views of the volcano, Belham Valley and the beach, there are 2 units: a guest room with kettle, toaster and fridge (from US$55), and a 1-bedroom apartment with kitchen and lounge (from US$75). Each has its own entrance and patio and there's a pool. It's a 5-min stroll to the Old Road Bay beach and car hire and trips can be arranged.

$$-$ Gingerbread Hill

St Peter's, T664-491 5812, www.gingerbreadhill.com.

David and Clover Lea run a delightful guesthouse with incredible views and lovely 3-acre garden. There are a few options for accommodation: a charming suite with rooftop deck (US$125), a 2-bed villa (US$125 for 2 plus US$25 per extra person), a twin/double cottage with mini-kitchen (US$65), and a small en suite 'backpackers' room (US$45). Family atmosphere, very friendly and hospitable. A 2-night minimum stay is required, breakfast is extra at the co-owned **Hilltop Coffee House**, a short walk away (see Restaurants, below).

$$-$ Grand View B&B

Baker Hill, T664-491 2284, www.mnigrandview.com.

On breezy Baker Hill, 6 rooms and 2 suites, 2 of the rooms share a bathroom and are cheaper (US$55), lunch and dinner with reservation. A little dated, but the view is grand, and the owner is knowledgeable and helpful. Food is local and tasty with herbs from the garden and the bar is lively, with darts and pool.

$ Hot Rock Youth Hostel

Flemings Rd, Salem, T664-496 1410, www.hotrockhostel.com.

This simple and spotless house has rooms with 2 or 4 bunk beds, shared bathrooms, a fully equipped kitchen, and lounge with sofas and floor cushions. It's within walking distance of the MVO, bus stop, restaurants and bars. Nothing fancy but super friendly and from only US$20 per person. Can arrange airport/ferry pickups.

$ Turtle Bay Apartments

Cedar Point, Woodlands, T664-491 4985, www.turtlebayapartments.com.

These 2 good-value apartments – Poolside and Seaview – are the upper and lower parts of a small villa, and there's a good-sized pool set in pretty flowering gardens with fruit trees. It's a 15-min walk to Woodlands Bay Beach, and while a car is useful, you can also walk to the bus stop on Woodlands Rd. Doubles from US$60.

Restaurants

$$$ Watermelon Cottage

Olveston Estate Drive, Olveston, T664-496 4131, www.watermeloncottagemontserrat.com. Dinner daily by reservation only.

Nestled next to a stream and surrounded by tropical vegetation with twinkly lights in the trees, this is a magical spot for dinner hosted by former cruise director and now chef Trevor Stephenson. There are just 12 tables and he provides a creative bistro-style menu depending on what's available. A sample might be coconut shrimp, beef tenderloin wrapped in bacon, freshly baked eclairs and Caribbean coffee with rum and whipped cream. He also has 1 B&B room in his house (US$80).

$$$ Ziggy's

Mahogany Loop, Woodlands, T664-491 8282, www.ziggysrestaurant.com. Dinner daily, by reservation only.

Right on top of the hill overlooking Salem (the 2nd turning on the right from the main road), this is the island's smartest restaurant and you dine by candlelight in a marquee with additional table areas in pergolas in a lovely forest setting. Ziggy has been serving great food since the early 1990s; dishes like lobster quadrille, butterfly shrimp, jerk pork, and chocolate sludge are beautifully presented and there's an excellent wine list.

$$$-$$ Olveston House

Olveston, T664-491 5210, www.olvestonhouse.com. Daily for overnight guests, otherwise Wed-Sat 1800-2100, bar until 2200, Sun lunch from 1200, reservations required and phone ahead to request breakfast, lunch or high tea at other times.

The restaurant at this charming guesthouse (see Where to stay, above) has tables on the veranda and a friendly pub-style bar where you can chat with the owners and staff and learn the musical history of Olveston House and George Martin. A short but tasty menu of international and Caribbean dishes (depending on what produce is available), barbecues on Wed, informal pub grub on Fri, traditional English roast on Sun lunchtime and great cocktails and rum punch.

$$ Pont's Beach View

Little Bay, T664-496 7788. Sun-Fri 1100-1500, owner/cook John may open for dinner if you phone ahead.

Carved into the side of the cliff at the southern end of Little Bay Beach, this has a wooden terrace above the beach and tables inside kept cool by the surrounding luxuriant plants. Lunches from the grill like chicken, fish and ribs are served with vegetables and their own barbecue sauce.

$$-$ Soca Cabana

Little Bay, just south of the ferry terminal, T664-493 1820, www.socacabana.com. Sun-Thu 0800-1600, Fri-Sat 0800-late.

With a cute terrace perched above Little Bay Beach and friendly staff, this classic beach bar serves lunches of tasty local fish, chicken, pork, and vegetable dishes, plus standard burgers and fries. It may be a bit odd on a hot day, but the chicken soup is quite delicious. Karaoke on Sat night or live music at weekends with dancing on the sand. The wooden bar came from George Martin's **AIR Studios Montserrat** (see box, page 78).

$$-$ Time Out

Little Bay, T664-491 9046. Mon and Thu 1100-2300, Fri 1100-0300, Sat 1200-0100.

Beach bar and grill restaurant on Little Bay Beach with pleasant tables on a terrace and a menu including barbecue chicken and ribs, burgers, fish of the day and a small but decent selection of pastas. Plenty of cocktails and on Fri there's a DJ and dancing.

$ Hilltop Coffee House and Family Centre

Fogarthy Hill, St Peter's, T664-496 8765, see Facebook. Daily 0700-1500.

David and Clover Lea, of **Gingerbread Hill** fame (see above), run this café and gift shop at the start of the Oriole Walkway Trail (see page 79). One wall is devoted to the volcano, which David has filmed and photographed for years, another to album covers of musicians who recorded at **AIR Studios** (see box, page 78), and another to the late Arrow (a Montserrat-born musician who wrote and recorded the infamous Caribbean tune *Hot Hot Hot* in 1984). There is also table tennis, Wi-Fi, comfy seating and a balcony with ocean views. Good local juices, coffee or tea accompany pies, pastries and quiche.

$ JavaLava Art Café

St Peter's Main Rd, St Peter's, T664-491 5252, see Facebook. Mon-Sat 0800-1500, open until 2100 for dinner Tue and Thu.

Opposite St Peter's Anglican Church, this welcoming café offers breakfast and brunches of pancakes, bagels and omelettes, lunchtime-filled paninis and a hot daily special, smoothies and home-made buttery pastries. The frappucinos are the talk of the island. Wine is also served and there's free Wi-Fi.

$ Sips & Bites

Up from Carr's Bay on Davy Hill Rd, T664-491 8110. Daily 0800-2100.

In a lovely location overlooking the bay with distance views of Nevis, offers a delicious daily changing menu of island cuisine, and is well-known for its breaded baked chicken, stewed fish, spare ribs and hot wings. Also serves meat patties, sausage rolls and cheese sticks with juices, coffee or tea, as takeaway breakfasts, and there's a bar. Check out the interesting old pictures of Plymouth on the walls.

$ The Attic

Olveston Estate Dr, Olveston, T664-491 2008. Mon-Fri 0800-1600.

In a jaunty wooden house. Popular for rotis and quesadillas, fried chicken/fish and ribs, and very good local juices (guava, blackberry, soursop and lime) and drinks such as ginger beer, tamarind or sorrel, plus there's cold beer.

$ The People's Place

Fogarthy Hill, St Peter's, T664-491 8528. Open 'any day, any time'.

A roadside shack, next to **Hilltop Coffee House**, painted bright blue, popular and a friendly local lunch stop (owner John is here almost every day). Eat indoors or outside if it isn't too windy on the hilltop for the fantastic views, or have a takeaway. There's limited choice but what you get is tasty, filling and plentiful. Good roti, goat water and fish, washed down with a cold **Carib** or rum and coconut water.

$ Tina's Restaurant

Brades Main Rd, Cudjoe Head, T664-491 3538. Daily 1100-2200.

Nothing special to look at in a wooden building in a car park, but very popular with locals for food such as soups (pumpkin is especially good), curried goat, chicken, fish and pork chops, with traditional vegetables such as breadfruit, plantain and, often, a solid dumpling.

Bars and clubs

Most bars and rum shops are in Little Bay, Cudjoe Head, Salem and St John's. They are small, forcing people outside to drink and play dominoes, and stay open until the last guests leave. The Fri night lime (see box, page 23) after work is the busiest night. Somewhere will have live music Fri or Sat nights, and sometimes a DJ, maybe from Antigua. Ask at the tourist office for a recommendation of a taxi/minivan driver to take you on a rum shop tour.

Festivals

17 Mar St Patrick's Festival is a week-long celebration highlighting Montserrat's African and Irish heritage, which culminates on St Patrick's Day. The celebration also commemorates the thwarted slave uprising which was planned on that very day, back in 1768. Highlights of the festival include African and Irish music performances, a freedom run, and a recreated slave village and feast. For more information on the event, visit www.visitmontserrat.com.

Jun Queen's Birthday, middle Mon (a public holiday), Salem Park. Celebrated with parades, salutes and the raising of flags from service officers and school cadet groups and often the police marching band from Antigua and soldiers from St Kitts and Nevis participate.

Shopping

Arts and crafts

The best places to buy locally made arts and crafts and books are the Montserrat National Trust gift shops either at the National Museum of Montserrat or the Montserrat National Trust Botanical Garden.

Last Chance Souvenir Shop, *at the airport, T664-491 2752. Mon-Sat 0800-1800.* Good choice of high-quality souvenirs such as volcano photos, ceramics, rum and hot local sauces.

Luv Cotton Store, *Salem, in front of Gary Moore's Wide Awake Bar, T664-491 3906/496 7022. Mon-Sat 0930-1700.* Doris Dorsett works with Sea Island Cotton, which was produced on Montserrat in the early part of the 20th century and exported to Britain. Doris learned her weaving skills at a government training centre which closed because of Hurricane Hugo in 1989. Handwoven on a loom, she now produces lovely soft scarves, shawls, table placemats and small rugs. Call ahead to make sure she's open.

Food

The **Public Market** building in Little Bay, which was built along with other new buildings post-eruptions, is underused and often closed. Very little agricultural produce is grown on the island, and most fruit and vegetables are brought across from other islands.

Angelo's Int Ltd Supermarket, *Brades Main Rd, Brades, T664-491 6176. Mon-Sat 0800-0830, Sun 1000-1400, 1800-2030.* Stocks a good range including frozen food and imported fruit and veg, toiletries, alcoholic and non-alcoholic drinks.

Ashok's Supermarket, *Brades Main Rd, Brades, T664-4917868. Mon-Sat 0830-2230, Sun 0930-1530 and 1700-2200.* Reasonable selection of groceries and some wines, plus cheap Indian takeaway snacks and curries.

Stamps

Montserrat Philatelic Bureau, *in the government headquarters building, 7 Farara Plaza, Brades, T664-491 2042. Mon-Fri 0830-1600.* Montserrat's postage stamps have traditionally been collectors' items. The island has issued its own stamps since 1876 and there are 6 issues a year and a definitive issue every 4-5 years.

What to do

Birdwatching and hiking

Montserrat National Trust, *at the museum in Little Bay, T664-491 3086, www.montserrat nationaltrust.ms.* Birding and hiking guides can be arranged to go with you on the trails in the Centre Hills, US$15-25 per person, per hr depending on group size, and they also sell a trails map for US$3.70. With luck you'll get Philemon 'Mapeye' Murrain, who has worked for the Trust as a botanist for more than 25 years. He's a certified tour guide and is also the official guide for the Trust's Botanical Garden. The Trust usually organizes a hike on the 3rd Sun morning of each month, contact them or check the Facebook page.

Scriber's Adventure Tours, *Woodlands, T664-491 3412, www.scribersadventures.com.* Legendary tour guide, former forest ranger, and really nice guy, James 'Scriber' Daley got his nickname from his childhood penchant for 'describing' everything. He can arrange a number of hiking tours for birdwatching, and bat-watching (there are 10 species on

Montserrat). He is a master at mimicking the calling sounds of various birds including the Montserrat oriole.

Diving, snorkelling and kayaking

The volcano has had an unexpected benefit for Montserrat's underwater life, as the Maritime Exclusion Zone has meant no one has gone into the area for some years. Pyroclastic flows chucked huge boulders into the sea off the south coast which formed new substrata for reefs. These waters are teeming with fish, coral and sponges and their larvae have drifted with the currents to the reefs of the north where there are 30 or so accessible diving and snorkelling sites; ones close to the shore can also be explored by kayak. Additionally around the top of the island cliffs drop steeply to a sandy bottom at about 60 ft and here divers can find schools of reef fish and pelagics, although there can also be strong currents.

Aqua Montserrat, *Little Bay Beach, T664-496 9255, www.aquamontserrat.com. Mon-Sat except Wed, 1000-1600, Sun 1200-1700.* Offers guided snorkelling trips off the beach with underwater photos, US$30 for 1 hr, snorkelling and kayaking, US$55 for 2 hrs, and rents out snorkelling gear, US$9.25 per hr, and single/double kayaks from US$15 per hr.

Scuba Montserrat, *near the ferry terminal at Little Bay, T664-496 7807, www.scubamontserrat.com.* Run by Andrew Myers and Emmy Aston, who provide courses, diving and snorkelling excursions, kayaking, beach picnics, volcano boat tours and equipment rental. PADI Open Water course US$600, 2-tank dive US$88, single-tank shore dive with guide US$35, snorkelling boat trip US$35 (equipment rental US$10), boat transfer to Rendezvous Bay US$15, round trip US$25, 2-seater inflatable kayaks, US$15 per hr.

Transport

Note At the time of writing, and since Apr 2016, the Antigua–Montserrat ferry was not operating. A new tender has been posted for a company to take over the service and resume as soon as possible. Flights with **FlyMontserrat** are presently more frequent than in the regular schedule below, as residents of Montserrat are being offering government-subsidised tickets until the ferry service is replaced. For updates contact **FlyMontserrat**, the tourist offices in St John's in Antigua (see Tourist information, page 51), and see www.visitmontserrat.com.

Air

John A Osborne Airport was named after a former chief minister of Montserrat.

FlyMontserrat (VC Bird International Airport, Antigua, T268-562 7605; Montserrat, T664-491 3434; www.flymontserrat.com) operates the only scheduled flight (20 mins), which depart daily from Antigua at 0910, 1600 and 1715, returning from Montserrat at 0730, 1200 and 1530. Fares are US$77 one-way. Reconfirm within 24 hrs as the flights can be cancelled or times altered. The planes are very small; sometimes just 7-seaters, so luggage space is restricted and everything (including you) will be weighed. If all the above goes well, it is a spectacular flight with marvellous views. You can also charter a plane with **FlyMontserrat**, or with **ABM Air Montserrat** (Antigua T268-562 7183/8033, Montserrat T664-491 4200/2533, www.montserrat-flights.com), or a helicopter with **Caribbean Helicopters** (see page 68); work out the costs, sometimes chartering can be cost effective if there are 5 or more people with a lot of luggage. For transport from the airport, see Finding your feet, page 75.

Departure taxes are in included in fares when departing from Antigua, but the departure tax from Montserrat by air is payable at the airport: US$13 for Caricom nationals and US$21 for all other nationals, and by ferry at the port, US$4.

Bus and taxi

Minivans run up and down the main road between Salem in the southwest and Lookout in the north via Brades. They have green licence plates beginning with 'H', and fares are set at US$1.10 per journey; for an extra US$1.10, drivers will go 'off-route', and for the right price they will convert to taxis. Ask at the tourist office or your accommodation for a recommendation of a driver for an island tour; the standard hourly rate is US$22 and 4 hrs should be plenty unless you want to stop for lunch too.

Car hire

If you are driving, the roads are fairly good, but narrow and twisty, so be careful, especially on inclines. You can obtain a local 3-month driver's permit for US$18.50 at the police stations in Brades or Salem. Some small jeeps and saloon cars are available, US$45-50 per day, discount for 3-7 days hire, plus the optional collision damage waiver premium at US$12-15 per day. Ask the tourist office for recommendations or try:

Gage's Car Rental (Lookout, T664-493 5821, www.gagescarrental.com) or **Tip Top Enterprises** (Woodlands, T664-496 1842/392 1842, www.tiptopcarrentals.com).

St Kitts & Nevis

NAGICO
BUY SELL TRADE QUICK CASH
GOLD

St Kitts & Nevis

The islands of St Kitts (officially named St Christopher) and Nevis are in the north part of the Leeward Islands. Slightly off the beaten track, neither island is overrun with tourists; St Kitts is developing its southern peninsula where there are sandy beaches, but most of the island is untouched. Rugged volcanic peaks, forests and old fortresses produce spectacular views, and hiking is very rewarding. Two miles away, the conical island of Nevis is smaller and very desirable. Plantation houses on both islands have been converted into some of the most romantic hotels in the Caribbean, and are very popular with honeymooners.

While one federation, the sister islands are quite different. St Kitts, the larger, is more cosmopolitan and lively, receiving international flights and the largest cruise ships, while Nevis is quieter and more sedate, receiving regional flights and smaller craft.

Wherever you go on these two small islands there are breathtaking, panoramic views of the sea, mountains, cultivated fields and small villages.

rugged volcanoes and attractive beaches

St Kitts is made up of three groups of volcano peaks split by deep ravines and a low-lying peninsula in the southeast where there are salt ponds and fine beaches. The dormant volcano, Mount Liamuiga (3792 ft, pronounced Lie-a-mee-ga) occupies the central part of the island. The mountain was previously named Mount Misery by the British, but has now reverted to its Carib name, meaning 'fertile land'.

St Kitts was the last 'sugar island' in the Leewards group, but the industry operated at a loss and finally closed in 2005. Evidence of sugar cane is everywhere and in the foothills of

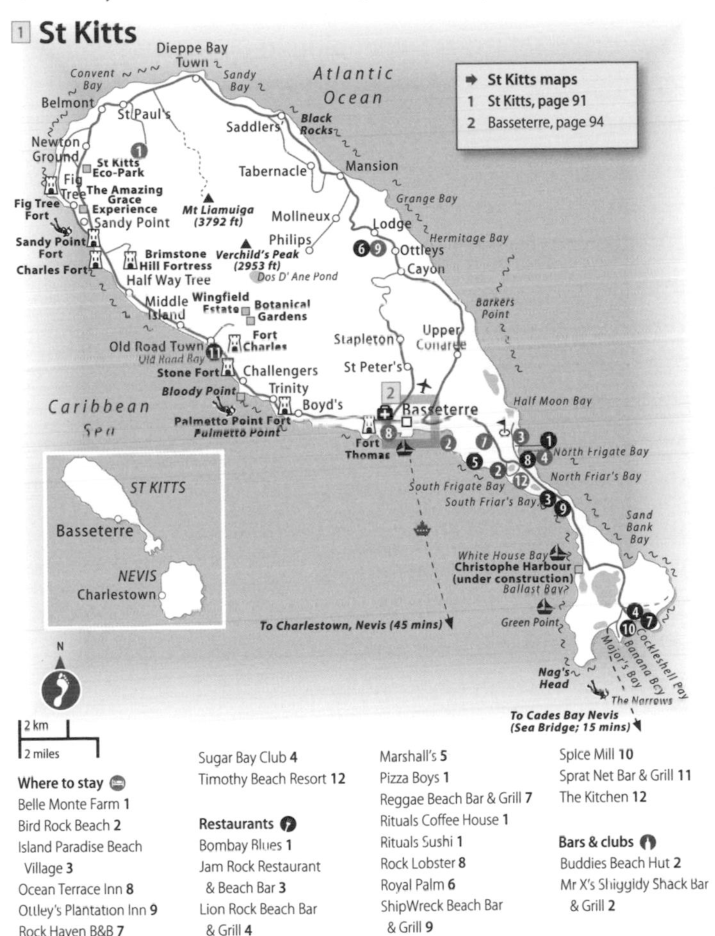

Essential St Kitts

Finding your feet

Robert L Bradshaw International Airport is just over 2 miles north of Basseterre. Taxis meet every flight and charge fixed rates; there's board displaying these outside along with a taxi dispatcher kiosk for the **St Kitts Taxi Association** (T869-465 8487; after hours T869-465 7818). Rates (for one to four people) are US$10 to Basseterre, Frigate Bay (north and south) US$16, Friars Bay (north and south) US$20, and down to Cockleshell Bay or Major's Bay (for the ferry to Cades Bay on Nevis) US$28. There's a 50% surcharge between 2200-0600. Alternatively, if you don't have much luggage you can walk between the airport and Basseterre, about 45 minutes, or on return to the airport, get a bus along the main road part way and walk the last five minutes; some buses might go right up to the terminal.

Cruise ships arrive at **Porte Zante** in Basseterre, a pedestrian area with shopping malls and restaurants that comes out on Bay Road in the middle of town. It also has the Port Zante Marina for yachts (www.portzantemarina.com) and is port of entry with customs and immigration facilities (Monday-Friday 0800-1600, overtime charged at weekends and after hours). Ferries from Nevis arrive and depart from the ferry terminal a little to the west of Port Zante on Bay Road, also home to the main bus terminal and taxi stand (with a board displaying taxi rates). The **Sea Bridge** car and passenger ferry arrives on the southeast peninsula at Major's Bay. See Transport, page 124.

Best restaurants

Ballahoo, page 115
Bombay Blues, page 116
Marshall's, page 116
Spice Mill, page 116
Reggae Beach Bar & Grill, page 117

Best strolls

Streets of Basseterre, page 93
Gardens at Romney Manor, page 96
Fort at Brimstone Hill, page 98
Beach at Cockleshell Bay, page 102
Lawns at Ottley's Plantation Inn, page 112

Getting around

The combined bus (minivans) and ferry terminal is on Bay Road in Basseterre where there is also a good food and beverage vendors' market. Cars can be hired and the main road around St Kitts is mostly very good. St Kitts is famous for not having any traffic lights (although town planners like roundabouts). A clockwise route around the island is best to see the historical sites as it will get you to Romney Manor and Brimstone Hill Fortress in the bright morning sun and maybe to **Ottley's Plantation Inn** on the east side for a late lunch or afternoon drink. If you book a day tour, this is the route most drivers will take.

Alternatively, a cheaper way is to take a minivan from Basseterre to Dieppe Bay Town or Saddlers (where you'll have to change) and then back to Basseterre along the Atlantic coast. The disadvantages of this is there are some long, hot and steep walks from the road up to the sites, particularly to Brimstone Hill.

the mountains, particularly in the north, you will see the grassland tracts that were once covered extensively with sugar cane plantations, and on the Atlantic coast catch glimpses of the narrow-gauge railway that was used to transport it from the fields (now the Sugar Train; see box, page 99). Disused sugar mills are dotted around as well as the plantation Great Houses. Some are now abandoned and ruined, some are in private hands, while **Ottley's** is open to the public as a fine and atmospheric hotel.

The decline in the sugar industry has thrown St Kitts into the arms of the tourist industry instead. Basseterre, and St Kitts in general, is heavily dependent on cruise ship tourism; three to four ships visit at a time in season (November to March), which can equate to a rather staggering 12,000 passengers per day. All the shops, arcades and stalls open when a ship is in port and the place is lively and vibrant, yet everything can seem dead and dull when there isn't. However, on the southeast peninsula, there is a great deal of development, such as the Christophe Harbour with its yacht marina and luxury villas, and the new **Park Hyatt St Kitts** in Banana Bay, which may be open by the time you read this.

Basseterre

The port of Basseterre, the capital and largest town, was founded in 1727 and named by the French (it means 'lower ground'). It has a slightly ramshackle appearance, but is a charming and relaxed place to wander around. Earthquakes, hurricanes and finally a disastrous fire destroyed the original town in 1867 and consequently it was rebuilt. There is a complete mishmash of architectural styles from elegant Georgian buildings with arcades, verandas and jalousies, mostly in good condition, to ugly 20th-century concrete block houses.

In the heart of Basseterre, an old waterfront warehouse on Bay Road has been converted into the **Pelican Mall**, a shopping and recreational complex, which also houses the St Kitts Tourism Authority. Behind is **Port Zante**, which was built in 1995 on 15 acres of reclaimed land along the waterfront between Brumbill Street and College Street. It is home to the cruise ship port, capable of accommodating the largest ships afloat, together with a marina, and lots of duty-free and souvenir shops, cafés and restaurants. Like other cruise ship terminals in the Caribbean, it can be very crowded when passengers come ashore, but otherwise it's fairly quiet (and shops may even close). You may be able to negotiate discounts on which the shopkeepers call 'dry days'.

At the south end of Fort Street on Bay Road is the imposing façade of the **Old Treasury Building**, with a dome covering an arched gateway. This building replaced a wooden building with an arched gateway, once the entrance to the town after you had disembarked from your ship at Treasury Pier. It was built in 1894 and the construction was financed by unused deposits on return voyages for indentured Portuguese labourers, most of who chose to stay on the island rather than return at the end of their contract. It has been converted into the **National Museum** ⓘ *T869-465 5584, www.stkittsheritage.com, Mon-Fri 0915-1700, Sat 0915-1300, US$3, children under 12 free*, which has a small, interesting display of old photographs and artefacts dealing with early occupations of the island, colonial and sugar history, and the journey to independence, together with exhibits on culture and arts. The gift shop sells copies of historic prints, books, postcards, handicrafts and jewellery to raise funds for the St Christopher National Trust, which also has its offices here.

Opposite the museum on Fort Street is the **Circus**, styled after London's Piccadilly Circus (but looking nothing like it). In the centre of the historic district of town, just back from Bay Road, it's lined with shops, restaurants and banks. It's at its busiest on Friday afternoon when locals come to lime (see box, page 23), and is as good a spot for people-watching as the London original. In its centre, the handsome green **Berkeley Memorial Drinking Fountain and Clock** (1891) is a memorial to Thomas Berkeley, former president of the General Legislative Council.

Head north up Fort Street, turn left at the main thoroughfare (Cayon Street) and you will come to **St George's Anglican Church** ⓣ *T869-465-2167, www.stkittsanglicanchurch.org, open most days 0800-1600, donation appreciated*, set in its own large garden, with a massive, square buttressed tower. In the early stages of the French occupation of Basseterre, it was originally a Roman Catholic Church built by the Jesuits and called Notre Dame, which was razed to the ground by the English in 1706. Rebuilt four years later and renamed St George's, it suffered damage from hurricanes and earthquakes on several occasions. It, too, was a victim of the 1867 fire. It was rebuilt in 1869 and contains some attractive stained glass windows. Further hurricane damage since the end of the 1980s has led to ongoing repair works. Amazingly, the original wooden pipe organ inside has survived each reincarnation. There is a fine view of the town from the tower, the tallest structure in Basseterre, accessed via five flights of very steep stairs which are almost ladders.

Independence Square was built in the 1730s and is surrounded now by a low white fence; eight gates let paths converge on a fountain in the middle of the square (it looks like the Union Jack when seen from the air). There are gaily painted muses on top of the

fountain. Originally designed for slave auctions and council meetings and called Pall Mall Square, it was renamed after independence in 1983 and now contains many plants, spacious lawns and lovely old trees. It is surrounded by 18th-century houses and, at its east end, the **Basseterre Co-Cathedral of Immaculate Conception** with its twin towers and impressive palm trees out front. Built in 1927, it is surprisingly plain inside. The first Catholic church was built in 1856 when an influx of Portuguese from Madeira after 1835 increased demand for services and this is its replacement. At 10 North Independence Square Street you can visit the very attractive and colourfully painted shuttered building housing the **Gallery Café** ⓘ *T869-465 7701, see Facebook, Mon-Sat 0900-1600*, to see artist Rosey Cameron-Smith's paintings and prints of local views and customs, as well as an impressive selection of work by other artists. While the walls are covered with larger pieces, there are plenty of affordable watercolours, small prints, gift cards and glassware. The café itself has comfortable sofas, good coffees, teas and juices, snacks like bagels and homemade pastries, and there are often yoga classes held here.

On South Independence Square Street is one of the best examples of 18th-century English colonial architecture, known as **Georgian House**. It probably once held slaves in its cellars, either prior to or post auction before being transferred to the plantations. It was built around 1790 and by 1836 it was the home of a merchant, James Berridge, whose fleet traded throughout the Caribbean and up the eastern seaboard of the USA and Canada. Berridge came to St Kitts in 1794 at the age of 20 "with no resources but his own abilities", but by 1812 he was not only a thriving merchant but also treasurer of the island's government, lieutenant colonel of the Windward Regiment of Foot and aide de camp to the governor.

West and north coasts

Most tours and cruise ship excursions take a clockwise route around the island taking in the magnificent Brimstone Hill Fortress, the lovely botanical gardens at Romney Manor and other sites on the west coast overlooking the Caribbean Sea. This part of shoreline is guarded by no less than seven **forts** and taking the road out of Basseterre, you will pass the sites of Fort Thomas, Palmetto Point Fort, Stone Fort, Fort Charles, Charles Fort, Sandy Point Fort and Fig Tree Fort. Little remains of any of them but the drive has plenty of historic interest. Once around the northern tip of the island, the Atlantic side of the island is wilder and offers good views of the coast with its palm trees bending into the wind. If you are following the route in a hire car, allow a leisurely day for the loop from Basseterre or Frigate Bay.

Basseterre to Old Road Town Heading west from Basseterre along the Caribbean coast, you come to the village of **Boyd's** where the 18th century **Fairview Great House** was built in 1701 for a French army commanding officer. It was surrounded by a wall with a gun emplacement at the edge of the property, a feature not seen at plantation houses inland or on the east coast. Although it was restored and opened to the public in 2011, it sadly closed again in 2016; perhaps the new owners will recommence tours in the future.

Beyond the village of Trinity, at **Bloody Point** is a sign board and white cross marks the site of what is now termed as the Kalinago Genocide. By 1626 both the British and the French settlements were expanding at such a rate that the Caribs began to perceive a threat to its very existence on the island. Joining forces with Caribs from other islands, Chief Tegremare prepared to attack the European settlements. Despite growing animosity between the French and the British, the two mounted a combined, pre-emptive attack on

BACKGROUND

St Kitts

Recorded history of St Kitts began when it was documented in Christopher Columbus' second voyage in 1493 when he sailed past but did not land. He named it St Christopher; possibly after himself, or after the patron saint of travellers, as it is said that he thought the island resembled the shape of St Christopher carrying Christ on his shoulder. It was only centuries later that it was affectionately nicknamed St Kitts.

At Columbus' time the islands were inhabited by the Arawaks and Carib people, and the first European settlement was in 1624 when the British arrived and founded the first non-Spanish European colony in the Caribbean. But French settlers quickly followed in 1627. Within a year, an early eruption of violence wiped out the entire native population of Arawaks and Caribs, and once the English and French had the island to themselves, they developed their sugar and tobacco plantations unheeded and brought in African slaves.

The Treaty of Versailles of 1783 granted St Kitts along with Nevis to Britain. The islands, along with Anguilla, united in 1882 and were part of the colony of the Leeward Islands (1871–1956) and of the West Indies Federation (1958–62). In 1967, St Kitts-Nevis-Anguilla became a self-governing state in association with Great Britain. Anguilla separated from the federation in 1980 and in 1983 St Kitts and Nevis gained full independence.

the Caribs. Over 2000 were massacred at Bloody Point, and legend has it so much blood spilled that it ran for three days straight; hence the name.

In Challengers Village is another plantation house, **Clay Villa** ⓘ *T869-465 2353, www.clayvilla.com, tours by appointment*. The 1763 house and gardens covering 10 acres are a family home, but there is a small museum and the owners give a very informative tour followed by delicious rum or fruit punch. There is an emphasis on the Amerindian heritage, partly because this was a free working estate which never used African slaves. Profits from tours go towards local good causes, mainly animal welfare.

Old Road Town and around Old Road Bay is believed to be the original landing point for the English sea captain and explorer, Sir Thomas Warner, in 1623. After checking several other islands in the Caribbean, it was Warner that decided that St Kitts would be the best site for an English colony. He had noted its strategic central position, fertile soil, abundant fresh water and large salt deposits. It became the first permanent European settlement in the Leeward Islands, and the settlers were at first on good terms with the island's Carib inhabitants, though such friendship lasted only a very few years. Rather than cultivating sugar, it was tobacco that had drawn Warner to the island, and it was the island's tobacco crop that first supported the settlement. The Warner family estate served as the capital of St Kitts until 1727, when it was moved to Basseterre.

At Old Road Town turn right up to Wingfield Estate, from where the road also then winds around to **Romney Manor**. It is believed that the Carib chief, Tegreman, previously had his village on what are now the grounds of the house, and as you approach, the remains of large stones with drawings, or petroglyphs, can be seen. At **Wingfield Estate** you can see the remains of old sugar machinery and buildings, including a 17th-century rum distillery, and the only aqueduct on the island. The estate dates from 1625 and was the first land granted in the English West Indies. Initially it grew tobacco and indigo, but from 1640 onwards it concentrated on sugar and rum. As technology developed, sugar was crushed first by animal power, then water power and eventually a steam engine, evidence of which can all be seen. It is free to walk around and there are display boards with information about each component.

Adjacent to Wingfield Estate, the **Botanical Gardens of Romney Manor and Caribelle Batik** ⓘ *T869-465 6253, www.caribellebatikstkitts.com, Mon-Fri, 0830-1600, daily when cruise ships are in, US$2.80, children under 11 free,* are today a joint attraction. Dating to the early 17th century, Romney Manor was once owned by Sam Jefferson, great-great-grandfather of Thomas Jefferson, the third president of the US. It was bought and renamed by Lord Romney in the late 17th century and was one of the most important sugar producers on the island. It remained in the Romney family for more than 200 years, and in 1834 the Romney Estate was the first to emancipate its slaves, despite contrary instructions from the British Parliament.

Unfortunately, Romney Manor was destroyed by fire in 1995, although the old bell tower still stands. This is in fact unusual; given that the ringing of the bell signalled every aspect of the life of a slave, they represented oppression, and many bell towers on plantations were destroyed after emancipation. The Romney family, however, were considered as benevolent masters and the ex-slaves allowed the tower to remain.

The gardens have been restored beautifully and are now a major attraction on island tours and cruise ship trips. They feature springy green lawns, fountains, terraces, labelled palms and other trees and coastal views. There is an enormous saman tree, believed to date from around 1600-1650, grown from seeds brought from South America by Arawak Indians, which has a girth of 23 ft and a remarkable canopy that spans three quarters of an acre. **Caribelle Batik** has a well-stocked shop where the cloths (no two pieces are the same) are made into clothing, wall hangings depicting Kittian scenes, bags, purses and wraps, and you can watch the artists producing the colourful and highly attractive material. A guide will explain the process.

Wingfield Estate is also the home of **Sky Safari Tours** ⓘ *T869-466 4259, www.skysafaristkitts.com, daily 0800-1500, tours normally run at 0900, 1030, 1200 and 1400, but schedules may change to accommodate cruise ship groups, reservations are essential, minimum age 6, closed shoes essential, US$89, children under 15 US$65,* a zip-line excursion through the rainforest with stunning views over the island down to Brimstone Hill Fortress and the sea. There is a short training line, then you are taken up the mountain in an open-air truck (look for green vervet monkeys along the way), from where you harness up for three breathtaking traverses across a small valley, followed by a double line race to the end; the highest point is 250 ft above the ground. Staff are friendly, entertaining and safety-conscious, but guests always wish there were more runs.

At the top and the end of the road to Wingfield Estate is the trailhead for a difficult half-day hike up to the attractive but secluded freshwater **Dos d'Ane Pond** on the lower slopes of **Verchild's Peak**. The trail itself is easy to find and follow but a sturdy vehicle with reasonable clearance is needed to get to the trailhead itself. From the start the trail begins to ascend quickly. It begins up a short but steep ghaut then becomes a more gradual switch-back trail, ascending the ridge of the mountain. The pond at the top sits at about 2460 ft, has a small but picturesque waterfall, is surrounded by emerald-green rainforest, and has a magical other-worldly feel about it. But it's likely to be shrouded in cloud – even glimpsing the opposite side of the pond can be difficult – and the walk can be wet and muddy. Allow about five hours for the return trip, go well-equipped and hike in a group.

At the village of **Middle Island**, you will see, on your right and slightly up the hill, the **St Thomas Church** at the head of an avenue of dead or dying royal palms. Here is the grave of Sir Thomas Warner who died on 10 March 1649, and the raised tomb is inscribed 'General of y Caribee'. There is also a bronze plaque with a copy of the inscription inside the church. Other early tombs are of Captain John Pogson (1656) and Sir Charles Payne, 'Major General of Leeward Carribee Islands', who was buried in 1744. The next village, **Half Way Tree**, is so called to avoid disputes. Warner and the French colonists chose a tamarind tree here in 1625 to mark the border between their territories. As the colonies grew and became increasingly prosperous, this border was sorely tested.

Brimstone Hill ⓘ *T869-465 2609, www.brimstonehillfortress.org, daily 0930-1730, US$10, children under 14 US$6.30, refundable deposit for audio guide US$4.80; allow up to 2 hrs.* Just before Sandy Point is the turn-off up to the impressive bastion which is the **Brimstone Hill Fortress**, although you will have seen it from along the coast road long before you arrive. It is one of the 'Gibraltars of the West Indies' (a title it shares with Les Saintes, off Guadeloupe), and sprawls over 38 acres on the slopes of a limestone hill 800 ft above the sea. It commands an incredible view of St Kitts and Nevis and on clear days you can see St Eustatius (5 miles), Saba (20 miles), Montserrat (40 miles), St Barts (40 miles), St Martin (45 miles) and Anguilla (67 miles). The site was inaugurated as a national park by Queen Elizabeth II in 1985 and gained UNESCO World Heritage Site status in 1999. The English mounted the first cannon on Brimstone Hill in 1690 in an attempt to force the French from Fort Charles below. The British released the potential of the hill as a place of defence and proceeded to fortify it; it was designed by British army engineers and built by African slaves. In 1782 it was besieged by 8000 French troops and the 1000 or so British fought for a month before surrendering. A year later the Treaty of Versailles returned the island to Britain and Brimstone was re-occupied by British troops until the fortress was abandoned in 1852.

It was constructed out of local limestone and volcanic stones and was designed along classic defensive lines. The five bastions overlook each other and also guard the only road as it zigzags up to the parade ground. The entrance is at the Barrier Redan where payment is made. Pass the Magazine Bastion but stop at the Orillon Bastion which contains the massive ordnance store (165 ft long with walls at least 6 ft thick). The hospital was located here and under the south wall is a small cemetery. You then arrive at the Prince of Wales Bastion (note the graffitied name of J Sutherland, 93rd Highlanders 24 October 1822 on the wall next to one of the cannons) from where there are good views over to the parade ground. Park at the parade ground where there is a small snack bar and good gift shop in the warrant officer's quarters. Stop for a good video introduction at the visitor centre, and then walk up the narrow and quite steep ramp to Fort George, the Citadel and the highest defensive position. From here are the best views, which are simply outstanding. You can climb up to the turrets lined with replica cannons and down to the barrack rooms which have informative display boards.

Tip...

You can get off a minibus on the main road, but the 1½-mile walk up to the fortress is extremely steep, hot and for fit hikers only; try instead to persuade the driver to take you 'off route' up to the entrance.

ON THE ROAD

The Sugar Train

The sugar industry was revolutionized in St Kitts when first the estates moved from wind to steam power in 1870 and then a central sugar factory was built in Basseterre in 1912. A narrow-gauge railway was built in 1912-1926 to deliver cane from the fields to the central sugar mill and it was the beginning of the end for all the small estate-based sugar mills dotted around the island. Many sail-less windmills still stand as relics of the old ways. Although the track initially ran as two spurs either side of the island, planters soon saw the sense of abandoning other delivery systems and it was extended to be a circular route all round the coast. With the decline in the sugar industry in the late 20th century, the track fell into disrepair, although parts of it remained in use until 2005 when the industry finally closed.

Today a tourist train, the **St Kitts Scenic Railway** (T869-465 7263, www.stkittsscenicrailway.com), operates on 18 miles of renovated track up the Atlantic coast from Needsmust station near the airport to La Vallee Station in Newton Ground on the northwestern tip of the island. With guided commentary and drinks, the rail journey takes two hours and is part of a tour that includes another 45 minutes by bus; they also run in reverse, and between them, they make a complete 30-mile circle around the island.

The railway lies mostly on the uphill side of the main island road, although in many places it runs along the coast. It has double decker carriages with an upper open-air viewing deck and the lower, enclosed, air-conditioned level. However, it only operates when there is a cruise ship in port, but anyone can join; book in advance and check what the cruise ship schedule is at the tourist office. It costs US$89, children (3-11) US$45, under 2s free.

Sandy Point Beyond Brimstone Hill, Sandy Point is the second largest town on the island and was established in the 1620s. It was one of the busiest ports in the region with hundreds of warehouses lining the shoreline. But after 1727, when the bulk of commercial activity moved to Basseterre, the port diminished in importance. In 1984, it was closed entirely following the impact of Hurricane Klaus. Once there were two forts here, Sandy Point Fort and Charles Fort (the latter named after King Charles II sent £500 to assist in its construction), which were built around 1670, although nothing remains of them now.

The Amazing Grace Experience ⓘ *Crab Hill, Sandy Point, T869-465 1122, www.amazinggraceexperience.com, Mon-Fri 0900-1600, Sat 1000-1300, later on Sat and Sun by appointment, US$7, children under 12 free,* opened in 2012 in the Lighthouse Baptist Church. and honours the man who wrote the lyrics to *Amazing Grace*. John Newton (1725-1807), a slave trader, became a reformed man during a visit to St Kitts in 1754. While anchored at Sandy Point to deliver West African slaves and collect sugar from the island, he had profound conversations with a Scottish ship's captain, Alexander Clunie that brought him to understand "the security of the covenant of grace". He subsequently joined the clergy, became actively involved in the abolitionist movement and wrote several hymns with the poet William Cowper, including *Amazing Grace*. It was written to illustrate a sermon on New Year's Day 1773, nearly 20 years after his visit to the island. The music most closely associated with the hymn, *New Britain*, was not added until 1835. It is a small but interesting exhibition which does its best to link the hymn to St Kitts through information panels and a 10-minute film. Just beyond on the right is another newish attraction, **St Kitts Eco-Park** ⓘ *Sir Gillies Estate, Sandy Point, T869-465 8755, www.ecopark.kn, Mon-Sat 0900-1600, US$4.80, children (6-12) US$2.40, under 5s free.* It opened in 2014 and is a joint project between St Kitts and Taiwan designed to promote green initiatives and enhance local agricultural skills. The 20-acre site has well-laid out gardens and orchards planted with plants, fruit trees and crops, and a key feature is a massive greenhouse where plants are grown in a cooled climate (and also hosts local weddings). It's still very much a work in progress, despite all the grand buildings at the entrance, but the guides here will explain how the plants are used on the island in food, tea and as herbal remedies. There is also a watchtower for an overview and children will enjoy the maze.

North and east coast

From Sandy Point the road winds its way around the northern top of the island through the villages of Newton Ground and St Paul's to **Dieppe Bay Town**, founded in 1625 by French settlers led by Pierre D'Esnambuc, where there is a palm-lined black-sand beach. It has been moved around by hurricanes but it is still a good place to stroll, with lots of sandpipers and herons and a view of The Quill on St Eustatius in the distance. The waves crashing over the offshore reef is supposedly where the Caribbean Sea meets the Atlantic Ocean.

Pass through Saddlers to the **Black Rocks**. Here lava flowed into the sea from Mount Liamuiga some 1800 years ago, providing interesting rock formations that have been pounded and eroded by the sea into sharp edges. The main road continues southeast along the Atlantic coast. Many island tours stop at **Ottley's Plantation Inn** (see page 112), an 1832 Great House and named after first owner, English sugar planter Drewry Ottley, and now a luxury hotel and a beautiful and atmospheric place to go for lunch, coffee or dinner if you aren't staying there. The road then continues through Cayon back to Basseterre or Frigate Bay past the Robert L Bradshaw International Airport.

Southeast peninsula

The southeast spit of land, the tail of the tadpole that is St Kitts, is where you find the island's sandy beaches and salt ponds, and is the closest point to Nevis which lies across The Narrows at its most southerly point. To get there, turn off the roundabout at the end of Wellington Road (opposite the turning to the airport) and turn left. This leads to the narrow spit of land sandwiched between North and South Frigate Bays, and then the six-mile Dr Kennedy A Simmonds Highway runs to Major's Bay along the backbone of the peninsula. It's a lovely drive with views down from the hills into the coves on both the Caribbean and Atlantic sides and Nevis at the end.

Frigate Bay Frigate Bay is the name of the two bays close together where the peninsula narrows. North Frigate Bay is on the Atlantic, South Frigate Bay on the Caribbean, about half a mile apart and divided by a huge roundabout on Dr Kennedy A Simmonds Highway. This area is where most if the island's tourist development is located. **North Frigate Bay** is dominated by the huge **St Kitts Marriott Resort & Royal Beach Casino** and adjacent **Royal St Kitts Golf Club**, and between the roundabout and the road that goes to the Marriot are several other resorts and condominium complexes, restaurants, and some shops around the **Sugar Bay Club**. Breakers have been built along this stretch of coast so that guests can

ON THE ROAD

Mount Liamuiga

St Kitts is dominated by the southeast range of mountains (1159 ft), the higher central range which contains Verchild's Peak (2953 ft), and the even higher northwest range where the extinct volcano Mount Liamuiga (3792 ft) is not only the highest point in St Kitts and Nevis, but in the entire Leeward Islands, as well as one of the tallest peaks in the eastern Caribbean archipelago. The Caribs knew their island as Liamuiga, or 'fertile land', a reference to the productive volcanic soil. It stands majestically above the rainforests that are now expanding over the tracts of disused land where sugar cane was once cultivated.

Its peak is topped by a wide summit crater, and the last eruption of the volcano was believed to be about 1800 years ago. Liamuiga attracts a lot of rain and is usually shrouded with cloud, and it was formerly named Mount Misery; it was renamed on the date of St Kitts' independence, 19 September, 1983. Cloud allowing, from the summit, it is possible to see the entire island and across to Nevis, Saba, St Barts, Saint Martin/Sint Maarten and Antigua.

Guided hikes are organized to the summit, or you can go unguided, and the trail is signposted off the main road near the village of St Paul's. You can drive part way on a dirt track; it's a long, gradual incline but smaller cars in good shape can usually make it, but if it has rained, there are several large mud puddles to negotiate. There is a car park where the road ends at the trailhead at 1500 ft. From here the two-hour ascent covers about 3½ miles and climbs through a cathedral-like rainforest with magnificent trees.

The first third of the trail is a gradual incline with some stairs and rope handholds. The rope may seem unnecessary when it's dry, but this section can get extremely muddy after a large rainfall. The second third begins when you reach a riverbed and it becomes much steeper, and the final third levels out and actually starts going back down in parts. But the last half a mile is a scramble, with rocks and tree roots and is very steep and slippery. It then emerges on the rim of the half-mile-wide volcanic crater where there are two viewpoints with ropes and ladders to get you to the top of rocks to look down at the lost green world at the base 700 ft below. For a more challenging hike, allow another two hours to climb in and out of the crater (again steep and rope-assisted; being with a guide is most certainly advised), where you can see the small lake and fumaroles, which are small cracks filled with sulphuric mud and gases.

A good level of fitness is required, but the path is maintained and the higher you go the cooler it gets. Wear proper hiking shoes or boots, be prepared to get dirty and maybe take walking sticks, as well as a small backpack with water and snacks, and you'll have an excellent chance of conquering Mount Misery.

get into the water and a reef gives some protection, but generally beaches on the Atlantic, or windward, side are not safe for swimming and attract a lot of seaweed.

South Frigate Bay is a short walk from the roundabout and lies between the base of Sir Timothy's Hill on the eastern end and the base of another hill on the western end. It is dominated by the **Timothy Beach Resort** and a string of beach bars collectively known as 'The Strip'. Consequently it isn't the cleanest beach on the island and the beach loungers are shabby, but it is pleasant and there is good snorkelling around the rocks in front of the **Timothy Beach Resort**. If the sea is a bit rough, watch out for rocks when entering the water but once you get out a bit further there is sand underfoot.

> **Tip...**
> Thursday to Saturday are the best nights to come for partying and dancing on the beach at The Strip, when a stream of minibuses bring people out from Basseterre, or it's easy enough to walk from hotels in North Frigate Bay.

Friars Bay Like Frigate Bay, Friars Bay is split into north and south on either side of the peninsula, and again at their closest, they are less than a mile apart. **North Friars Bay** beach is very open and sandy but do not be tempted by its beauty and emptiness; it's deserted because the Atlantic here is treacherous, even in shallow areas. There are no facilities, no shade and no beach bar. **South Friars Bay** is a long stretch of sand with access at the north and south ends. Take the right fork in the track to the north end, where there are beach bars and dark sand which is cleaned regularly. What appear to be shacks quickly spring into life as bars according to demand, such as when a cruise ship is in port. It can get very busy at weekends and you can rent sun loungers and umbrellas. The sea is calm enough for swimming and snorkelling. Brown pelicans can be seen diving for fish and the view of cliffs and mountains is attractive.

White House Bay This bay on the Caribbean side is being developed as Christophe Harbour with a yacht marina and luxury development of villas; some of which are finished and occupied. You'll notice the roads leading off up into the gated communities in the hills. Once completed, the marina will include berths big enough to accommodate superyachts and a shore side marina village with shops and services.

Sand Bank Bay The road down the peninsula skirts the Great Salt Pond. Halfway round the pond turn left to reach horseshoe-shaped Sand Bank Bay, backed by sand dunes with hills at each end. There are no public facilities, although a few houses have been built, set back from the beach. There is a private beach club at one end, **The Pavilion**, part of the Christophe Harbour development, but otherwise it is just a wild, windy and empty beach apart from a few cows. It's a great place for picnics, but don't swim as there is an undertow.

Cockleshell Bay Continue on the main highway towards the end of the road at the **Sea Bridge** car and passenger ferry at Major's Bay (see page 103) and just before turn left for Cockleshell Bay. The beach here is a two-mile curving stretch of powdery-white sand, and is the closest point to Nevis with a stunning view across The Narrows. It is excellent for swimming which makes it the most popular beach on the southeast peninsula, and is a magnet for Kittitians out to party on weekends and public holidays, and a favourite for cruise ship excursions. But you can have the beach pretty much to yourself on weekdays in the quiet summer season.

There are varied beach bars, from the gourmet **Spice Mill Restaurant**, through to the unprepossessing **Lion Rock Beach Bar**

> **Tip...**
> No public buses run any further south than North Frigate Bay; a taxi from Basseterre to Cockleshell Bay costs about US$28, and from Frigate Bay US$26.

& Grill, known for its mean rum punch, and the barbecue-style **Reggae Beach Bar** with its rows of sun loungers and thatched umbrellas, from where water taxis go across to Nevis (see page 117). You can hire snorkelling gear and head for the rocks where there are lots of colourful fish, and women offer aloe vera massages on the beach. **St Kitts Water Sports** is here and offers a large range of activities (see page 123).

Banana Bay and Major's Bay Another left turn-off before Major's Bay is to Banana Bay, now the location for the new 124-room, luxury five-star **Park Hyatt St Kitts**, part of the Christophe Harbour development and the first Park Hyatt hotel in the Caribbean, which may well be open by the time you read this (www.stkitts.park.hyatt.com). The road ends at Major's Bay, 10 miles southeast from Robert L Bradshaw International Airport, which is a thin strip of land between the sea and the pond. The sand is mostly at the far end and it is rocky where the cars stop for the **Sea Bridge** car and passenger ferry between St Kitts and Nevis (see page 104). There is nothing else here apart from the ferry, but the water is calm and there's a lovely view of Nevis, which from this point is about 3½ miles away.

Nevis

small island with a low-key and easy-going atmosphere

Two miles across The Narrows from St Kitts is the beautiful little circular island of Nevis, which covers an area of 36 square miles. The central dormant volcano, Nevis Peak (3232 ft), is usually shrouded in white clouds and mist. It reminded Columbus of Spanish snow-capped mountains and so he called the island 'Las Nieves'. For the Kalinago (Caribs), it was Oualie, the land of beautiful water. Smaller than St Kitts, it is also quieter.

The delightful plantation inns have long been a favourite with the well-heeled British and the newer **Four Seasons Resort Nevis** now attracts golfing Americans. Like St Kitts, it's easily explored on an island tour, by bus or taxi, which can take in the major sites like the small but interesting museums, the pretty Botanical Gardens, the delightfully quaint capital of Charlestown with its Georgian-style buildings, with perhaps a stop for lunch at a beach-side restaurant or local rum shop.

Charlestown

The main town of Nevis is one of the best-preserved old towns in the Caribbean, with several interesting buildings dating from the 18th century. It is small and compact, on Gallows Bay, guarded by Fort Charles to the south and the long sweep of Pinney's Beach to the north. Nevis had the only court in the West Indies to try and hang pirates. Prisoners were taken from the courthouse across the swamp to where the gallows were set up, hence the name, Gallows Bay. After embarking from the ferry, you arrive on a pleasant waterfront area with a café/snack bar, seating for waiting passengers and a gateway leads a few steps into the centre of town. Alternatively, you can walk through the old stone **Cotton Ginnery**, which was where cotton was ginned and packed into bales before shipment to England, and now houses about half a dozen shops, the **Nevis Philatelic Bureau** (see page 121) and a cheerful restaurant.

The centre of town is dominated by **DR Walwyn Square**, where on one side the balconied **Old Customs/Treasury House**, built in 1837 and restored in 2002, is now the **tourist office** and headquarters for the Nevis Tourism Authority. The ground floor

Essential Nevis

Finding your feet

The small Vance W Amory International Airport is in the north of the island at Newcastle, 7 miles from Charlestown. A taxi dispatcher is in the car park and rates are set; to Charlestown US$19.50, the closer hotels like **Nisbet** and **Oualie**, US$10, and across the island to Montpelier or Hermitage US$25. A few buses (minivans) pull into the airport on their route around the island, but do not rely on them. The fare to Charlestown is US$1.50.

The ferry terminal is right in the middle of Charlestown; taxis wait on the street outside, or the bus stops are just around the corner. The **Sea Bridge** car and passenger ferry docks at Cades Bay, and on-demand water taxis from St Kitts at Cades Bay or **Oualie Beach Resort**, both on the island's northwest side. See Transport, page 126.

Best places to stay

Best stops on an island tour

Getting around

The main road around Nevis is only 20 miles, so it doesn't take long to circumnavigate, and there are taxis, hire cars, buses (minivans), or you can walk or hire a bike. Minivans start from the two bus stops in Charlestown, close to each other near DR Walwyn Square and a short walk from the ferry. Taxis offer leisurely island tours and drivers make good and friendly guides.

is constructed of stone, and the upper floor built of wood with clapboard sheathing. This style, known as blouse and skirt can be seen all over Charlestown, and often, like the tourist office, the upper wooden floor has a gallery or veranda featuring elaborate fretwork and wooden railings, which were added to buildings years after their original construction. Other fine examples are the nearby **Post Office** and **Main Street Grocery** opposite the police station. The **police station** itself is a handsome stone mansion dating from 1811, which at one time was on the outskirts of town and had a basement for police horse and carriages to shelter in.

Memorial Square, to the south of DR Walwyn Square, is larger and more impressive; the war memorial is in a small garden and commemorates the Nevisian soldiers who died during the First and Second World Wars. The **Courthouse** was constructed here in 1825 and used as the Nevis Government Headquarters, but were largely destroyed by fire in 1873 and subsequently rebuilt. It now houses the Nevis High Court and upstairs, the town library. The little square tower was erected in 1909 to 1910, and contains a clock which keeps accurate time with an elaborate pulley and chain system. You can see it, together with the weights, among the roof trusses in the **library** ⓘ *Mon-Fri 0900-1800, Sat 0900-1700*. Behind the square towards the waterfront, **Charlestown Public Market** ⓘ *Tue and Sat 0730-1500*, is where local farmers sell their produce. It can be fascinating to try and identify fruit and vegetables and there is usually a good range of ginger, chillies and other spices.

Other notable Charlestown buildings include the **Methodist Church** off Chapel Street. Ten years after emancipation, the freed slaves of Nevis using their own locally raised funds and labour, with European supervision, built it in 1844 on the site of previous wooden chapels; one built in 1794 and a replacement in 1802. The new church was large enough to hold 1500 worshippers, the basement was used as a school, and it is reported that children carried stones to assist with the construction. Next to it the **Methodist Manse** dates to the previous wooden church of 1802, another blouse and skirt building.

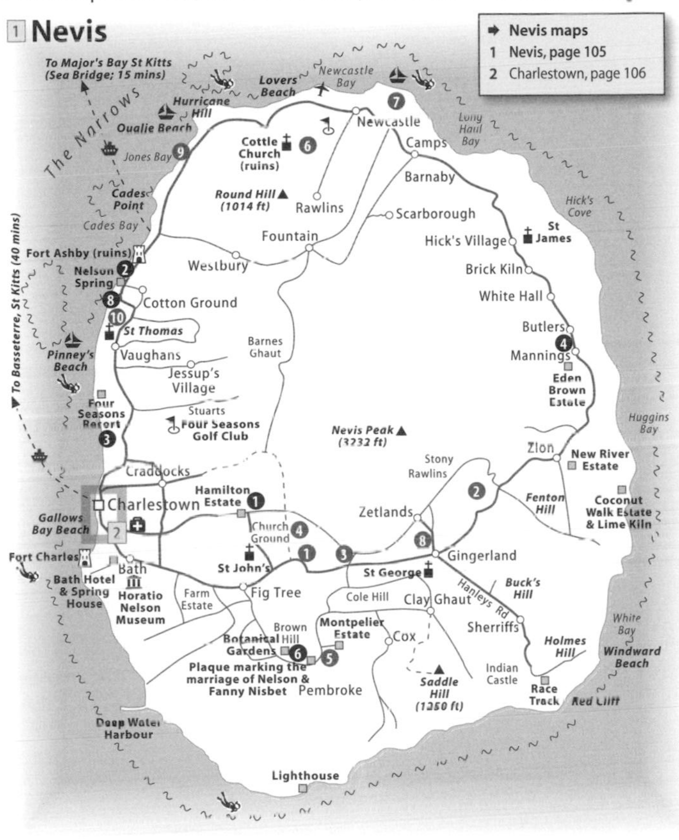

Where to stay
Banyan Tree B&B **1**
Golden Rock Plantation Inn **2**
Lindbergh Landing **4**
Montpelier Plantation **5**
Mount Nevis **6**
Nisbet Plantation Beach Club **7**
Old Manor **8**
Oualie Beach Resort **9**
Paradise Beach **10**
The Hermitage Plantation Inn **3**

Restaurants
Bananas Bistro **1**
Coconut Grove **2**
Double Deuce Restaurant & Bar **3**
Esme's Sunrise Snackette **4**
Lime Beach Bar **3**
Oasis in the Gardens **6**
Sunshine Beach Bar & Grill **3**
Yachtsman Grill **8**

On Main Street, surrounded by a stone wall, the pretty **St Paul's Anglican Church** was built about 1830 in a typical cruciform plan with gabled roof. The stained glass windows beside the altar are in memory of Reverend Daniel Gatward Davies, priest from 1812-1825, who converted slaves before emancipation. He went on to become the Bishop of Antigua. Next to the church is another stone building, which was the parish school.

The **Museum of Nevis History** ⓘ *between Main St and the sea, T869-469 5786, www.nevisheritage.org, Mon-Fri 0830-1600, Sat 1000-1300, US$4.80, children under 12 US$2.20,* next to the sea and set in an attractive garden, occupies the house that is the birthplace of Alexander Hamilton. The original house was built around 1680 but destroyed in the 1840s, probably by an earthquake. It was rebuilt in 1983 on the foundations and dedicated during the islands' Independence celebration in September of that year. The Nevis House of Assembly meets in the rooms upstairs, while the rather cramped museum occupies the ground floor. Alexander Hamilton, Nevis' most famous son, was born here on 11 January 1757. He lived on Nevis until he was eight years old before leaving for St Croix with his family. In later life he was a Founding Father of the United States, chief staff aide to General George Washington, and one of the most influential interpreters and promoters of the US Constitution. He was also an outspoken advocate of the emancipation of slavery. About half of the display is given over to memorabilia and pictures of his life. The rest contains examples of Amerindian pottery, African culture imported by the slaves, cooking implements and recipes, a rum still, the ceremonial clothes of the Warden which were worn on the Queen's birthday and Remembrance Day and a section on nature conservation.

2 Charlestown

➜ **Nevis maps**
1 Nevis, page 105
2 Charlestown, page 106

Restaurants
Café des Arts **1**
Wilma's Diner **2**

Along Government Road is the well-preserved **Jewish Cemetery**. The earliest evidence of a Jewish community on the island dates from 1677 to 1678, when there were four families. By the end of the century there were 17 households, a thriving synagogue and part of the main street was known as Jew Street, but invasion by the French in 1706 and 1783, hurricanes and the decline of the sugar industry in the 18th century led to an economic downturn and emigration. By the late 18th century only three Jewish households remained, and now there is no evidence of their presence except for the cemetery where 19 tombstones have survived, the first one is dated 1654 and the last one 1768. The engravings are written in English, Hebrew and Portuguese, since these were Sephardic Jews, who had come to Nevis from Brazil.

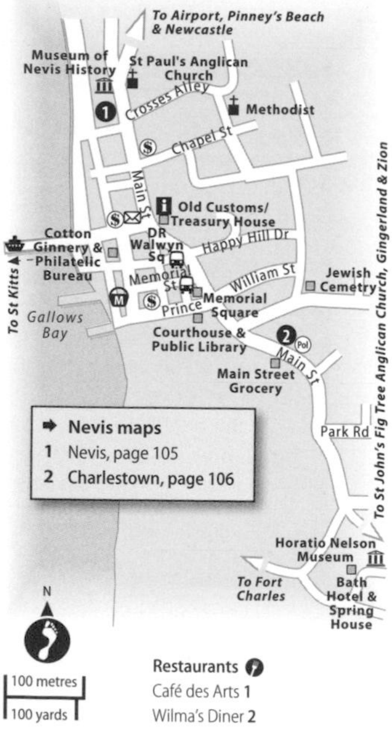

Around the island

Taking the road south out of Charlestown, you can visit the rather unkempt **Fort Charles**. Fork right at the fuel station and again at the mini-roundabout, keep right along the sea shore (rough track), and through gates at the end of the track. The fort is one of the oldest fortifications in the Leeward Islands and was built before 1690 and altered many times before being completed (1783-1790). It was named in honour of King Charles II, as was Charlestown, and it had mountings for 26 cannons, a considerable number for a small island. Not much remains now apart from some parts of the walls, the circular well and a small building that was the magazine. The gun emplacements looking across to St Kitts are being badly eroded by the sea, although some cannons have been dragged back to safer grounds. A detailed map of the Fort drawn in 1679 is at the Museum of Nevis History and shows the locations and dimensions of the original walls. The Nevis Council surrendered to the French here in 1782 during the siege of Brimstone Hill on St Kitts.

Back on the main road and only about half a mile outside Charlestown lies the former **Bath Hotel and Spring House**. Built by the Huggins family in 1778, it is reputed to be the oldest hotel in the Caribbean and in its day hosted many illustrious figures including the poet Samuel Taylor Coleridge, British Naval Admiral Horatio Nelson, Prince William Henry, the Duke of Clarence and King William IV of England. In the mid-19th century, a nine-hole golf course was built in the grounds, the first in the Caribbean and one of the earliest courses in the world. The hotel housed troops of the British West India Regiment in the First World War and again during the Second World War before being abandoned. Restored in the 1990s, it is now in use as government offices. The Spring House lies over a fault which supplies constant hot water at 42°C, but for a long time the pipes supplying the water were blocked. However, the pipes are currently being restored and parts are flowing again. They now supply a thermal dipping pool with the water, which is very clean because it's spring-fed. It is free to use (daylight hours) and is very hot; but once you've got used to it, it's soothing and a reputed tonic for all sorts of aches and pains. However, immersion is not recommended for people with a heart condition and no one should stay in for more than 15 minutes.

A friendly lady, Eldaria Jones, runs a little shop next to the pool called **Mobile Bare Necessities** ⓘ *usually open daily 0630-0730 when local people come to bathe and again 0930-1700*, and sells (and rents out) towels and slippers, and locally made herbal soaps, oils and sprays.

Close to the Bath Hotel and about 15 minutes' walk from Charlestown, the **Horatio Nelson Museum** ⓘ *Belle Vue, T869-469 0408, Mon-Fri 0900-1600, Sat 0900-1200, US$4.80, children under 12 US$2.20*, is based on a collection donated by Mr Robert Abrahams, an American who lived on the island. It is small, and it's a bit of a poorly presented mishmash of Nelson memorabilia, but it deals very well with Nelson's life and his short time on Nevis, a place so important to him and where he met his first wife Fanny Nisbet. Exhibits include letters, china, pictures, furniture and books (request to see the excellent collection of historical documents and display of 17th-century clay pipes) and a replica of Nelson's military uniform. Nelson was not always popular, having come to the island to enforce the Navigation Acts which forbade the newly independent American states trading with British colonies. In his ship *HMS Boreas,* he impounded four American ships and their cargoes. The Nevis merchants immediately claimed £40,000 losses against Nelson, who had to remain on board his ship for eight weeks to escape being put into gaol. It was only after Prince William, captain of *HMS Pegasus*, arrived in Antigua that Nelson gained social acceptability and married the widow, Fanny Herbert Nisbet who he had met at a dinner party on Nevis. Some reports say there were madly in love, other historians claim he married Fanny for her uncle's money; if it was the latter, this proved a disappointment as her uncle left the island and spent his wealth in London. The museum is hard to find because it's in a house in a residential area.

More evidence of the Nelson connection is found at the **St John's Fig Tree Anglican Church** about 2 miles on from the Bath Hotel. Originally built in 1680, the church was rebuilt in 1838 and again in 1895. The marriage certificate of Nelson and Fanny Nisbet is displayed here. There are interesting memorials to Fanny's father William Woodward and also to her first husband Dr Josiah Nisbet. Many died of fever during this period and if you lift the red carpet in the central aisles you can see old tombstones, many connected with the then leading family, the Herberts. The graveyard has many examples of tombstones in family groups dating from the 1780s. Nevis is divided into five parishes, each with its own Anglican church, but these make up a tiny fraction of the more than 80 churches for other denominations on the island. On Sunday church bells start ringing from 0600, calling the faithful to services lasting three hours or more, and it is a quiet day everywhere.

Slightly off the main road to the south lies **Montpelier Great House** where the marriage of Nelson and Mrs Nisbet actually took place. However, the ceremony was not actually in the house itself but in the grounds. If you walk down the hill from the entrance of the house towards the Botanical Gardens you will see a plaque set in a gatepost marking the event on 11 March 1787. The plantation is now a luxury hotel with pleasant gardens and lily ponds formed out of old sugar pans; a great place for lunch or a drink. Beyond the house lies **Saddle Hill** (1250 ft). It has the remains of a small fort, **Saddle Hill Battery**, and it is from here that Nelson is reputed to have walked the walls with his eyeglass watching for the French fleet in the 1780s. It is said that he devised a mirror signalling system between Saddle Hill on Nevis, St Kitts, Montserrat and Antigua so that if an enemy was sighted, the British West Indies Fleet could quickly leave English Harbour in Antigua. Nevisians also had a grandstand view from here of the siege of Brimstone Hill by the French in 1782. The track up the hill starts at Clay Ghaut, about a moderate 1½ miles, and although the fort is overgrown with scrub, many of the old stone walls are still visible and the views from 'Nelson's Lookout' marvellous.

Near Montpelier are the **Botanical Gardens** ⓘ *T869-469 3509, www.botanicalgardennevis.com, Mon-Sat 0900-1600, Sun 1130-1500 in high season and for groups, US$13, children (6-12) US$8, under 5s free*, 7 acres of well-laid out plants from around the world: cactus, bamboo, orchids, flowering trees and shrubs, heliconias and rose gardens, a mermaid fountain, a greenhouse with bridges, ponds, waterfall, and a gift shop. The landscaping is beautiful and it is the perfect spot for relaxation, with views reaching out across The Narrows to St Kitts. It is, however, somewhat overpriced, given that you can see everything in about one hour, so make an afternoon of it and bring a picnic. The **Oasis in the Gardens** restaurant (see page 118) is in a lovely wooden whitewashed replica of a Great House, with an upstairs terrace, so if you are having lunch or dinner here, you don't need to pay garden entry unless you want to walk around.

The small parish of **Gingerland** is reached after about 3 miles from the turn-off to Montpelier. Its rich soils made it the centre of the island's ginger root production (also cinnamon and nutmeg), but it is noteworthy for the very unusual octagonal Methodist church built in 1930 on the site of an original church dating to 1801. You turn right here along newly tarred Hanleys Road to reach the excellent **Windward Beach** on **White Bay**. Go all the way down to the bottom and turn left at Indian Castle on to a dirt road past the race course (on Black Bay) and Red Cliff. You have to park near the bluff where the dirt road peters out, and then walk down a short distance to get to the sand. Windward is a wild long, sandy beach, completely undeveloped with no facilities. Beware though, this is the

ON THE ROAD

Hiking Nevis Peak

A dormant volcano that perhaps last erupted some 100,000 years ago, 3232-ft-high Nevis Peak dominates the whole island, and is almost constantly shrouded in cloud. It is very steep and covered in dense forest, and reaching the top is much tougher than the ascent of Mount Liamuiga on St Kitts. Not a hike as such, more of a rugged, scrambling, muddy climb, rope-assisted in parts, it takes four to five hours to go up and down. The trailhead is at 1200 ft above Gingerland at the village of Zetlands.

The trail itself is unmarked (a guide is essential) and once into the forest, the incline becomes steep and slippery; you will need to use hands to grab tree roots, trunks and vines, and flat spots to rest and drink water are few and far between. The summit is not much more than a sudden break in the foliage and the inside of the caldera is permanently full of thick fog. But quite delightfully there is a box with a visitors' book to sign and you can take celebratory photos in front of a small St Kitts and Nevis flag. You may well want to record that fact that you've just climbed a near-vertical 2000 ft in two hours. Unfortunately, and like most mountain climbs, it's just as tough going back down.

Summiting Nevis is as adrenaline-charged as it is physically demanding, and in the event that the cloud does break, the views are simply outstanding; you can see most of the island, look down into Charlestown and across to St Kitts.

Wear decent hiking boots, take water and snacks and light rain gear. **Nevis Adventure Tours** (Newcastle, T869-765 4158, www.nevisadventuretours.com) and **Sunrise Tours** (Gingerland, T869-669 1227, www.nevisnaturetours.com) can organize the climb, which costs US$40-80 per person, depending on how many are in the group. They can also organize less strenuous rainforest hikes in the foothills, and a hike up Saddle Hill (see opposite).

Atlantic coast and the sea can be very rough and dangerous, but on quieter days, the surf is fun and there are views across to Montserrat, Redonda and Antigua in the distance. It's ideal for a picnic and an isolated walk.

The seaside **racetrack** itself has a small grandstand seating 200 with a rickety bar underneath and places for food vendors. For many years horseracing was a popular pastime in Nevis, with an average of four horses in each race, running around the mile-long track. It hasn't been going for a while due to lack of funding/sponsorship, but at the time of writing the government were refurbishing it and new toilet blocks had already been built and the car park cleared; check at the tourist office for information about upcoming races.

After Gingerland the land becomes more barren and this side of the island is much drier. Several sugar mills were built here because of the wind. One of the more interesting to visit is **New River Estate,** just to the right of the road at Zion, which was still processing sugar commercially until 1958 when it finally closed down; the last operating sugar facility on Nevis. With its machinery, elegant chimney, ruined great house with volcanic stone colonnade and rusting steam engine (manufactured in 1883), which was used to crush the cane, it gives a good glimpse of the days when sugar was so important to the island. Further on, **Eden Brown Estate**, built around 1740, was originally a sugar plantation, but cotton was grown here until the mid-1900s. It had a reputation of being haunted. A duel took place between the groom and the bride's brother at the wedding of Julia Huggins. The brother was killed and the fiancé fled the island to escape trial and execution. Heartbroken, Julia became a recluse and died in the Great House and her tortured ghost can reputedly still be heard today as she wanders through the ruins. They are in poor condition and care should be taken, but on a clear day Antigua and Montserrat can be seen.

Continuing down towards the sea from New River, you can follow the goat trail to **Coconut Walk Estate**, where among the ruins is the tallest surviving windmill tower in Nevis and a stone lime kiln.

The island road continues north through Butlers and Brick Kiln (known locally as Brick Lyn), past St James' Church (Hick's village), Long Haul Bay and Newcastle Bay, the location of the superb **Nisbet Plantation Beach Club.** Once a prominent 18th-century sugar plantation turned coconut plantation, it is the only historic estate on the island with a sea frontage. Nisbet is so called today as it was the ancestral home of Fanny Nisbet, owned by her parents William Woodward and Mary Herbert, and she lived in the Great House (1778) during the 18 months of marriage to her first husband, Dr Josiah Nisbet. Later, Nelson was apparently quite taken by Fanny's refinement and resourcefulness in operating such a large house. Today, as part of the luxury resort, it has been restored magnificently into a fine restaurant, one of the best on the island, and the crumbling remains of the sugar mill are at the entrance.

The road then goes through the small fishing community of Newcastle and past the airport. You could make a detour down a rickety, hole-ridden track to **Lovers Beach**, an undeveloped mile-long strip of sand, occasionally windy, but secluded and perfect for sunbathing in privacy. From here the road continues southwards through an increasingly fertile landscape, and there are fine views across The Narrows to the southeast peninsula of St Kitts, with **Booby Island** in the middle of the channel, the latter being mostly inhabited by brown pelicans (all birds are referred to as boobies by the local population). The small hill on your left is **Round Hill** (1014 ft). Under the hill lie the ruins of the beautiful and tiny **Cottle Church**. It was built by John Cottle, once the president of Nevis and a plantation owner, in 1824 as a place for his family and his slaves to worship together, although it was never consecrated as the practice was illegal at the time. It was severely damaged by the 1974 earthquake and Hurricane Hugo in 1989. But the site has been partially resorted to show off the remaining stone walls and rafters in a lovely grassy clearing. The owners of the **Oualie Beach Resort**, John and Karen, were the first couple to be married here and now it's regularly used for outdoor island weddings. The little font can be seen in the Museum of Nevis History (see page 106).

There is a small beach at **Mosquito Bay** and some good snorkelling under the cliffs of Hurricane Hill. The **Oualie Beach Resort** offers watersports including diving and snorkelling and water taxis go from here across to **Reggae Beach Bar & Grill** at Cockleshell Bay on St Kitts (see page 117). **Cades Bay** is where the **Sea Bridge** car and passenger ferry arrives and departs, and nearby, just off the island road, lies **Fort Ashby**, constructed in 1701 to protect Jamestown, the original settlement and former capital. The fort saw fierce action in February 1706, when the French with 14 ships attempted to land 3000 troops over five days. The determined fire from Fort Ashby, as well as from the other Nevis shore batteries, repelled them and the French withdrew. But in April they returned with 224 man-of-war frigates, and Fort Ashby was taken by French troops who attacked it from behind after only brief resistance. It is now in a very overgrown state with just some sections of wall remaining and some cannons. The outer wall used to be on the sea front but the shape of the coast has changed over the centuries and it is now inland.

Near here is a freshwater lagoon fed by **Nelson's Spring**. In the 1780s when Nelson was a captain in charge, he would periodically use the spring to fill his ships with fresh water; hence the name. Now it is worth seeing for its flowering water lilies, birds and butterflies. Drive past Nelson's Spring to **St Thomas's Church**. Built in 1643, this is the oldest church in Nevis and one of the oldest surviving in the Caribbean, where the cemetery has many tombstones bearing names of Nevis' early settlers dating back to 1649.

Almost back in Charlestown, after a full circuit of the island, you come to the beautiful 4-mile **Pinney's Beach**. The most popular beach on the island, backed along its entire length by a tangle of tall palm trees, it has soft, sugar-fine white sand and calm and shallow water perfect for swimming. There are many tracks leading down to it, often with a beach bar at the end of them, and the **Four Seasons Resort Nevis** lies in the middle of the beach. The sun loungers are for guests only, but the public has access to the beach and there are watersports available. Behind the resort is the **Four Seasons Golf Club and** course which straddles the island road. The manicured fairways and greens are in marked contrast with the quiet beauty of the rest of the island but the hotel's considerable efforts at landscaping have lessened its impact.

Listings St Kitts and Nevis *maps pages 91, 94, 105 and 106.*

Tourist information

St Kitts *map page 94.*

St Kitts Tourism Authority
Pelican Mall, Bay Rd, Basseterre, T869-465 4040, www.stkittstourism.kn. Mon-Fri 0730-1630.
This is the head office and has very helpful staff and a bunch of brochures and maps to pick up including ones with Nevis on the reverse side. They also operate a satellite kiosk in Port Zante, T869-467 1400, open whenever cruise ships are in.

Nevis *map page 106.*

Nevis Tourism Authority
Old Treasure Building, Main St, Charlestown, T869-469 7550, www.nevisisland.com. Mon-Fri 0800-1700.
Well-staffed and there are a number of leaflets and maps to pick up.

Where to stay

Unless otherwise stated, all hotel rooms have a/c, TV and Wi-Fi. On both St Kitts and Nevis, government hotel tax (10%), tourism levy (2%) and service (11%) is charged by all accommodation options, usually as a single charge of 23%. Check if this has been included in quoted rates.

St Kitts *map page 91.*
There aren't many places to stay on St Kitts; the overwhelming majority of visitors are cruise ship passengers. The 2 big resorts are the **St Kitts Marriott Resort & Royal Beach Casino** (www.marriott.com), and the soon-to-be opened **Park Hyatt St Kitts** (www.stkitts.park.hyatt.com). Villa rentals are listed on www.stkittstourism.kn, and **St Kitts and Nevis Island Homes** act as an agent, www.sknih.com.

Basseterre *map page 94.*

$$$ Ocean Terrace Inn (OTI)
Wigley Av, just outside the centre, T869-465 2754, www.oceanterraceinn.com.
This long-standing seaside hotel had a complete overhaul in 2015 and now offers 50 smart rooms in blocks climbing up the hillside (there are a quite a lot of steps), with patios or balconies, sofa beds and views of Basseterre and the bay. Nice pool with waterfall and sun loungers, **The Verandah** restaurant/bar with terrace, and **Fisherman's**

Wharf restaurant (see page 115) is across the road on the waterfront.

$$ Bird Rock Beach Hotel

South Pelican Dr, Bird Rock, T869-465 8914, www.birdrockbeach.com.

Located at Bird Rock, 2 miles southeast of Basseterre; follow Bay Rd and turn right along the shoreline. Far from fancy with dated 1980s decor, and while it overlooks the water, there's only a tiny beach, but the 46 rooms and apartments are roomy and comfortable enough. There are 3 restaurants, a beach bar and pool, and it's in a good location for diving and snorkelling. **Dive St Kitts** is based here, see page 122.

$ Seaview Inn

Bay Rd, Basseterre, T869-466 1635, www.seaviewinnstkitts.net.

There is no sea view despite the name and it being upstairs above shops, but if you need to stay in Basseterre, this is a great budget option (from US$65) right in the heart of things, a short walk from the ferry/bus terminal, and well run by Dominican-born Javier and his friendly team. With 10 small and simply furnished tiled rooms, and a bar/restaurant with a great balcony, perfect for people-watching on the main street.

West and north coasts *map page 91.*

$$$$ Belle Mont Farm

Kittitian Hill, St Paul's, T869-465 7388, www.bellemontfarm.com.

Lauded as one of the most exciting developments on St Kitts for a number of years, this occupies 400 acres of a former sugar plantation and now organic farmland in the foothills of Mount Liamuiga. The 84 cottages and villas feature private plunge pools, outdoor roll-top baths and decks with sweeping views across to the ocean on the northern tip of the island, with lots of character and style from colonial antique furniture to iPads loaded with movies. Facilities include a golf course, infinity pool, gym, spa and outstanding restaurant (see page 115).

$$$$ Ottley's Plantation Inn

Ottleys, T869-465 7234, www.ottleys.com.

Originally an 18th-century sugar plantation, this luxury hotel is set on 35 acres with views to the Atlantic, and 23 spacious and elegantly furnished rooms; 8 are in the 1832 Great House with its wraparound veranda and the rest are cottages, some with plunge pools, in the beautiful tropical gardens with sweeping lawns and palm trees. Large pool, floodlit tennis court, croquet lawn, nice walks in the area, and the spa is in a little chattel house in the trees. The excellent and atmospheric **Royal Palm** restaurant is built into the side of old sugar mill buildings and is open to non-guests (see page 116).

Southeast peninsula *map page 91.*

$$$ Rock Haven B&B

Scenic Dr, Frigate Bay, T869-465 5503, www.rock-haven.com.

A traditional, Caribbean-style home with views of both North and South Frigate bays, has 2 B&B rooms; 1 in the house that sleeps 2, the other with its own entrance, a kitchen, patio, and can sleep 3. Genial host Judith serves a substantial breakfast with home-made bread on the breezy sea-view balcony, and offers free airport and ferry transfers.

$$$ Timothy Beach Resort

South Frigate Bay, T869-465 8597, www.timothybeach.com.

The only hotel in this area actually on the Caribbean. Good value, unpretentious mid-range place with accommodating staff, and there are 60 various rooms and studios with kitchens, which can be connected to make apartments or a townhouse to sleep 2-10, with mountain or sea views. Pool, steps down to the sea, **The Dock** bar (see page 120) and **Sunset Café** for local food and burgers (see page 117), and right next to The Strip.

$$$-$$ Sugar Bay Club
North Frigate Bay, T869-465 8037, www.sugarbayclub.com.
Large place with 89 hotel rooms and apartments – at the time of writing going under extensive refurbishment so ask for a newly renovated one – all with balconies/ patios, some with Atlantic views. The property itself is a little featureless with concrete blocks scattered around the 2 pools, but facilities are excellent; 2 restaurants and **Ram's Supermarket** on site, and next to **Rituals Coffee House** and other restaurants, and a 10-min walk to The Strip.

$$ Island Paradise Beach Village
North Frigate Bay, T869-465 8035, www.islandparadisebeachvillage.com.
A little plain and unremarkable but this condo-rental property (each is individually owned and decorated) is well located just south of the **Marriot** and good value, with self-catering 1-, 2- and 3-bedroom units, pool and laundry room, set in pleasant gardens and short walk to the supermarket. There's a 3-night minimum stay.

Nevis *map page 105.*

$$$$ Four Seasons Resort Nevis
Pinney's Beach, www.fourseasons.com/nevis.
The island's 5-star all-inclusive option with 196 rooms/suites, 4 restaurants, 3 pools, 10 tennis courts, a dive shop golf course and spa. In quiet times they offer a B&B rate and you can visit to play golf (see page 124)

$$$$ Montpelier Plantation
St John's Parish, T869-469 3462, www.montpeliernevis.com.
Closed mid-Aug to early-Oct.
Beautiful old property on 60 acres of a former sugar estate, with a huge wild fig tree at its entrance, 19 luxury rooms scattered around the lovely gardens in cottages, each painted white with cool green or blue flourishes, a veranda and louvered windows. The pool area has a contemporary chic feel with the **Indigo** bar/restaurant, white couches and chilled music, while the main restaurant (page 118) is in the hugely atmospheric Great House. Tennis courts and shuttle to its private facility (bar, showers/ changing rooms) on Pinney's Beach.

$$$$ Nisbet Plantation Beach Club
St James's Parish, T869-469 9325, www.nisbetplantation.com.
Closed early Aug to end of Sep.
On a ½-mile beach close to the airport, this is the only plantation inn on the beach and has been a hotel since the 1950s; some of the excellent staff have been here many years. The 36 very comfortable rooms are in hexagonal cottages or double-storey suites in 30 acres of gardens fanning out from an impressive avenue of palms (where you can get married). Tennis courts, lovely pool area with decking, beach bar for lunch, and the main restaurant/bar is in the 1778 Great House (see page 118). Rates are inclusive of breakfast, afternoon tea and dinner; pay extra for lunch if you need it. Also offer a great rum shop tour on Fri afternoons.

$$$$ Paradise Beach Nevis
Paradise Estates, St Thomas's Parish, T869-469 7900, www.paradisebeachnevis.com.
These 7 3- and 4-bedroom contemporary villas sleep 6-8, or 2 couples, each with a pool and patio, located steps away from Pinney's Beach where there's a private beach bar with watersports. Luxuriously designed with thatched roofs and well-equipped kitchens and butler and chef service. Sophisticated and discreet, a top-end alternative to the larger resorts.

$$$$-$$$ Golden Rock Plantation Inn
St George's Parish, T869-469 3346, www.goldenrocknevis.com.
This 100-acre 18th-century plantation on a hillside has 11 charming rooms in cottages, simple but comfortable in wonderful gardens with fish ponds, no a/c but cool breezes at night, also a 2-storey suite in the old windmill for honeymooners/families, with antique furniture and 4-poster beds.

Ocean view all the way to Montserrat, pool (formerly the sugar mill cistern), and **The Rocks** restaurant is open to non-guests and a good place to stop for lunch, even just for a sandwich (lobster or snapper).

$$$$-$$$ The Hermitage Plantation Inn
St John's Parish, T869-469 3477, www.hermitagenevis.com.
In a peaceful rural setting with views down to the sea, and centred around the **Planter's House** (1680), believed to be the oldest wooden house on the island and today filled with antiques and curiosities. 17 rooms in pastel-painted, timber-framed garden cottages among mango and tamarind trees, each has 4-poster bed, veranda and hammock. Some are fairly small but are also cheaper. Tennis, pool, curio shop, horse-riding stables, and excellent meals taken on the house's wraparound porch; non-guests welcome (see page 118).

$$$ Banyan Tree B&B
Church Ground, T869-469 3449, www.banyantreebandb.com. Closed 15 Apr-15 Nov.
A relaxing and quiet rural place with 2 charming rooms in the guesthouse and a 1-bedroom suite with kitchenette in Bamboo House, all with verandas, 700 ft above sea level on a 6-acre farm growing flowers, spices (try the ginger tea) and raising Barbados black-belly sheep, lots of fruit trees and a 300-year-old banyan tree.

$$$ Mount Nevis
Shaws Rd, Newcastle, T869-469 9373, www.mountnevishotel.com.
Sitting on 17 acres on a hillside with views of St Kitts on what was a lime plantation dating to the 1800s, comfortable, quiet and peaceful with excellent service, 32 airy rooms in 4 pavilions with balconies, the suites have kitchens and sofa-beds. Pool, beach shuttle, open-air restaurant/bar and library.

$$$ Old Manor Hotel
Gingerland, T869-469 3445, www.oldmanornevis.com.
On a sugar plantation (1690), the 12 spacious rooms incorporate the stone walls of the old mill buildings, with wooden shutters and louvered windows, each with veranda, no a/c but delightfully breezy and cool sitting at 800 ft with views to Montserrat, old furnishings, and prints of maps on the walls, good restaurant, beach shuttle and pool in tropical gardens.

$$$ Oualie Beach Resort
St Thomas's Parish, T869-469 9735, www.oualiebeach.com.
On a calm, sheltered cove right on Oualie Beach, low-key resort surrounded by tropical gardens, 32 comfortable rooms in cottages in the sand with colourful artwork and views from the screened-in verandas, 2 with kitchens and sofa beds. Relaxed bar/restaurant under tamarind trees, which offers regular entertainment like a beach barbecue on Tue with a live band, dive shop and other watersports can be arranged.

$$ Lindbergh Landing
Church Ground, T869-469 3398, www.lindberghlandingnevis.com.
Sweet and cheerfully decorated little wooden cottages high on the hillside with views down to the coast, with kitchenettes, although breakfast is available too. The bar here is open to all (Thu and Sun from 1600, Fri-Sat from 1200) for cocktails, rum punch and wine accompanied by good music and some Nevisian snacks. Guided nature walks are offered on trails from the property. Get Spencer and Jacqueline to explain the odd name; the original land owner was inspired by Charles Lindbergh's transatlantic flight of 1927.

Restaurants

On both St Kitts and Nevis, government tax (10%), tourism levy (2%) and service (12%) are charged; this is a whopping 24% on top of menu prices. The government tax is usually included, but double check; most menus stipulate what is and what is not included.

Basseterre *map page 94.*

At the bus and ferry terminal there are several kiosks selling cheap snacks and cold soft drinks and beers; look out for delicious fried saltfish balls, Johnny cakes (dumplings) and banana bread.

$$$ Fisherman's Wharf

Bay Rd, part of Ocean Terrace Inn (OTI), T869-465 2754, www.fishermanswharfstkitts.com. Mon-Wed 1830-2230, Thu-Sat 1700-2230, Sun 1100-1430.

On a pier jutting out from Bay Rd, this has been going more than 30 years, and as the name suggests has a predominantly seafood menu and is famous for its conch chowder, but there are meat, poultry and vegetarian dishes too. Good lounge areas on decks and Happy Hour Thu-Sat 1700-1900. Also a good spot for sundowners as it faces west.

$$$-$$ Serendipity Restaurant & Lounge Bar

3 Wigley Av, T869-465 9999, www.serendipitystkitts.net. Mon-Fri 1130-1500, Mon-Sat 1800-2200.

Reservations recommended. Cheerfully decorated spot overlooking Basseterre Bay from the terrace, offers excellent service and a menu of Caribbean and European dishes. Lighter meals at lunch include salads, garlic prawns and mussels, burgers and pastas, while dinner has a more sophisticated choice including 'surf and turf' and some delicate desserts.

$$$-$ Ballahoo

Corner of Bank St and Fort St at The Circus, T869-465 4197, www.ballahoo.net. Mon-Wed 0800-1500, Thu-Sat 0800-2100.

This great central meeting place has a fun, laid-back atmosphere and an always interesting view of The Circus from the balcony. Run by a French couple, the menu offers both Gallic favourites such as French onion soup, and steak au poivre and Caribbean flavours like conch chowder and grilled red snapper. Good choice of filling sandwiches for lunch, excellent croissants for breakfast and a French wine list at the lively bar.

$$ Sweet Cane

Port Zante, T869-665 7628. Mon-Sat 1100-2100.

In a convenient (if not entrancing) location in Port Zante, with bright and cheerful decor and a few pavement tables, and a varied and good value menu that has something for everyone, from simple soup of the day, burgers and lasagne, to Cajun grouper, jerk chicken and beef in red wine sauce.

$$-$ Lemongrass

Corner of Bay Rd and Fort St, T869-465 0143, see Facebook. Mon-Sat 1100-2100.

Popular with the office trade as well as visitors, the covered balcony of this Asian restaurant is a good place to observe the bustle of the street below. The coconut shrimp and grilled chicken/fish are well presented and tasty, and there are also snacks like spare ribs, satay and spring rolls. It suffers from slow service though.

$ El Fredo's

Bay Rd on the corner with Sandown, T869-466 8871. Mon-Sat 1100-1600.

This small, wood-framed courtyard restaurant is a good local lunch spot, serving typical dishes such as goat water, curried conch, oxtail and steamed fresh fish served with traditional accompaniments like plantain, yam, cassava and sweet potato. Also try the juices made from local herbs and fruits, such as sorrel, guava and soursop.

West and north coasts *map page 91.*

$$$ The Kitchen

At Belle Mont Farm, Kittitian Hill, St Paul's, T869-465 7388, www.bellemontfarm.com. Daily 1030-1430, 1600-2200.

Reservations required. Run by a French chef, this new restaurant is part of the **Belle Mont Farm** luxurious resort and has panoramic views over the north of the island and airy, industrial-look interiors. The farm-to-table 4- to 7-course lunch and dinner menus change daily and feature organic vegetables, lobster and lamb. Superb choice of fine wines, champagne and cocktails at **The Mill Bar**.

$$$-$$ Royal Palm

At Ottley's Plantation Inn, Ottleys, T869-465 7234, www.ottleys.com. Open 0800-2000.

Set within the arched stone walls of the old sugar factory at this luxury hotel, the civilized Royal Palm has elegant tables, potted plants and a view to the coast. The menu has contemporary Caribbean dishes such as Kittitian beef patties, flying fish tempura, coconut shrimp or lamb curries, and soursop ice cream. Have a formal lunch or dinner (reservations recommended) or stop in for a casual brunch or afternoon tea.

$ Sprat Net Bar & Grill

Old Road Town, T869-466 7535, see Facebook. Wed-Sun 1800-2300.

Wedged between the sea and the island's coastal road, people come from all over the island to this rustic beach hut for their fresh fish and goat water, good atmosphere and reasonably priced food. If you're lucky there'll be lobster (**$$**) with baked potato, corn, and fried Johnny cakes. Watch your fish being cooked on an open grill and eat at wooden picnic tables. An adjacent hut serves pizza.

Southeast peninsula *map page 91.*

$$$ Marshall's

Fort Tyson Rise, South Frigate Bay, T869-466 8245, www.marshallsdining.com. Daily 1800-2200.

With a sophisticated setting and romantic poolside dining, an ocean view and great sunsets, this restaurant has been going for more than 20 years. The menu features Caribbean staples, seafood including lobster thermidor and grilled swordfish, meat and poultry dishes, cocktails and wines, and some inventive desserts. Pricey but one of the best restaurants on the island.

$$$-$ Rock Lobster

North Frigate Bay, T869-466 1092. Bar from 1500, dinner 1700-2130 except Wed.

Inside and outside seating in a quaint and casual house. The name speaks for itself – the lobster rocks! But the menu has a wide choice for most budgets including fish, seafood platters, tapas, steaks, nachos, and fruity cocktails, wine and beer.

$$ Bombay Blues

At the Sugar Bay Club, North Frigate Bay, T869-466 0166, see Facebook. Tue-Sun 1200-1430, 1700-2200.

This is the place to come if you crave an authentic Indian curry, with good use of seasonings in all the usual offerings; tandoori, tikka, vindaloo, masala, buttery naans, plenty of vegetarian dishes and an excellent Sun buffet (1230-1430) on the outdoor upstairs balcony. Everything is cooked from scratch and arrives steaming hot in copper pots.

$$ Lion Rock Beach Bar & Grill

Cockleshell Bay, T869-663 8711. Daily 1030-1730.

This unprepossessing shack is popular with both the cruise ship crowd and locals for a game of dominos and a cold beer. Run by Lion and Angela who cook up heaped plates of fish, jerk chicken, shrimps and ribs with coconut rice and grilled plantain, accompanied by a killer rum punch with grated nutmeg. Bottles of Lion's famous barbecue sauce are for sale and you can rent sun loungers.

$$ Rituals Sushi

North Frigate Bay, T869-466 0161. Tue-Sat 1200-2200.

Next to **Rituals Coffee House** (see below), offers a small but good selection of Japanese dishes (the sushi is super-fresh), kimono-clad waitresses, and the choice of eating on a pleasant patio, in the elegant, Asian-themed interior, or takeaway.

$$ Spice Mill

Cockleshell Bay, T869-765 6706, www.spicemillrestaurant.com. Daily 1130-2130, closes 1630 on Thu, reduced hours out of season; phone ahead.

With a fine view of Nevis, this upmarket beach bar/restaurant offers seafood, pizzas from the wood-fired oven and creamy pastas. Free Wi-Fi, you can rent beach loungers or luxurious day-beds for 2, plus watersports equipment can be hired from a hut nearby. On Sun afternoon in high season there's a band or DJ.

$$-$ Jam Rock

South Friars Bay, T869-469 1608, www.jamrockbarandrestaurant.com. Daily 1100-2200.

In the middle of South Friars Bay beach, this easy-going beach bar is Jamaican-owned so expect tasty jerk chicken and pork and mutton curry with rice and peas, but there's also fish (the grouper is excellent), and delicious conch fritters to snack on. Diners sit at wooden tables beneath a corrugated metal roof.

$$-$ Reggae Beach Bar & Grill

Cockleshell Bay, T869-762 5050, www.reggaebeachbar.com. Daily 1030-1800, open until 2200 on Fri for the 'lobster-fest' dinner.

This has everything you would expect of a fun Caribbean beach bar: good food, mostly fish, shrimp, conch and lobster but also chicken, burgers, sandwiches and vegetarian options, frozen cocktails and fruit smoothies. Beach loungers, snorkelling gear, and kayaks are for hire. There are panoramic views across to Nevis, and naturally a reggae soundtrack.

$ Rituals Coffee House

North Frigate Bay, T869-466 8443. Daily 0700-2200.

Fantastic range of coffees with syrups and whipped cream, smoothies and vanilla chai, food includes toasted bagels, hot and cold wraps and paninis, good cookies and cakes and free Wi-Fi. Part of a quality Trinidad chain, another component is **Pizza Boys** (T869-465 0107, daily 1000-2200), just up the road on the other side of Sugar Bay Club; eat in or takeaway.

$ ShipWreck Beach Bar & Grill

South Friars Bay, T869-764 7200, www.shipwreckstkitts.com. Daily 1000-sunset.

Set on the rocks at the east end of the beach, this friendly spot is popular with visitors and resident expats; the look is decidedly scruffy castaway, with ramshackle wooden decking, and fishing nets hanging from the rafters, but always a great atmosphere, rents out snorkelling gear, sun loungers, and serves the likes of fish tacos, barbecue wings, conch fritters and grilled mahi mahi. Live music on Sun from 1600.

$ Sunset Café

At Timothy Beach Resort, South Frigate Bay, T869-465 8597, www.timothybeach.com. Daily 0730-2130.

A casual open-sided place with picnic benches along the beach offering simple dishes like burgers, chicken and seafood rotis, and fish and chips, has free Wi-Fi, and as the name suggests, good sunset views. On Sun (1900-2130) is a West Indian buffet for US$24.

Nevis *map page 106.*

$$$ Bananas Bistro

Upper Hamilton Estate, above Church Ground, T869-469 1891, www.bananasrestaurantnevis.com. Mon-Sat 1230-1530 and 1800-2200, reservations recommended for dinner.

Set in a lush garden, in an attractive wooden house with wraparound veranda, very romantic at night, and inside, the walls are covered with art work from Caribbean-wide artists (which is also for sale). British chef and former dancer Gillian Smith serves up delicious meals including lobster in season, a wonderful mix of local specialities, together with Asian, Mediterranean and veggie options. Service is most hospitable.

$$$ Coconut Grove

Nelson's Spring, T869-469 1020, www.neviscoconutgrove.com. Lunch and dinner by reservation only, closed Aug-Oct.

Open-air under a thatched roof on the beach with lush sofas, an infinity swimming pool, and great views of St Kitts and the sunset, gourmet restaurant and wine bar with a varied list from around the world and a sommelier, the French cuisine and local seafood are a wonderful marriage. High end with prices to match but a great place for a special meal and very romantic.

$$$ Montpelier Plantation

T869-469 3462, www.montpeliernevis.com.

The stylish **Indigo** bar/restaurant (daily 1200-1500) is next to the large pool and has relaxed couches, sun loungers, café tables and a menu of light meals, cocktails and coffees. The main dining area in the Great House (reservations only) features fine artwork, a broad veranda with views, luxurious lounge/bar that serves fine wines and aged rums, and offers a 3-4 course dinner; examples might be spiny lobster tail, goat's cheese and serrano ham, yellowfin tuna or pork tenderloin, or you can eat at a table set up inside the old sugar mill, beautifully romantic and lit with candles.

$$$ Nisbet Plantation Beach Club

St James Parish, T869-469 9325, www.nisbetplantation.com.

Reservations only. Stop here for a leisurely lunch on an island tour, or enjoy an atmospheric dinner in an elegant and historic setting in the 1778 Great House; you can climb the steps to the top of the crumbling sugar mill outside. The 3-course dinners are superb and feature a combination of local food like breadfruit soup or grilled grouper as well as fillet steak or rack of lamb and delicious desserts. Superb service from the barman who has been here more than 30 years.

$$$-$ The Hermitage Plantation Inn

St John's Parish, T869-469 3477, www.hermitagenevis.com. Daily 0800-1030, 1200-1430 and 1800-2100.

A gracious, colonial dining porch wraps around the historic house at this hotel and is open to non-guests. Inventive chicken, lamb and pork dishes, home-grown produce and seafood delivered every morning. Wed night Caribbean barbecue and pig roast, one of the most popular events on the island, Fri Italian night, and an excellent pub serving rum punch made from a 350-year-old recipe. Reservations preferred.

$$ Oasis in the Gardens

At the Botanical Gardens, T869-469 3509, www.botanicalgardennevis.com. Mon-Sat 1000-1700, stays open for dinner Fri until 2100 and Sun 1130-1500 in high season and for groups.

In the upper part of the Great House, serving Thai food with a long menu of hot and sweet and sour dishes, well-presented and charming ambience at wrought-iron tables on the balcony with panoramic views of Nevis Peak, a popular lunch spot or for a drink during a tour of the gardens.

$$ Yachtsman Grill

Cotton Ground, T869-469 1382, www.yachtsmangrill.com. Daily 1200-2200, Apr-Oct Thu-Sat.

Modern and smart serving good quality, fresh food, more upmarket than most other beach bars, with items such as seared tuna on the menu as well as lobster (you choose from the tank), plus burgers and pizza, good wines and cocktails and there's a swimming pool. Happy hour 1600-1900, Fri evening live music.

$$-$ Double Deuce Restaurant & Bar

Pinney's Beach, T869-469 2222, www.doubledeucenevis.com. Tue-Sun 0900-until the last customer leaves.

Specializes in local seafood such as mahi mahi, lobster, snapper, conch as well as really good burgers and barbecue ribs. Karaoke Thu from 2100, Sat dance night from 2200, Sun is roast beef and Yorkshire pudding. Also table tennis, pool tables, darts board, a swimming pool, Wi-Fi and book exchange library.

$$-$ Lime Beach Bar

Pinney's Beach, T869-469 1147. Daily 1100-2300.

An upscale beach bar as popular with **Four Seasons** guests as it is with locals, with a sunny deck and upstairs lounge area, offers simple but good fare off the grill, including burgers, fish, chicken and lobster, live band Fri night.

$$-$ Sunshine Beach Bar & Grill

Pinney's Beach, www.sunshinesnevis.com. Daily from 1100 with lunch 1200-1530, dinner 1800-2130, bar later.

Casual beach bar, colourful and laid back with friendly staff. Salads, burgers, wings, ribs, lobster sandwich or food from the grill: fish, chicken, lobster, shrimp. The signature cocktail is a 'killer bee': rum with passion fruit.

$ Café des Arts

Between the museum and waterfront, Charlestown, T869-667 8768. Mon-Fri 1000-1400, and Fri from 1800 for Burger Night.

A charming shaded café that looks out over the bay at Charlestown good for salads, sandwiches, quiche; try the home-made lemonade. Tables are outside under the trees and parasols.

$ Esme's Sunrise Snackette

St James's Parish, just south of Butlers, T869-664 6446, see Facebook. Mon-Sat from 0600, Sun from 1400 until the last person leaves.

Really open from sunrise, this little rum shop is great to stop at on an island tour with car park, sunny deck and ocean views, pool table, hot meals like goat water and conch or pig feed soup, coconut Johnny cakes and snacks at the small shop, and lots to drink. Live string band every Sat from 2000.

$ Wilma's Diner

Next to the police station, Main St, Charleston, T869-663 8010. Mon-Sat 1000-1400.

Local lunchtime spot where the menu changes daily but expect the likes of fried snapper or grouper, baked or stewed chicken, barbecue pork ribs, served with rice and peas, coleslaw, plantain, sweet potato, breadfruit, coconut dumplings and green salad. Will open up for dinner for a group to try a feast of local specialities.

Bars and clubs

Basseterre *map page 94.*

Rum Barrel

Port Zante, Basseterre, T869-466 9852. Mon-Sat 0800-2300.

Great place for people-watching as this open-sided bar with wooden stools and tables is close to where the cruise ship passengers disembark. Popular Fri afterwork liming spot (see box, page 23) for Kittitians when there is often a DJ raising the decibel level.

Twist

Port Zante, Basseterre, T869-466 7440, see Facebook. Mon-Sat 1200-0200, Sun 1200-2400.

Upstairs sports bar with TVs showing major sporting events, plus a pool table and table football for entertainment. Food is available, from pizza and wings to Indian and Chinese dishes, but caters for cruise ship passengers so is overpriced for the quality; there's a good choice of drinks though from many Caribbean rums to fruity cocktails.

Southeast peninsula *map page 91.*

South Frigate Bay is lined with bars, familiarly known as 'The Strip'. You can wander along the beach doing a pub crawl, choosing the atmosphere that suits you. Some have live music or a DJ some nights, or there might be volleyball matches and other entertainment, such as the fire show at **Mr X's** on Thu night.

Buddies Beach Hut

South Frigate Bay, T869-465 2839, www.buddiesbeachhut.com. Tue-Thu, Sat and Sun 1700-2400, Fri 1600-0200.

One of the biggest establishments on The Strip offering a good-value cook-up of spare ribs, chicken, lobster, fish and burgers with fries, garlic bread, rice and crispy vegetables. Bar downstairs, dance floor upstairs and Fri is the liveliest, with things heating up from 2000.

Mr X's Shiggidy Shack Bar & Grill
South Frigate Bay, T869-465 0673, see Facebook. Mon-Fri 1000-2400, Sat-Sun 0800-2400.
One of the best-known beach bars on The Strip, a simple wood-and-palm leaf shack, Mr X's has a friendly atmosphere and soon fills up if there's a cruise ship visiting. During the day and early evening the menu features burgers, ribs and fish dishes. Thu night is the time to go if you want to party, when there is a bonfire and live band on the beach.

The Dock
Part of the Timothy Beach Resort, South Frigate Bay, T869-465 8597. Daily 1500-0200.
One of the pit-stops along The Strip, with bright rope lights adding a party mood, popular with both locals and visitors, Sun is the main night, when there's a live band playing reggae, soca or R&B (usually 2100-2400). During happy hour (Mon-Fri 1700-1800) beers and house-brand mixed drinks are half-price and they give you a bucket of ice to stock pile.

Nevis *map page 106.*
The hotels usually have live music 1 night a week in season, although things get quieter in the summer. The beach bars along Pinney's Beach and some restaurants also offer live bands or a DJ or karaoke 1 or more nights a week.

Entertainment

St Kitts *map page 91.*

Casinos

Royal Beach Casino, *at the Marriot, North Frigate Bay, T869-466 5555, www.royalbeachcasino.com.* Gaming tables (from 1600, depending on demand and season), slot machines (Mon-Thu 1200-0200, Fri 1200-0400, Sat 1000-0400, Sun 1000-0200) and kiosks for betting on sports, this is a glitzy Vegas-style vast casino, offering free drinks for gamblers.

Cinemas

St Kitts Megaplex 7, *Cayon Rd, Basseterre, T869-466 4777, www.caribbeancinemas.com.* This complex has 7 screens, kiosks for drinks and popcorn, and movies showing daily 1400-2100.

Festivals

St Kitts *map page 91.*
Jun St Kitts Music Festival, 3rd or 4th weekend, Warner Park Stadium, Basseterre, www.stkittsmusicfestival.net. Attracting about 3000 people each night, this features a diverse line-up of music including R&B, jazz, hip-hop, reggae, soca, calypso and gospel performances over 3 nights with musicians coming from across the Caribbean.

Nevis *map page 106.*
Mar Annual Nevis to St Kitts Cross Channel Swim, usually 3rd weekend, Oualie Beach Resort, www.nevistostkittscrosschannelswim.com. The annual 2.6-mile open water swim across The Narrows (the shortest route between Nevis and St Kitts) starts at Oualie Beach on Nevis and finishes at the **Reggae Beach Bar & Grill** at Cockleshell Bay on St Kitts. Those who don't want to swim competitively can use fins and snorkels to assist.
Apr Nevis Blues Festival, usually 2nd weekend, Oualie Beach Resort, www.nevisbluesfestival.com. On a stage set up on the beach, 2 nights of music from international visiting bands with bars and barbecues.
Sep Nevis Marathon and Running Festival, usually the 2nd weekend, www.nevismarathon.com. Incorporates a marathon, half marathon and shorter distances of 10 km and 5 km. The full marathon and marathon relay course circles the entire island.
Nov Nevis International Triathlon, usually the 2nd Sat, Oualie Beach Resort, organized by the **Nevis Cycle & Triathlon Club**, www.neviscycleclub.com. Comprising a 2-km

swim, a bike ride taking in 2 laps of the island, and 21-km run, followed by a beach bash.

Shopping

St Kitts *maps pages 91 and 94.*
The area around the cruise ship docks, Pelican Mall and Port Zante are busy with shops. Some are duty free and sell jewellery, liquor, watches and leather goods. The **Amina Craft Market** at the back of Pelican Mall sells (some tacky) cruise ships souvenirs. This pedestrianized area is open Mon-Fri 0900-1730, Sat 0900-1300, longer hours and Sun when cruise ships are in, and conversely, some shops/vendors may close if they aren't. Go to **Caribelle Batik**, at Romney Manor (see page 96), for a huge range of batik clothing and to see the way it is made.

Food

The small corrugated-iron-roofed **Basseterre Market** is on Bay Rd and is open Wed-Sat mornings, but the busiest is Sat. It's good for fruit and vegetables and also has fish and meat stalls. There are plenty of small grocery shops in Basseterre, but **Ram's Supermarket** is the best on the island. It's in 3 locations: Bay Rd, Basseterre, T869-465 2145; Bird Rock, T869-466 6055; and at Sugar Bay Club, North Frigate Bay, T869-465 3433; they also have a duty-free booze shop in Port Zante; www.ramstrading.com. All are open Mon-Thu 0800-1900, Fri-Sat 0800-2000, Sun 0900-1300.

Stamps

St Kitts Philatelic Bureau, *Pelican Mall, T869-465 2521. Mon-Wed, Fri-Sat 0800-1200, 1300-1500, Thu 0800-1100.*

Nevis *maps pages 105 and 106.*

Art and crafts

Eva Wilkin Gallery, *Clay Ghaut, Gingerland, T869-469 2673. Mon-Fri 1000-1500, but hours are irregular, so phone first.* Started by Howard and Marlene Paine, this has an exhibition in an 18th-century windmill of paintings and drawings by Nevisian Eva Wilkin MBE (whose studio it was until her death in 1989), prints of which are available. Next to the windmill is a shop selling antique furniture, maps and other bits and pieces.

Nevis Craft House, *Cotton Ginnery, Charlestown, T869-469 5505. Mon-Thu 0900-1600, Fri 0900-1530.* The outlet for a government training facility selling leatherwork, ceramics, wooden bowls, baskets and paintings.

Nevis Handicraft Co-operative, *DR Walwyn Square, Charlestown, T869-469 1746. Mon-Sat 0930-1630.* Has a small but good collection of locally produced items such as paintings, batiks and preserves including hot pepper sauce.

Newcastle Pottery, *Newcastle, T869-469 9746. Mon-Fri 0900-1600.* About 1 mile east of the airport on the main road, this small pottery makes red clay artefacts including bowls, light holders and candlesticks. You can watch potters at work on the wheels and at the kilns fired by burning coconut husks.

Food

The **Charlestown Public Market** is good for fruit and vegetables, fresh fish and meat but is only open on Tue and Sat mornings. There are a couple of small grocery shops in Charlestown including **BestBuy** and **SuperFoods**, but the biggest and best supermarket on the island is **Ram's Supermarket** (Stoney Grove, to the east of the Bath Hotel, but can be reached via Government Rd in Charlestown, T869-469 7777, www.ramstrading.com. Mon-Thu 0830-1900, Fri-Sat 0830-2000, Sun 0900-1300).

Stamps

Nevis Philatelic Bureau, *Cotton Ginnery, Charlestown, T869-469 5535. Mon-Fri 0800-1600.* Nevis produces many commemorative, special event and definitive issues of the island's fauna and flora, undersea life and history.

What to do

St Kitts *maps pages 91 and 94.*

Cricket

Warner Park Sporting Complex is in Basseterre. It was one of Caribbean's 7 stadiums built for the 2007 Cricket World Cup and is named after Sir Thomas Warner, who established the first English colony on St Kitts. Capacity is 8000 and it's a multi-sport facility and home ground to the St Kitts and Nevis Patriots national cricket team. Contact **St Kitts Cricket Association**, T869-466 4589, Facebook, for details of fixtures.

Diving and snorkelling

Most dive sites are on the Caribbean side, where the reefs start in shallow water and fall off to 70-100 ft. Between the 2 islands there is a shelf in only 25 ft of water, while off the southeast peninsula is also black coral and wrecks which attract abundant fish and other sea creatures of all sizes and colours. Some offshore reefs are shallow enough for snorkelling although the best snorkelling around St Kitts is accessible by boat. Single dives from US$75, 2-tank dives US$105, night dives US$85, PADI Discover Scuba US$120, PADI Open Water course US$420. Snorkelling trips by boat from US$30, 2-2½ hrs, or US$50, 3½ hrs, for a speedboat trip to reefs around the southeast peninsula. You can also rent out snorkelling gear for the day or week, and masks, fins and flippers can be hired from a number of beach bars on the southeast peninsula for snorkelling off the beach.

Dive St Kitts, *Bird Rock Beach Hotel, South Pelican Dr, Bird Rock, T869-465 8914, www.divestkitts.com.*

Kenneth's Dive Centre, *Bay Rd, Basseterre, T869-465 2670, www.kennethdivecenter.net.*

Pro Divers St Kitts, *Fisherman's Wharf, Basseterre, T869-660 3483, www.prodiversstkitts.com.*

Fishing

The deeper waters around the island are home to barracuda, kingfish, bonito, mahi mahi and marlin. In shallower waters are snapper, jacks and grouper. For fishing charters, expect to pay around US$150, 4 hrs, to US$290 8 hrs, prices are per person, minimum 4. Both these companies can also organize snorkelling trips and sightseeing trips around the island or to Nevis by boat.

Speedy 4 Charters, *Frigate Bay, T869-662 3453, www.speedy4charters.com.*

VIP Charters, *Frigate Bay, T869-762 5410, www.vipcharters.net.*

Golf

The **Christophe Harbour Golf Club** at Christophe Harbour on the southeast peninsula (www.christopheharbour.com) is presently under construction. Golfers staying on St Kitts can also go across for the day to the **Four Seasons Golf Club** on Nevis (see below). For more information on the options on both islands, visit www.golfstkittsandnevis.com.

Irie Fields Golf Club, *Belle Mont Farm, Kittitian Hill, St Paul's, T869-465 7388, www.bellemontfarm.com.* The par 71, 18-hole course at this new luxurious resort has been designed by European PGA Tour and Ryder Cup star Ian Woosnam. Every hole is surrounded by organic crops and fruit trees; it is being lauded as the world's first 'edible' golf course. Due to open Dec 2016.

Royal St Kitts Golf Club, *North Frigate Bay, T869-466 2700, www.royalstkittsgolfclub.com. Daily 0630-1830.* An 18-hole championship golf course on 125 acres, with 2 holes on the Caribbean and 3 holes on the Atlantic. A full round is generally 4½ hrs, with drinks and snacks available at the Clubhouse Grille overlooking the 18th green, and there's a well-stocked pro shop. Green fees are US$165 for 18 holes, club rental US$64, although rates drop in low season (1 Jun-31 Oct) and are discounted for guests staying at the nearby Marriott.

Hiking

Greg's Safaris, *T869-465 4121, www.gregsafaris.com.* Founding members of the

St Christopher National Trust, this company offers a number of tours, popular with cruise ship passengers so there are often large groups and not all involving hiking. It's a great and experienced operator for the full-day Mount Liamuiga hike, US$110, children under 12 US$80, but no small children allowed. The full day trip with transfers is 7-9 hrs, and the hike duration is 4-5 hrs; a picnic lunch is included on the crater rim. Also offers a combined trip to visit Romney Manor/Caribelle Batik followed by a hike around the Wingfield Estate; US$70, children under 12 US$50, 4 hrs.

Sailing

These companies offer a number of cruises on either sailing or motorized catamarans from snorkelling and lunch, US$65 for 4 hrs, and sunset cocktail cruises, US$50 for 2½ hrs, to leisurely trips with time on the beach at Cockleshell Bay or Pinney's Beach on Nevis, from US$45-90 for 4-6 hrs, or you can charter a vessel for the whole day from US$400. All go from the marina at Port Zante. Contact in advance to see what options are going on what days, as there is usually a minimum number, and if a cruise ship group is booked on, it's possible to join in.

Blue Water Safaris, *T869-466 4933, www.bluewatersafaris.com.*

Leeward Island Charters, *T869-465 7474, www.leewardislandschartersstkitts.com.*

Purple Turtle Charters, *T869-766 0011, www.ptcharters.com.*

Tour operators

Many taxi and tour operators offer island tours in minibuses and will pick up from hotels, the airport and Port Zante. The standard rates for a full day around-the-island tour is US$81.50 per person up to 4, US$57 per extra person. But other options include a shorter tour just up to Romney Manor/Caribelle Batik and Brimstone Hill, from US$60 per person, or a tour of the southeast peninsula from US$40 per person with lots of stopping time. In the event you are on a cruise ship, it's a lot less expensive to pre-organize a tour independently than book a shore excursion from the tour desk on the boat.

Caribbean Journey Masters, *T869-466 8110, www.caribbeanjourneymasters.com.*

Kittitian Taxi and Tours, *T869-762 8994, www.kittitiantaxiandtours.com.*

Properway Tours & Taxi, *T869-669 8570, www.properwaytours.com.*

Rose & Jim's Taxi & Tour Service, *T869-465 4694, www.roseandjimstaxi.com.*

St Kitts Captain Sunshine's Tour Services, *T869-762 4663, www.stkittscaptainsunshine.com.*

St Kitts Island Paradise Tours, *T869-466 3028, www.stkittsislandparadisetours.com.*

Tatem's Taxi and Tours, *T869-662 1129, www.stkittsnevistaxitours.com.*

Turtle-watching

St Kitts Sea Turtle Monitoring Network, *T869-764 6664, www.stkittsturtles.org.* This community-based non-profit organization monitors nesting sea turtles (green, hawksbill and leatherback) that come ashore during the nesting season. Visitors can join the research teams (15 Apr-15 Jun) from 0800 until midnight under the supervision of a guide on one of the nesting beaches. Only 10 people are permitted per night so book well in advance; US$60, children (under 12) free.

Watersports

St Kitts Water Sports, *Cockleshell Bay, next to Reggae Beach Bar & Grill, T869-762 3543, www.stkittswatersports.com. Open most days in high season and when cruise ships are in, but phone ahead at quiet times.* Lots of activities and toys to play with here on a day on the beach at Cockleshell Bay including fly-boarding, jet-skiing, snorkelling, stand-up paddle-boarding (SUP), kayaking, wakeboarding, water-skiing, tubing and paragliding. You can rent equipment, instruction is available, and some tours are on offer like 2-hr SUP or glass-bottomed kayaking guided excursions around the southeast peninsula. Check the website; 1-day packages are also available.

Nevis *maps pages 105 and 106.*

Diving and snorkelling

Snorkelling around Nevis is not as good as St Kitts; the island lacks a comprehensive offshore reef system so there isn't much to see underwater from the beaches. The best places are around the man-made jetties at resorts such as at **Nisbet**, **Four Seasons** or **Oualie Beach**. There are, however, numerous dive sites offshore. One of the best is Nag's Head, just off Oualie Beach, a schooling ground for big fish such as king mackerel, barracuda, jacks and yellowtail snappers. From Jan to Apr humpback whales and dolphins may be seen. Some dive operators in St Kitts visit the sites around Nevis (see above).

Scuba Safaris, *Oualie Beach Resort, T869-469 9518, www.divenevis.com.* A PADI 5-star resort run by Ellis Chaderton, prices are from a 1-day dive package for US$110 to a 4-day PADI Open Water course for US$550.

Fishing

Caribbean Catch Fishing & Boat Charters, *T869-760 8776, www.caribbeancatch.com.* Half- and full-day fishing charters for snapper, wahoo, mahi mahi and king mackerel on the *Cast Away* or hire the boat for sunset cruises or snorkelling trips.

Golf

Cat Ghaut Chip 'n' Putt Course, *Shaws Rd, Newcastle, opposite the entrance to the Mount Nevis Hotel, T869-469 9826/469 9325.* Set on Roger and Peggy Staiger's beautiful 14-acre property, this 9-hole course is a lot of fun and takes about 2 hrs. When you get there, you can pick up clubs and balls at 'The Putty Haus', where there's an honesty box to post the fee of US$9.25 per person. The greens may be a bit rough, but the setting is lovely, with views of the Atlantic and Nevis Peak. Roger ('Tiger') has spent years planting many species of tropical trees, shrubs and flowers on the grounds, and there is also a (free) nature/jogging trail.

Four Seasons Golf Club, *at Four Seasons Resort Nevis, T869-469 1111, www.fourseasons.com.* An excellent 18-hole, par 71 championship course designed by Robert Trent Jones Jr. It is beautifully maintained, offers fabulous views, and there's a pro-shop, driving range, putting green, and instruction is available. But green fees for non-guests are a whopping US$200 for 18 holes, US$120 for 9 holes, and club rental is US$50. Golfers fly in from other islands to play here.

Horse riding

Nevis Equestrian Centre, *Main Rd, Clifton Estate, Cotton Ground, T869-662 9118, www.nevishorseback.com.* Offers horse trails for novices and experienced riders and children over 6; the most popular are the 90-min rides at 0900 and 1400 through villages and on the beach for US$74, but they can organize sunset trips, a 6-hr cross island ride, but don't try that if you're not used to riding.

Transport

St Kitts *map page 91.*

Air

Named after the first premier of St Kitts and Nevis at the time of independence, **Robert L Bradshaw International Airport** is just over 2 miles north of Basseterre. There are duty-free and gift shops and a café, but they tend to open for long-haul flights only. There's a **St Kitts-Nevis-Anguilla National Bank** exchange bureau (Mon-Thu 0830-1330, Fri 0830-1530) with an ATM. See Finding your feet, page 92, for details of transport from the airport.

It receives flights from the UK, Canada and US as well as numerous regional flights from within the Caribbean region (see Getting there, page 129). There are no domestic flights between St Kitts and Nevis, but see box, opposite, for details of ferries between the islands. Departure tax from St Kitts is US$22, payable at the airport desk.

ON THE WATER

Ferries between St Kitts and Nevis

The crossing between Basseterre on St Kitts and Charlestown on Nevis takes 40 minutes and provides beautiful views of both islands. There are five ferries: *Mark Twain*, *Sea Hustler*, *Caribe Breeze*, *Caribe Queen* and *Caribe Surf*, and between them they go roughly every one to two hours, Monday-Saturday between 0600 and 1800, and four to five times on a Sunday. To check times, visit the Nevis Disaster Management Department on Facebook; although rather ominously sounding, this government department updates the ferry schedule first thing every morning on its Facebook page.

At Basseterre, the combined and well-organized ferry and bus terminal is on Bay Road and there's a covered waiting area with bench seating, ticket offices, kiosks for food and drinks, and taxis are available. At Charlestown, the ferry pier is right in the middle of the tiny town, with a shaded seating area and a good kiosk for snacks and drinks (try the delicious fresh juices). Taxis wait on the street outside, or the bus stops are nearby. The one-way ferry fare is US$9.25, children under 12 US$5.55, plus US$0.40 port tax per person.

The **Sea Bridge** car and passenger ferry (T869-765 7053/662 7002) links the two islands across The Narrows, the name of the strait that separates them, which at its narrowest is 2 miles wide, although the ferry route is 3½ miles. It runs between Major's Bay on the southeast peninsula of St Kitts and Cades Bay on the northwest side of Nevis and takes about 10-15 minutes. Departures are from St Kitts: Monday-Friday, on the hour, every two hours, 0800-1900, Saturday 0800, 1300 and 1900; from Nevis, Monday-Friday, on the hour, every two hours, 0700-1800, Saturday 0700, 1200 and 1800; US$28 for one car and a driver and US$7.40 for each additional passenger. Tickets can only be purchased from the quay just prior to departure, and as the boat is fairly small, it's best to turn up with a car about an hour in advance.

The big hotels on Nevis, **Four Seasons Resort Nevis**, **Nisbet Plantation Beach Club** and **Montpelier**, organize boats exclusively for guests and the arrangement is for representatives to meet them at the airport on St Kitts and accompany them on a transfer down to Major's Bay and then get the boat across The Narrows; an exciting boat journey in the dark for those arriving on late flights. You can also get water taxis between the **Reggae Beach Bar & Grill** in Cockleshell Bay (see page 117) on the southeast peninsula of St Kitts to the jetty at Cades Bay or **Oualie Beach Resort** on Nevis; one-way US$81.50 for up to four people, US$20 per extra person.

Bus

Buses (minivans) are identified by their green 'H' registration plate. The combined bus and ferry terminal is on Bay Road in Basseterre, and elsewhere you flag them down with a wave. They follow set routes (more or less) around the island either clockwise from Basseterre to Dieppe Bay Town or Saddlers, or an anti-clockwise direction from Basseterre to Saddlers or Dieppe Bay Town. To do an around-the-island you'll have to change at these places. They go as far south as South Frigate Bay but not to North Frigate Bay (although it's easy enough to get off at the roundabout near South Frigate Bay and walk), and they don't go to the southeast peninsula. They generally run from very early in the morning until 0800 or 2100, later at weekends on the route between South Frigate Bay (where the bars are) and town. Fares are US$0.90-2.20 depending on distance.

Car hire

Drivers must be over 25 and a local driver's permit, US$23 valid for 3 months, must be purchased on presentation of a foreign (not international) licence; the car hire companies will arrange this. A list of hire companies can be found on the website of the **St Kitts Tourism Authority** (www.stkittstourism.kn) or drop into the tourist offices in Basseterre and they'll phone one for you. The car hire companies can arrange pick-ups/drop-offs at the airport and hotels. Rates are from US$45 for a small car up to US$75 for a jeep/SUV per day; US$300-400 per week. Basic hire generally only includes statutory 3rd-party insurance; it is advised to take out the optional collision damage waiver premium at US$10-15 per day as even the smallest accident can be very expensive. See page 133, for further details about hiring a car and driving.

Taxi

Taxis have a yellow 'T' registration plate. There are taxi ranks at the airport, the **Circus** and **Pelican Mall** in Basseterre, and there's a stand in North Frigate Bay between the **Marriot** and the **Sugar Bay Club**, or any hotel or restaurant can call one for you. Fares are set by the **Ministry of Tourism** and **St Kitts Taxi Association** (T869-465 8487; after hours T869-465 7818). Sample fares are the airport to Basseterre US$10, to Frigate Bay (north and south) US$16, and down to Cockleshell Bay or Major's Bay (for the ferry to Cades Bay on Nevis) US$28. The official rate per hour is US$30, for day tours by taxi; see Tour operators above. There's a 50% surcharge between 2200-0600.

Nevis *map page 106.*

Air

Named after a former Premier of Nevis, the airport is modern but tiny; there is a kiosk for drinks/snacks, an ATM and that's about it. You are most likely to meet all the airport staff in the central seating area waiting for the flights. With plenty of time, you can easily catch a bus (minivan) back to the airport. For details of transport from the airport, see page 104.

It is not large enough to receive long-haul flights and there are no domestic flights between St Kitts and Nevis. Those arriving on flights into St Kitts from the UK, Canada and US go by ferry or boat between the 2 islands (see box, page 125). However, Nevis does receive a number of flights from neighbouring islands, St Barts, Saint Martin/Sint Maarten, Antigua and San Juan in Puerto Rico, which means you can get to Nevis without going to St Kitts first. **Note** On departing, airport departure taxes are not include in fares from Nevis and you pay these at the desk in the airport. They are US$17 per person, plus US$1.85 security fee, and US$1.50 environment levy. Anyone over 12 must pay.

Bike hire

Both places listed below rent out bikes from US$30 for the day, and do deals for more than 3 days' hire. You can get a minivan to both to pick them up, and they can also organize island tours by bike. The 20-mile circular road is ideal for a bike tour, although it can be hilly, and you can pull off to the sugar mills and beaches, or more adventurous mountain bikers can opt for trails up into the hills.

Bike Nevis, Oualie Beach Resort, T869-664 2843, www.bikenevis.com. Daily 0900-1700. Owned by Winston Crooke.

Nevis Adventure Tours/Green Edge Bike Shop, Newcastle, T869-765 4158, www.nevisadventuretours.com. Mon-Sat 1000-1700. Owned by Reggie Douglas.

Bus

Buses (minivans) have green licence plates starting with the letter 'H' or 'HA'. They run around the island main road and can be flagged down anywhere. There are 2 bus stops in Charlestown, close to each other near DR Walwyn Square and a short walk from the ferry. One is on the south side of the square and is where minivans park that go in a clockwise direction around the island to Butlers; the other is just further down Main St where minivans go to/from Zion in the anti-clockwise direction, the 2-3 miles part of the island where most people live. There is a gap between Butlers and Zion of about 1¾ miles but these are the 2 bus routes; there is always the option of paying extra on either route to go between these points or walking. They mostly depart when full, or at least with enough passengers to make it worthwhile for the driver, and cost US$0.90-1.50 depending on the distance; an island tour is possible, if time consuming.

Car hire

You will need a local driver's permit, US$23 valid for 3 months, to drive on Nevis; the car hire companies will arrange this. There's a list of car hire companies on the website of the **Nevis Tourism Authority** (www.nevisisland.com), and they can arrange pick-ups/drop-offs at the airport and hotels. Rates are similar to St Kitts, see above.

Taxi

Taxis have a yellow 'T' registration plate. Fares are set by the **Ministry of Tourism**, and start from US$5.90 for a short distance say from Charlestown to Pinney's Beach to US$25 for a journey from one side of the island to the other; 50% surcharge 2200-0600. For island tours the set rate is US$74 for the day or US$50 for 2 hrs and US$30 per hr. You can pick them up at the airport or in Charlestown, any hotel or restaurant will phone one, and the island is so small they may stop if they see you standing somewhere.

Practicalities

Getting there

Air

Antigua and Barbuda

VC Bird International Airport is in the northeast corner of Antigua, allowing passengers with window seats an enticing view of the coastline and multi-hued waters around the island as the plane comes in to land. It is well served with flights from Europe and North America, and you can often pick up good-value deals on package holidays. It also has good connections with other Caribbean islands for a two-centre holiday or some island-hopping by air. See also Transport, page 69.

Antigua's sister island of Barbuda has a tiny airport near the main village of Codrington, which doesn't receive international flights but is served by an inter-island flight from Antigua. See also Transport, page 70.

Flights from the UK and Europe British Airways ⓘ *www.britishairways.com*, fly six times a week, and **Virgin Atlantic** ⓘ *www.virgin-atlantic.com*, three times a week direct to Antigua from London Gatwick (just over eight hours) and both offer connecting services to and from Europe. **Thomas Cook Airlines** ⓘ *www.thomascookairlines.com*, fly seasonally (November-March) to Antigua once a week from London Heathrow, Manchester, Birmingham and Bristol. **Condor** ⓘ *www.condor.com*, fly seasonally (December-April) once a week from Frankfurt via the Dominican Republic. Europeans also have the option of flying with **KLM** or **Air France** to Saint Martin/Sint Maarten, connecting to Antigua with the Caribbean regional airline LIAT ⓘ *Leeward Islands Air Transport; www.liat.com.*

Flights from North America American Airlines ⓘ *www.aa.com*, fly to Antigua from Miami, **Delta** ⓘ *www.delta.com*, from Atlanta, and **United Airlines** ⓘ *www.united.com*, from New York/Newark. From Canada, **Air Canada** ⓘ *www.aircanada.com*, fly from Toronto, and **WestJet** ⓘ *www.westjet.com*, from Toronto seasonally (November-March). The other option for North Americans is to fly with **Caribbean Airlines** ⓘ *www.caribbean-airlines.com*, from New York, Orlando, Fort Lauderdale, Miami or Toronto to either Trinidad or Jamaica, from where Caribbean Airlines fly to Antigua.

Flights from the Caribbean LIAT connects much of the Caribbean and has its hub in Antigua. To/from Antigua it has direct flights with Anguilla, Barbados, Dominica, Dominican Republic, Guadeloupe, Nevis, Puerto Rico, Saint Martin/Sint Maarten, St Kitts, St Lucia, St Thomas, St Vincent, Tortola and Trinidad. Connecting flights also go to Curaçao, Grenada, Martinique, St Croix, Tobago and Guyana in South America. **Caribbean Airlines** ⓘ *www.caribbean-airlines.com*, has direct flights to/from Antigua and Trinidad and Jamaica. **Winair** ⓘ *www.fly-winair.sx*, has direct flights to/from Antigua and Saint Martin/Sint Maarten.

Montserrat

The only scheduled flight connection with the island is the daily service to/from Antigua with **FlyMontserrat** ⓘ *www.flymontserrat.com*. You can also charter a plane from Antigua with **FlyMontserrat** or with **ABM Air Montserrat** ⓘ *www.montserrat-flights.com*, or a helicopter with **Caribbean Helicopters** ⓘ *www.caribbeanhelicopters.com*. See also Transport, page 86.

St Kitts

Robert L Bradshaw International Airport on St Kitts is in the middle of the island, close to the capital, Basseterre, and on arrival you get a good view of the Caribbean coastline including several historic fortresses. See Transport, page 124, for airport facilities, and Finding your feet, page 92, for transport from the airport.

The airport has a reasonable amount of international flights. Many cruise ships passengers, if not starting their cruises in Miami, will get on/off a ship in St Kitts because of the good flight connections with the US during the winter cruise ship season.

Flights from the UK and Europe **British Airways** ⓘ *www.britishairways.com*, fly twice a week direct to/from St Kitts and three of their six weekly flights into Antigua continue on to St Kitts, which effectively makes the service five times a week from London Gatwick. The option with **Virgin Atlantic** ⓘ *www.virgin-atlantic.com*, is to fly to Antigua, three times a week from London Gatwick and then connect to St Kitts with **LIAT**. The same goes with **Condor** from Frankfurt to Antigua. From Amsterdam with **KLM** or Paris with **Air France**, you can fly to Saint Martin/Sint Maarten and then connect to St Kitts with **Winair**, who also have a direct flight between Saint Martin/Sint Maarten and Nevis.

Flights from North America **American Airlines** ⓘ *www.aa.com*, fly from Miami daily and New York/JFK twice weekly, **Delta** ⓘ *www.delta.com*, from Atlanta weekly, and **United Airlines** ⓘ *www.united.com*, from Charlotte and New York/Newark weekly (December-April). From Canada, **Air Canada** ⓘ *www.aircanada.com*, fly from Toronto weekly (December-April). Another option for North Americans is to fly into Antigua and connect to St Kitts with **LIAT**, or to Puerto Rico (with **American Airlines, Delta, JetBlue, Southwest Airlines, United Airlines** and **Air Canada**) and connect to St Kitts with **Seaborne Airlines** ⓘ *www.seaborneairlines.com*.

Flights from the Caribbean **Seaborne Airlines** fly to/from Puerto Rico, **LIAT** to/from Antigua and Winair to/from Saint Martin/Sint Maarten. For other destinations you'll have to change on one of these islands.

Nevis

The small **Vance W Amory International Airport** is in the north of the island at Newcastle, 7 miles from Charlestown; see Transport, page 126. There are no flights between St Kitts and Nevis and many visitors from Europe and North America fly to St Kitts and get a ferry or water taxi over (see box, page 125, for the options). However, there are a couple of possibilities within the Caribbean which means you don't have to go to St Kitts first to get to Nevis, or are useful if you're island-hopping.

Tip...

Flights on the small airlines between the islands of the Caribbean are generally reliable, but schedules may change and they tend to run on 'island time' (an acronym for **LIAT** is "Leave Island Any Time"). But this has got its advantages too; they could wait for you if an international connection is delayed.

Flights from the Caribbean Both **LIAT** and **FlyMontserrat** have direct flights between Nevis and Antigua, and **Winair** between Saint Martin/Sint Maarten, so going via either of these from Europe or North America is an option. For North Americans another route is to fly to Puerto Rico and get a direct flight from there to Nevis with **Seaborne Airlines** or **Tradewind Aviation** ⓘ *www.flytradewind.com.*

Tip...

Most of regional airlines also offer charter services for island hopping; for a group taking the maximum amount of seats in a small plane seating five to 12, it's worth considering the costs as they can be competitive against paying for the same amount of scheduled flights.

Sea

Large cruise ships call at St John's in Antigua and Basseterre in St Kitts, both of which have cruise ships terminals with shops and restaurants, while smaller ships visit Nevis and Montserrat. Although there is a domestic ferry service between St Kitts and Nevis (see box, page 125), there are no long-distance ferry services except for one between Antigua and Montserrat. However, at the time of writing, and since April 2016, the Antigua–Montserrat ferry hasn't been operating; see Note under Monserrat Transport, page 86.

Yachts meander between these islands, and there are several ports of entry. A clearance out certificate from your last port is required, and at most customs and immigration facilities are open Monday-Friday 0800-1600. An overtime fee is applicable for processing at weekends, public holidays and 1600-0800, so it's worth arriving during normal working hours. There are four ports of entry in Antigua: Heritage Quay, St John's Deep Water Harbour, English Harbour and Jolly Harbour. Yachts wishing to visit Barbuda must clear in at Antigua prior to proceeding to Barbuda. Little Bay is the port of entry in Montserrat; Basseterre in St Kitts, although Christophe Harbour will be a port of entry (it is currently under construction); and in Nevis, Charlestown (although the same country, you must either clear at both Basseterre and Charlestown or get a permit to sail between the two).

Getting around

Air

LIAT fly between Antigua and both St Kitts and Nevis, **FlyMontserrat** between Antigua and Montserrat, and **LIAT** and **FlyMontserrat** between Antigua and Nevis. The only inter-island domestic service in this region is the scheduled 20-minute daily flight between Antigua and Barbuda with **FlyMontserrat**.

You can also charter a plane or helicopter from Antigua, and some of Barbuda's upmarket resorts arrange air transfers. It is often the case that you will have to stay on Antigua overnight before flying to Barbuda as international flights mostly arrive there later in the day. There are no domestic flights between St Kitts and Nevis.

Road

On all the islands the main roads are in reasonable condition and connect most points, which make it relatively easy to get around. On the larger islands of Antigua and St Kitts there are perimeter roads that more or less follow the coastline, as well as across island roads serving the residential areas. Barbuda has one short road with dirt tracks leading off it to beaches; Montserrat has a single, hilly main road that winds along the east and west coasts and across the middle, while Nevis has one 20-mile paved road around the island with smaller access roads off it.

Car hire, regular taxis, buses, or an island tour with a taxi or tour operator are the options of getting around by road. Hitchhiking is not advised; neither is giving lifts to strangers.

Bus

Buses (always small vehicles known as minivans with 12-17 seats) operate on all the islands. They are all privately owned but usually belong to an association of drivers and are registered as public service vehicles with the necessary insurance and licences. From the public terminals, such as the ones in St John's on Antigua and Basseterre on St Kitts, they radiate out on fixed routes around the islands. They set off when full, or at least when they have enough passengers to make it worthwhile for the driver. They run frequently during the day, but rarely after dark or on Sunday. A bus may be flagged down anywhere along its route and will drop passengers off anywhere on request. Fares range from US$0.90-2.50, depending on distance, and you can pay for an extra seat if you have luggage. There is usually the option of paying extra for a short deviation ('off route'), and most will convert to a taxi for the appropriate rate. Minivans are a cheap and colourful means of transport, but they primarily serve the needs of local people (getting them between work and home). As such they may not always be useful for tourists; for example, on Antigua there is no service out to the airport or to the northwest where many of the resorts are, and on St Kitts, buses similarly avoid the areas where tourists might want to go, such as the beaches on the southeast peninsula.

Car

Driving on any of the islands is not especially challenging. There are few roads, and even less signposts, but wandering from your intended route is seldom more than a minor inconvenience and you can never get really lost on an island. Some roads along the coasts can be narrow and winding, and on secondary and rural access roads look out for potholes, deep storm drains at the edges, as well as speed bumps or dips. Driving is on the left, and cars are right-hand drive. All passengers must wear seatbelts in the front and back seats, and the use of mobile phones is illegal while driving, except in 'hands-free' mode.

In the towns, petrol stations are located on main thoroughfares, but are scarce in rural areas (on Barbuda, there is one; while Montserrat and Nevis have two each).

Car hire is readily available; the minimum age is usually 25, you need to have a full driving licence (it does not have to be an international licence, your home country one will do as long as it's got a photograph, with an English translation if necessary), and a credit card. If it's not busy, then you should be able to arrange a car almost immediately. Deals can be made for more than three days. Basic hire generally only includes statutory third-party insurance; it is advised to take out the optional collision damage waiver premium at US$15-20 per day as even the smallest accident can be very expensive. A local driver's permit valid for three months is required, which the car hire companies organize; Antigua and Barbuda US$20, Montserrat US$18.50, and St Kitts and Nevis US$23.

Fact...

There are numerous car hire companies in Antigua and several in St Kitts, but only a couple of small outfits with a few cars on the smaller islands of Montserrat, Barbuda and Nevis; nor is there a need for car hire, when you can cover the small distances by walking or on short bus or taxi rides.

Taxi

Taxis are plentiful but are expensive and rates are set by the government and taxi associations on each island so there is no negotiation. You can pay the equivalent of about US$10 for a short ride of no more than 10 minutes to US$50 for a 30-minute drive or 15-20 miles (for four people). However, it may still be cheaper to take the odd taxi ride than it is to hire a car on the smaller islands. Lists of fares are available at the airports and tourist offices.

Any hotel can phone a taxi for you and, if you find a driver you like, get their card and phone number, and he/she may also offer to be your driver on a tour of the Islands, which is usually informative and fun. Always book ahead if you have a flight to catch.

Sea

Antigua and Barbuda are connected by ferry, the **Barbuda Express** ⓘ *www.barbudaexpress.com*, which also arranges a day tour of Barbuda, see page 70. The Antigua–Montserrat ferry is currently not in operation (see page 131). There is a variety of sea transport between St Kitts and Nevis including regular ferries between Basseterre on St Kitts and Charlestown on Nevis (40 minutes), and a car ferry, water taxis and hotel transfer boats on the shortest routes between the two islands at the southeast of St Kitts and the northwest of Nevis (a distance of 3-4 miles, which takes just over 10 minutes); see box, page 125.

Essentials A-Z

Accident and emergency

Antigua and Barbuda

Police/ambulance T911 or T999. **Fire** St John's T268-462 0044, All Saints T268-462 5988. **Sea rescue** T268-562 1234.

Montserrat

Police T999. **Fire** T911. In the event of volcanic activity an island-wide siren system will sound.

St Kitts and Nevis

Police/ambulance T911. **Fire** T333 (St Kitts), T869-469 3444 (Nevis).

Customs and duty free

Generally duty free imports are 200 cigarettes or 50 cigars or 250 g tobacco, 1.5 litres wine or spirits, 50 ml of perfume and 250 ml of eau de toilette. Once in the islands, be careful about accepting any wildlife-derived object from villagers and guides. These could include coral or shell souvenirs. If you were to buy such items, you should always consider the environmental and social impact of your purchase. Attempts to smuggle controlled products can result in confiscation, fines and imprisonment under the **Convention on Trade in Endangered Species** (CITES), www.cites.org.

Departure tax

Antigua and Barbuda

Airport departure taxes are included in all tickets.

Montserrat

Departure tax by air is US$13 for Caricom residents and US$21 for visitors, and by ferry US$4.

St Kitts and Nevis

Departure tax from St Kitts is US$22, and from Nevis, US$20.50, which includes an environmental levy and airport security tax.

Disabled travellers

Wheelchairs are not accommodated on public road transport and the towns have very uneven pavements. However, modern resorts and hotels have rooms with disabled facilities and it's easy enough to get around on an organized tour, in a rented vehicle or by boat. Local people will do their very best to help.

Dress

Beachwear is for the beach (and beach bars), and it is advised to wear casual attire when visiting towns/villages and going into restaurants. Topless sunbathing is not permitted on Montserrat, St Kitts and Nevis. However, on Antigua and Barbuda it is deemed OK at some resorts, although not always by the pool; make sure you find out if there are any rules. Some boat captains are fine if day trippers go topless. There is one nudist beach on Antigua south of the **Hawksbill by Rex Resorts** on the northwest coast. In the evening dress is not formal, although many local people dress up for 'liming' (see box, page 23) or parties. Light cotton clothing is best for the tropical weather but pack a sweater, cardigan or wrap for cool evenings and some long sleeves and trousers to ward off mosquitoes and sandflies.

Drugs

Do not be tempted to dabble in narcotics, all are illegal and law does not allow for 'personal possession'; if any is found on a yacht, the governments can confiscate the vessel. Larger amounts of marijuana or any amount of cocaine will get you charged with trafficking and penalties are very severe. If you are offered drugs on the beach, in a rum shop or at a party, be warned; some visitors have been found themselves arrested a few minutes later.

Electricity

An international multi-adaptor is recommended to cover all eventualities, but many hotels and resorts have adaptors for UK, European and US visitors.

Antigua and Barbuda

230 volts/60 cycles. Flat blade 2-pin plugs are used and some resorts popular with British holidaymakers also have 3-rectangular-pin plug sockets.

Montserrat

230 volts/60 cycles. Flat blade 2-pin plugs are used.

St Kitts and Nevis

230 volts/60 cycles. Plugs with either 3 round pins or 3 flat pins are used.

Embassies and consulates

For a full list of embassies and consulates see www.embassy.goabroad.com.

Health

See your GP or travel clinic at least 6 weeks before departure for general advice on travel risks and vaccinations. Make sure you have sufficient medical travel insurance, get a dental check, know your own blood group and, if you suffer a long-term condition such as diabetes or epilepsy, obtain a **Medic Alert bracelet** (www.medicalert.org.uk). If you wear glasses, take a copy of your prescription. No special vaccinations are required, but a yellow fever inoculation certificate must be produced on arrival if you have arrived within 5 days of leaving an area affected with yellow fever.

Warning...
Although a rare occurrence, while swimming watch out for Portuguese man-o-war jellyfish as their tentacles can inflict a painful sting, and be wary of treading on sea urchins as a spine in the foot is nasty.

It is essential to have travel insurance as hospital bills need to be paid at the time of admittance, so keep all paperwork to make a claim.

Insect-borne risks

The major risks posed in the region are those caused by insect disease carriers such as mosquitoes and sand flies. The key parasitic and viral diseases are **dengue fever** and **chikungunya** (also known as chik V). Also spread by mosquitos, cases of the **Zika virus** have also been reported in in the Caribbean from early 2016. However, the risk of contracting any of these is very low, although it is always a good idea to protect yourself against mosquitoes; try to wear clothes that cover arms and legs at dusk and dawn (when mosquitoes are most active) and also use effective mosquito repellent. Rooms with a/c or fans also help ward off mosquitoes at night.

Stomach issues

Some form of **diarrhoea** or intestinal upset may occur for some holidaymakers. The standard advice is always to wash your hands before eating and to be careful with drinking water and ice. Tap water on all the islands is generally very good, but if any doubt buy bottled water. Food can also pose a problem; be wary of salads if you don't know whether they have been washed or not. Symptoms should be relatively short lived. Adults can use an anti-diarrhoeal medication to control the symptoms but only for up to 24 hrs. In addition, keep well hydrated by drinking

WARNING

Little Apple of Death

The manchineel tree (*Hippomane mancinella*) has a range across the Caribbean from South Florida to northern South America. It is an endangered species, but is also considered the most dangerous tree on earth, and the Spanish dubbed it *manzanilla de la muerte* 'little apple of death'. Resembling a small green crab-apple, the fruits are the most obvious threat, and can cause hours of agony – and potentially death – with a single bite. But all parts of this tree contain strong toxins, and interaction with, and ingestion of, any part including the bark and leaves may be lethal.

Even without touching the tree itself, people (and car paint) have been burned by the thick, caustic sap as rain washes it off branches overhead. You can find the manchineel at many locations on the islands, especially along the beaches – do not shelter under them from the sun or when it's raining. Plant toxins typically evolve for defence, but it's unknown why the manchineel went to such extremes.

plenty of fluids and eat bland foods. Oral rehydration sachets are a useful way to keep well hydrated. These should always be used when treating children and the elderly.

Sun

Protect yourself adequately against the sun. Apply a high-factor sunscreen (greater than SPF15) and also make sure it screens against UVB. Prevent **heat exhaustion** and **heatstroke** by drinking enough fluids throughout the day (your urine will be pale if you are drinking enough). Symptoms of heat exhaustion and heatstroke include dizziness, tiredness and headache. Use rehydration salts mixed with water to replenish fluids and salts and find somewhere cool and shady to recover. If you suspect heatstroke rather than heat exhaustion, you need to cool the body down quickly (cold showers are particularly effective).

Medical facilities

There are hospitals, medical centres and clinics, while the larger hotels have doctors on call. For diving emergencies, the nearest hyperbaric chambers are Dominica and St Eustatius.

Antigua Mount St John's Medical Centre, Michael's Mount, St John's, T268-484 2700, www.msjmc.org. The main facility on the island with 24-hr A&E department and helicopter air-ambulance.

Barbuda Spring View Hospital, Codrington, T268-460 0409. A very small clinic with one resident doctor; adequate for minor injuries otherwise more serious medical emergencies are transferred by air to Antigua.

Montserrat Glendon Hospital, St John's, T664-491 2802. A small facility for most routine and surgical emergencies; serious medical cases are taken by helicopter to Antigua or Guadeloupe.

St Kitts Joseph N France (JNF) General Hospital, Cayon St, Basseterre, T869-465 2551. The main facility on the island with 24-hr A&E department; serious cases may require medical air evacuation to Antigua or Miami in the US.

Nevis Alexandra Hospital, Government Rd, Charlestown, T869-469 5473. A small hospital with ambulance service but any serious medical emergencies will be transferred by boat to St Kitts, or if that is not possible, by air to Puerto Rico.

Useful websites

www.btha.org British Travel Health Association.
www.cdc.gov US government site that gives excellent advice on travel health and details of disease outbreaks.
www.fco.gov.uk British Foreign and Commonwealth Office travel site has useful information on each country, people, climate and a list of UK embassies/consulates.
www.fitfortravel.nhs.uk A-Z of vaccine/ health advice for each country.
www.travelhealth.co.uk Independent travel health site with advice on vaccination, travel insurance and health risks.
www.who.int World Health Organization, updates of disease outbreaks.

Insurance

Before departure, it is vital to take out comprehensive travel insurance. There is a wide variety of policies to choose from, so shop around. At the very least, the policy should cover medical expenses, including repatriation to your home country in the event of a medical emergency. There is no substitute for suitable precautions against petty crime, but if you do have something stolen, report the incident to the nearest police station and ensure you get a police report and case number. You will need these to make any claim from your insurance company.

Language

English is the official language.

LGBT travellers

Technically same-sex relationships are illegal on all these islands but it is not enforced and there's a relaxed attitude in the tourism industry, although public displays of affection are ill-advised.

Money

US$1 = EC$2.67; UK£1 = EC$3.58; €1 = EC$3 (Jul 2016)

Currency

The currency on Antigua and Barbuda, Montserrat, and St Kitts and Nevis is the East Caribbean dollar (EC$ or XCD). Notes are for EC$5, 10, 20, 50 and 100. Coins 5, 10, 25 cents, EC$1 and 2. US dollar cash is widely accepted by businesses at the official fixed exchange rate of US$1 = EC$2.67, although most prefer to deal in East Caribbean dollars, and you will receive any change in East Caribbean dollars. Hotel rates, air fares and sometimes activities such as diving and tours, are quoted in US dollars, but you can pay in either. On departure change East Caribbean dollars back into US dollars or other currencies if possible; on Antigua and St Kitts there are foreign exchange bureaux at the airports, but not on Montserrat and Nevis. You can however use East Caribbean dollars to pay departure taxes where applicable.

If travelling elsewhere in the Caribbean, East Caribbean dollars are also used in Anguilla, Dominica, Grenada, St Lucia and St Vincent and the Grenadines.

Changing money

The easiest currencies to exchange are US and Canadian dollars, UK pounds and euros. Antigua's **VC Bird International Airport** has ATMs and foreign exchange bureaux, and there are banks and ATMs in St John's and English Harbour. Barbuda has only 1 bank with ATM, but it is not to be relied on so take sufficient East Caribbean dollars cash. There are no facilities at the airport in Montserrat and only 2 banks/ATMs in Brades. On St Kitts, **Robert L Bradshaw International Airport** has an exchange bureau and ATM and there are banks/ATMs in Basseterre. On Nevis, **Vance W Amory International Airport** has an ATM but no foreign exchange bureau, and there are banks/ATMs in Charlestown. On all the islands, if travelling outside the main towns, make sure you have sufficient cash as not all places have card machines.

ATMs generally only dispatch notes in increments of EC$100, which are often too large for people to have change – break bigger notes when you can and save small change for bus fares, snacks and drinks and the like.

Credit, debit and currency cards

Credit and debit cards are widely accepted by the larger hotels, shops and restaurants, airlines, car hire firms and tour operators. An additional levy of 5% may be charged by some businesses, so check first if paying a sizeable bill. **Visa** is the most widely accepted card, followed by **MasterCard**; **AMEX** and **Diners** far less so.

Pre-paid currency cards allow you to preload money from your bank account, fixed at the day's exchange rate. They look like a credit or debit card and are issued by specialist money changing companies, such as **Travelex** and **Caxton FX**. You can top up and check your balance by phone, online and sometimes by text.

Opening hours

In the rural areas and on the smaller islands, small grocery shops and kiosks are often open daily, but more like when the vendor feels like it – 'any day, any time'.

Antigua and Barbuda

Banks: Mon-Thu 0800-1400; Fri 0800-1600. **Bank of Antigua** opens Sat 0800-1200. **Shops**: Generally Mon-Sat 0800-1700, although the larger supermarkets open until at least 1900 and all day on Sun too. Shops at Redcliffe Quay and Heritage Quay in St John's will be open whenever there is a cruise ship in port.

Montserrat

Banks: There are only 2 banks, the **Royal Bank of Canada** and the **Bank of Montserrat**, both in Brades, Mon-Fri 0800-1400. **Shops**: Generally 0800-1600, but often close early Wed and Sat afternoons. The small grocery stores and supermarkets will open later in the evening and on Sun mornings.

St Kitts and Nevis

Banks: Mon-Thu 0800-1400; Fri 0800-1600. In Basseterre some open Sat 0830-1100. **Shops**: Generally Mon-Sat 0800-1600, some close for lunch 1200-1300 and Thu afternoon, but the larger supermarkets open until at least 1900 and on Sun 0900-1300. Shops at Porte Zante and Pelican Mall in Basseterre will be open whenever cruise ships are in port.

Post and courier services

There are branches of **DHL** in St John's on Antigua, Little Bay on Montserrat, Basseterre on St Kitts and Charlestown on Nevis; www.dhl.com.vc. **FedEx**, is in St Johns and English Harbour in Antigua, Basseterre on St Kitts and Charlestown on Nevis; www.fedex.com.

Antigua and Barbuda

There are 4 post offices on Antigua; at the airport, High St in St John's, Friar's Hill Rd north of St John's and Nelson's Dockyard. In Barbuda the post office is in Codrington. Open Mon-Fri 0815-1200, 1300-1530, Sat 0900-1200.

Montserrat

The main post office is in Brades and there's a sub-post office in Salem. Open Mon-Fri 0815-1600.

St Kitts and Nevis

In St Kitts post offices are located in Basseterre, Cayon, Dieppe Bay Town, Old Road Town and Sandy Point. On Nevis, the post office is on Main St in Charlestown. Open Mon-Fri 0800-1500, except Thu 0800-1100, Sat 0900-1200.

Public holidays

Antigua and Barbuda

New Year's Day (1 Jan), **Good Fri**, **Easter Mon**, **Labour Day** (1st Mon in May), **Whit Mon** (7th Mon after Easter), **Independence Day** (1 Nov), **National Heroes Day** (9 Dec), **Christmas Day** (25 Dec) and **Boxing Day** (26 Dec).

Montserrat

New Year's Day (1 Jan), **St Patrick's Day** (17 Mar), **Good Fri**, **Easter Mon**, **Labour Day** (1st Mon in May), **Whit Mon** (7th Mon after Easter), **Queen's birthday** (middle Mon in Jun), **Aug Mon/Emancipation Day** (1st Mon in Aug), **Christmas Day** (25 Dec), **Boxing Day** (26 Dec).

St Kitts and Nevis

New Year's Day (1 Jan), **Carnival Day/ Las' Lap** (2 Jan), **Good Fri**, **Easter Mon**, **Labour Day** (1st Mon in May), **Whit Mon** (7th Mon after Easter), **Aug Mon/ Emancipation Day** (beginning of Aug), **National Heroes Day** (16 Sep), **Independence Day** (19 Sep), **Christmas Day** (25 Dec), **Boxing Day** (26 Dec).

Safety

The people of these islands are, as a rule, exceptionally friendly, honest and ready to help you. Most visitors will not experience any issues and will have a safe and enjoyable stay, so there is no need to get paranoid about your safety. The general common sense rules apply to prevent petty theft: don't exhibit anything valuable and keep wallets and purses out of sight; do not leave your possessions unattended on the beach; use a hotel safe to store valuables, money and passports; lock hotel room doors as noisy fans and a/c can provide cover for sneak thieves; don't leave items on hotel or villa balconies when you go out; at night, avoid deserted areas, including the beaches, and always take taxis. If you are driving, avoid travel outside major populated areas at night as erratic driving by others can be a problem, avoid stopping if at all possible and keep doors and windows locked. If you are staying on a yacht you should make sure it is secure, day or night.

Tax

Antigua and Barbuda

Hotel sales tax (12%) and service (10%) is charged by all accommodation options, usually as a single charge of 22%. Check if this has been included in quoted rates. VAT on restaurant bills is 15%, but this is nearly always included in menu prices; 10% service charge is however usually added to the bill.

Montserrat

Government hotel tax is 10% (guesthouses, B&Bs and villas 7%), and there's a 10% service charge. Check if these have been included in quoted rates. Restaurants add on 10% service charge.

St Kitts and Nevis

Government hotel tax (10%), tourism levy (2%) and service (11%) are charged by all accommodation options, usually as a single charge of 23%. Check if this has been included in quoted rates. In restaurants, government tax (10%), tourism levy (2%) and service (12%) are charged; this is a sizable 24% on top of menu prices. The government tax is usually included, but double check; most menus stipulate what is and what is not included.

Telephone and internet

The international code for Antigua and Barbuda is 268, for Montserrat 664 and for St Kitts and Nevis 869; followed by a 7-digit number. **Digicel**, www.digicelgroup.com, and **Flow**, www.discoverflow.co, are Caribbean-wide cellular and internet providers. Local SIM cards and start-up packs are available to purchase at phone shops.

You'll find these in the major towns on each island, and you can top up via phone, the websites or buy credit at small shops.

Almost all hotels have free Wi-Fi, as well as many restaurants and coffee shops, even beach bars. However, some all-inclusive resorts (especially on Antigua) may not in fact include Wi-Fi in their all-inclusive rates; this can be one of the 'optional' extras and could cost up to US$40 for a week.

Time

Atlantic standard time, 4 hrs behind GMT, 1 hr ahead of EST.

Tipping

Tipping is not mandatary given that service charge is added to hotel and restaurant bills and taxi fares are set by the governments and taxi associations. However, given that Antigua and St Kitts receive so many thousands of cruise ship passengers (the majority from the US) a tipping culture is prevalent on these islands. By all means tip if you want to show your appreciation for extra helpful waiting staff in restaurants, a tour guide that has been informative, or a taxi driver that has helped with luggage, and it is most appreciated. However, be wary of over-tipping, which may make it difficult for the next person. An amount of 10% is about right and only for good service.

Tourist information

All the tourist information offices on each island are in Listings in the relevant chapters. Good free maps for all the islands are published by the tourism associations, and private publishers produce ones paid for by advertisers; they can be easily found at the tourist offices and on reception desks of hotels.

The following websites are very useful resources before you go:

Antigua and Barbuda

Antigua & Barbuda Buzz, www.visitantiguabarbuda.com.
Antigua & Barbuda Tourism Authority, www.antigua-barbuda.org.
Antigua Hotels & Tourist Association, www.antiguahotels.org.
Antigua Nice, www.antiguanice.com.
Barbudful, www.barbudaful.net.

Montserrat

Montserrat Tourism, www.visitmontserrat.com.

St Kitts and Nevis

St Kitts Tourism Authority, www.stkittstourism.kn.
Nevis Tourism Authority, www.nevisisland.com.
Government of St Kitts and Nevis, www.gov.kn.

Visas and immigration

For all the islands, visitors must have a passport valid for 6 months after the date of entry and adequate unused pages for stamps. Even though you may not always get asked for it, all travellers need to be able to produce a return or onward ticket, proof that they can support themselves during their stay (a credit card will suffice), and an address at which they will be staying (the hotel on your 1st night should be enough). Those in transit or visiting from a cruise ship for less than 24 hrs don't need visas, even if they are nationalities that are required to get one to stay longer.

Antigua and Barbuda

Visas are not required for tourist visits of up to 6 months for almost all nationalities including citizens of the USA, UK, EU, most Commonwealth countries, South Africa and the Caribbean. For those that do require visas, they are not available at the port of entry and eVisas must be acquired online with a credit card in advance of arrival; cost varies depending on nationality. **Department of Immigration Antigua and Barbuda**; www.immigration.gov.ag.

Montserrat

Visas are not required for tourist visits of up to 90 days for almost all nationalities including citizens of the USA, UK, EU, most Commonwealth countries, South Africa and the Caribbean. For those that do require visas, they are not available at the port of entry and eVisas must be acquired online in advance, US$50 for all nationalities. **Government of Montserrat**; www.immigration.ms.

St Kitts and Nevis

Visas are not required for tourist visits of up to 90 days for almost all nationalities including citizens of the USA, UK, EU, most Commonwealth countries, South Africa and the Caribbean (with the exception of the Dominican Republic and Haiti). For those that do require visas, they are not available at the port of entry and eVisas must be acquired online in advance, US$100 for all nationalities and for a maximum length of stay of 30 days. **Government of St Kitts and Nevis**; www.evisa.gov.kn.

Weights and measures

Imperial.

Index

*Entries in **bold** refer to maps*

FOOTPRINT Features

Credits

Footprint credits

Editor: Jo Williams
Production and layout: Emma Bryers
Maps: Kevin Feeney
Colour section: Patrick Dawson

Publisher: Felicity Laughton
Patrick Dawson
Marketing: Kirsty Holmes
Sales: Diane McEntee
Advertising and content partnerships:
Debbie Wylde

Photography credits

Front cover: Rich Carey/Shutterstock.com
Back cover top: Robert Harding Productions/SuperStock.com
Back cover bottom: Verena Matthew/Shutterstock.com
Inside front cover: Nico Tondini/SuperStock.com, Gavin Hellier/SuperStock.com, Travel Pictures Ltd/SuperStock.com, Jean-Pierre De Mann/SuperStock.com.

Colour section

Page 1: BlueOrange Studio/Shutterstock.com.
Page 2: Radius/SuperStock.com.
Page 4: Bildagentur Zoonar GmbH/Shutterstock.com, PlusONE/Shutterstock.com, Firecrest Pictures/SuperStock.com.
Page 5: Miguel Sobreira/SuperStock.com.
Page 6: Adrian Reynolds/Shutterstock.com..
Page 7: Shane P White, Travelshots/SuperStock.com, Don Mammoser/Shutterstock.com.
Page 8: Michael Runkel/SuperStock.com.

Duotones

Page 26: fotoswiat/Shutterstock.com.
Page 72: fotogestoeber/Shutterstock.com.
Page 88: GlenroyBlanchette/Shutterstock.com.

Printed in Spain by GraphyCems

Publishing information

Footprint Antigua, Montserrat, St Kitts & Nevis
2nd edition

ISBN: 978 1 911082 06 4
CIP DATA: A catalogue record for this book is available from the British Library

Published by Footprint
6 Riverside Court
Lower Bristol Road
Bath BA2 3DZ, UK
T +44 (0)1225 469141
F +44 (0)1225 469461
footprinttravelguides.com

Distributed in the USA by
National Book Network, Inc.

Every effort has been made to ensure that the facts in this guidebook are accurate. However, travellers should still obtain advice from consulates, airlines, etc about travel and visa requirements before travelling. The authors and publishers cannot accept responsibility for any loss, injury or inconvenience however caused.

BACKGROUND

English Harbour

In the early 18th century, the British Royal Navy recognized the strategic importance of English Harbour in protecting ships from hurricanes and for monitoring French naval activity; its position on the south side of the island meant it was well positioned to observe the French island of Guadeloupe. By 1723 it was in regular use and officers petitioned for the building of maintenance facilities, as it was the only harbour in the Eastern Caribbean large and sheltered enough for safe repairs prior to the return voyage across the Atlantic to Britain, particularly for battle-damaged vessels.

In 1728 the first dockyard, St Helena, was built on the east side of the harbour and had a capstan house (where ships were careened, or were turned on their sides, for cleaning, caulking, or repairs), a stone storehouse for supplies, and three wooden sheds for careening gear. Operations soon outgrew the small dockyard and the western side of the harbour was developed from the 1740s, when slave labourers from the plantations in the vicinity were sent to work on the dockyard.

Most of the buildings seen today were constructed during a building programme between 1785 and 1794; these include the Engineer's Offices, Pitch and Tar Store, Copper and Lumber Store, Capstan House, Saw Pit Shed and Blacksmith's Shop. This construction overlapped with Horatio Nelson's tenure in the dockyard from 1784 to 1787. He served as captain of HMS Boreas, and was sent to Antigua at the head of the Squadron of the Leeward Islands to develop the naval facilities at English Harbour and to enforce British shipping laws in the colonies.

The Sail Loft was built in 1797, the Pay Master's Office around 1806, the Officers' Quarters building in 1821, and the Clerk's House and Admiral's House in 1855. However, after peace was established among the islands after about 1815, and with the growing use of steamships, the dockyard's importance declined, and in 1889 the Royal Navy officially closed it. Restoration began in 1951 and a decade later it was opened to the public and renamed Nelson's Dockyard in honour of the years he spent in Antigua.

buildings of the dockyard and on to the waterfront area with the jetties and berths of the yacht marina.

The **Dockyard Museum**, located in the former Admiral's House (1855), has exhibits on the history of the dockyard and a bust of Nelson above the entrance. Also here is a good gift shop. Behind it is an old stone kitchen, which still serves as the small **Dockyard Bakery** selling bread and pastries. The **Copper and Lumber Store** (1789) was built to store the lumber and sheets of copper required for repairing and maintaining the wooden sailing ships of the time, and sailors from ships being repaired sometimes permitted to sleep upstairs. Its walls are 3 ft thick and built entirely of yellow bricks imported from Britain as ship ballast. It is now a hotel (see page 54), pub and restaurant (see page 60). Other buildings to look out for are the Officers' Quarters building (1821), now an art gallery, and the Pay Master's Office (1806), now a supermarket and liquor store catering to yachties.

A footpath leads from the dinghy dock in the marina around the bay to **Fort Berkeley** at the harbour mouth. It is well worth the walk for the wonderful views; it only takes about 10-15 minutes including some wooden steps over the hilly parts. Constructed in 1704, long

a yachting mecca, good nightlife and a colonial naval stronghold

The southeast is the area of most historical interest, with the old naval dockyard in English Harbour which had major strategic importance in the 17th and 18th centuries. It lies just to the east of Falmouth Harbour, a magnet for yachts from all over the world and many world-class yacht races are held here.

Yachtsmen and women need entertainment and there are several good hotels, lots of restaurants, bars and nightlife in both Falmouth Harbour and English Harbour, which are also the best places to arrange a wide range of watersports. Former military buildings dot the hillsides up to the top of Shirley Heights, from where you get a spectacular view of the coastline, popular with visitors on Sunday for a barbecue, steelpan bands and reggae.

Falmouth Harbour

You can come from the interior of the island via **Liberta**, the third largest town in Antigua whose name is derived from it being a place of freed or liberated slaves. This brings you to the northern shore of Falmouth Harbour and the village of the same name. From here Dockyard Drive winds its way around this picturesque naturally sheltered horseshoe-shaped bay, which is full of yachts at several marinas, while luxurious villas are dotted around the gentle hills. Some of the most prestigious yachts in the world come here during the winter season, especially for events such as the **International Yacht Show** in December, and the **Antigua Classic Regatta** and **Antigua Sailing Week** in April (see Festivals, page 12). The **Falmouth Harbour Marina** ⓘ *www.antigua-marina.com*, has berths big enough to accommodate superyachts up to 330 ft in length, while on the south side the **Antigua Yacht Club Marina** ⓘ *www.aycmarina.com*, has an attractive wooden jetty over the water with shops catering to yachties selling sailing gear and swimwear, a supermarket, and cafés offering excellent coffees and cocktails (at Seabreeze Café/ Gelateria, try the delicious homemade Italian *gelato*). It's a pleasant place to come for a drink and watch the comings and goings of the yacht crowd, and any would-be crew can have a look at the vast noticeboard here. Bars and restaurants line Dockyard Drive, especially around the junction where it heads south the short distance to English Harbour.

Follow the road past the Antigua Yacht Club Marina over a small hill to **Pigeon Beach**, a five- to 10-minute walk, which is a lovely stretch of sand with good views into Falmouth Harbour and a favourite spot for the local community as well as visitors. West-facing, it's perfect for a sundowner at either the delightful beach bar at the north end, **Bumpkins Beach Bar** (T268-562 2522, Monday-Wednesday 1100-1800, Thursday-Sunday 1100-2200), which is famous for its banana piña coladas, strong rum punch and jerk chicken on the large wooden veranda, or at the good restaurant at the other end, **Catherine's Café Plage**, see page 60.

For a good view of Falmouth Harbour, and English Harbour beyond, hike to the top of 700-ft-high **Monk's Hill** and the remains of **Fort George**, an important and large defence post built in the 1680s. The perimeter of the massive fortifications exceeded over a mile, but the low remains of the walls are now overgrown. The views are tremendous and you get views of

Tip...

Bus No 17 from the West Bus Station in St John's will get you down to Falmouth and English harbours; the furthest point on this bus route is the petrol station on Dockyard Drive at the junction with English Harbour.

much of the island along the hike. Although the track is very steep at times, and the acacia thorns are rife; wear good shoes. It starts at Cobbs Cross junction, and follows the eastern side of the primary school fence and then and keep walking up towards the mobile phone antennas on top of Monk's Hill and you will get to the fort. The distance is about 2 miles from the junction.

English Harbour and Nelson's Dockyard

T268-481 5028, www.nationalparksantigua.com. Between 0800-1800 the entrance fee to the restored dockyard, and all other sites such as Shirley Heights and Dow's Hill, is US$8, under

3 Falmouth Harbour & English Harbour

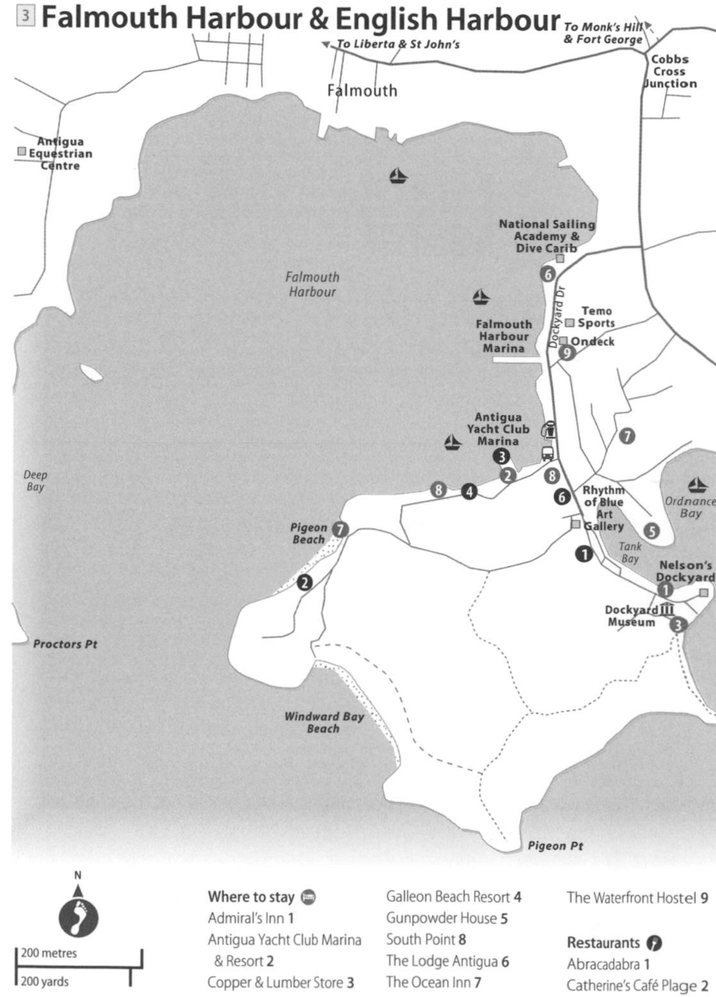

Where to stay
Admiral's Inn 1
Antigua Yacht Club Marina & Resort 2
Copper & Lumber Store 3
Galleon Beach Resort 4
Gunpowder House 5
South Point 8
The Lodge Antigua 6
The Ocean Inn 7
The Waterfront Hostel 9

Restaurants
Abracadabra 1
Catherine's Café Plage 2
Cloggy's Café 3
Club Sushi 4
Shirley Heights Lookout 5
Trappas Restaurant & Bar 6

Bars & clubs
Bumpkins Beach Bar 7
Life on the Corner 8

12s free, but there is no charge if you are staying at the hotels, visiting the restaura evening, or have a yacht moored in the marina (for which there is a fee in any case tours are available on request.

On the eastern side of Falmouth Harbour is **English Harbour** (a five-minute wa Dockyard Drive from the Antigua Yacht Club Marina junction), which is another a yachting centre and takes its name from the deep-water sheltered bay in which t Navy established its base of operations for the area during the 18th century. N restored, Nelson's Dockyard is the only existing Georgian Naval Dockyard in the and the major sites around its sho hillsides are part of the 15 square m the **Nelson's Dockyard National P** includes the marina, once a moori battleships, now yachts; restored bui in the historic naval dockyard, so them now restaurants, cafés, hotel shops; the Dockyard Museum, v Nelson's telescope and tea caddy a display; Dow's Hill, where visitors watch a 15-minute presentation on history of the island at the Interpreta Centre; and the old observation point signal station at Shirley Heights. See box, page 42.

The main entrance and information centre is at the end of Dockyard Drive, from where you first walk through a covere vendor's market selling souvenirs (the are toilets and a Bank of Antigua ATM her and then the route goes though the **Pill Restaurants** of the Admiral's Inn hotel. T Georgian brick building dating from 1 was once a store room for pitch, turpen and lead, while upstairs were the of for Royal Navy engineers. Here look for its boat and mast yard, slipway boathouse pillars; although still star they suffered earthquake damage i 19th century. From the hotel, path out attractively throughout the oth

Tip...
From in front of the Copper & Lumb Store Hotel, you can catch water ta over to the splendid Galleon Beach Freeman's Bay (US$3.70) or negoti to do a little harbour tour by wate

ON THE ROAD

Hiking to Shirley Heights

A pleasant walk from Falmouth Harbour is up Shirley Heights Road; a popular activity for locals at the weekend. Take the road inland from near Falmouth Harbour Marina and next to The Waterfront Hostel, turn right again at the next junction and you're on Shirley Heights Road. There are a couple of crossroads leading downhill to the right as you climb, the first to the slipway and the dockyard on the eastern side of English Harbour, the second to Galleon Beach, then it goes past Dow's Hill and up to Shirley Heights. The distance is about 4½ miles and takes about an hour. The Lookout Trail goes down between Shirley Heights and Freeman's Bay near the Galleon Beach Resort; covering a distance of about two thirds of a mile, it's a nice easy trail going down (though a steep sharp shock going up). From here you can follow a shore trail to reach the site of former Fort Charlotte, built to guard the eastern side of the entrance to English Harbour. It's a peaceful spot, where the regatta flagpole is hoisted during yacht races. You can then return to Galleon Beach from where you can get a water taxi across to Nelson's Dockyard.

before the dockyard was built, at one time the fort was defended by no less than 25 large cannons to protect English Harbour and was a crucial part of an island-wide defence network. Today, some of the well-preserved walls remain and a couple of replica cannons look southwards. It's also a good spot to watch racing yachts in events such as **Antigua Sailing Week** (see Festivals, page 12). A new path has recently been carved out from here around Pigeon Point and you can walk all the way to Pigeon Beach on Falmouth Harbour; from Fort Berkeley it's about 1 mile but allow 30-45 minutes as it's a bit rocky in places.

The other components of Nelson's Dockyard National Park are on the road up to Shirley Heights overlooking the harbour on the eastern side. To get there, Shirley Heights Road goes up from Falmouth Harbour off Dockyard Drive and winds up the hill. On the way, and on the left, a small branch road goes to the **Dow's Hill Interpretation Centre** ⓘ *T268-481 5045, www.nationalparksantigua.com, daily 0900-1700, US$5, under 12s free, or is covered by the Nelson's Dockyard ticket*, which offers an interesting 15-minute multimedia show every 15 minutes on the history of the island right back to the Amerindian era. It also has a viewing platform.

The rambling 18th-century ruins of fortifications, gun emplacements and military buildings at **Shirley Heights** were all part of a signal station from which a system of flags was used by day and guns by night to convey messages to St John's by way of Fort George on Monk's Hill. Today it is best known for breathtaking views over English and Falmouth harbours from its summit at 490 ft and its Sunday night party (see box, page 63). The site is named for General Thomas Shirley, Governor of the Leeward Islands (1781–1788) when the area was fortified. The complex included a guard house, magazine and kitchen, officers' quarters, adjoining parade grounds, a 40-bed hospital, canteen and a cemetery. Some buildings, such as officers' quarters, are still standing, restored but roofless, giving an idea of their former grandeur. The lookout point, or **Battery**, at the south end is now the **Shirley Heights Lookout** bar and restaurant (T268-728 0636, www.shirleyheightslookout.com, daily 0900-2200, except Monday when it closes at sunset), which is where the Sunday party is held from 1600. It also offers drinks, snacks and Caribbean meals.

A car is essential for exploring the villages in the northeast and east of Antigua because there are no buses. You can approach from either Falmouth Harbour in the southeast, via either Willoughby Bay or All Saints, or across the island from St John's. Parham is the site of the first settlement on the island and the area is full of secluded bays, shielded by numerous islands offshore, now either protected as nature reserves or the locations of all-inclusive resorts. There are a few things to see and do; you can go kayaking in the mangroves or visit the stingrays kept in a shallow area at the mouth of a bay off Seatons. Evidence of past dependence on sugar can be seen by visiting Betty's Hope, where the mill has been restored and opened to visitors.

St John's to Willikies

If you are driving from St John's, take Old Parham Road and then Sir George Walter Highway towards the airport. Take the right fork which runs alongside the runway and after about 1½ miles take a right turn down a small road to **St George's Church**, on **Fitches Creek Bay**. Built in 1687, it is in a beautiful location, and with interesting gravestones, including the marble tombstone of the first English settler to be buried within a place of worship in 1659. It was remodelled in 1735. From here, a rough coast road leads to **Parham**, which was the first British settlement on the island (1632) and has an attractive and unusual octagonal church, **St Peter's Anglican Church**, which dates from the 1840s, surrounded by flamboyant trees. Designed by Thomas Weekes in the Palladian style, it dates from the 1840s and features a ribbed wooden ceiling and stucco walls. Parham was once the main port, exporting sugar from some 20 sugar estates, but after 1920 it ceased to be a port of entry and its fortunes declined along with those of sugar. On Market Street are the remains of imposing Georgian buildings.

From Parham go due south and then east at the petrol station through Pares to **Willikies**. On this road, just past Pares village, is a sign to **Betty's Hope** ⓘ *visitor centre Mon and Wed-Sat 0830-1600, for a guided tour contact the Museum of Antigua and Barbuda (see page 32), T268-462 4930, entry by donation*, a ruined sugar estate built in 1650 and owned by the Codrington family 1674-1944. Restoration was carried out by the Museum of Antigua and Barbuda in St John's and it was officially opened in 1995. One of the twin windmills can sometimes be seen working. The visitor centre tells the story of life on a sugar plantation and is well worth a visit. Sir Christopher Codrington established the first large sugar estate in Antigua in 1674 and leased Barbuda to raise provisions for his plantations. Forests were cleared for sugar cane production and slave labour was imported. Today many Antiguans blame frequent droughts on the island's lack of trees to attract rainfall, and ruined mill towers of sugar plantations stand as testament to the barrenness. A map of the remaining 112 mills can be seen at the visitor centre.

At **Seatons**, you can get a boat out into a shallow area at the edge of Mercer's Creek Bay to what is known as **Stingray City** ⓘ *T268-562 7297, www.stingraycityantigua.com, daily tours 0900, 1100, 1300 and 1500, US$50 per person, no children under 4*. Southern stingrays can be seen in a large pen on a sandbank in the sea (there are also a few huge starfish). You are given snorkelling gear to get into the water and stand or swim with the rays or view them from a floating platform. They come up to be fed by the guides and you can

ON THE WATER

D-Boat

A fun day can be enjoyed on this retired 140-ft 1974 oil tanker, which has been turned into a water park and party boat for all ages, and is permanently moored by Maiden Island in the northeast. It has a giant inflatable waterslide and a rope swing into the sea, a trampoline in the water and sun decks. Other options are snorkelling on a nearby reef, going to the beach on Maiden Island, and for the extra entry fee (US$50) you can add a trip to Stingray City (see page 44). The price includes a five-minute round-trip ferry ride from Shell Beach Marina off Burma Road near the airport to D-Boat, the boat ride to and from Maiden Island or Stingray City, lunch of barbecue/burgers, salad and fries, and drinks; 1100-1700, US$110, children (2-12) US$70, under twos free. Cheaper options are for four hours (1100-1500) or without lunch. For more information T268-734 2628, see www.dboatantigua.com, or book through resorts.

hold them under the water; they are quite harmless and don't appear to be bothered by the attention. Fortunately there are no fences or cables to keep them in the pens. Stingray City is a popular activity, especially for children, and boat trips are also organized directly from some of the resorts.

Off the northeast coast of Antigua, to the west of Long and Maiden islands, is **Great Bird Island**, a 20-acre islet that is part of the North Sound National Park. It got its name when sailors noticed that an extraordinary number of birds lived on the island and there are still colonies of red-billed tropic birds, West Indian whistling ducks, brown pelicans and magnificent frigate birds. Boat parties come here for the two pristine beaches on the island and the mangroves and reef offer some of the best snorkelling around Antigua.

Also at the jetty in Mercers Creek at Seatons is **Antigua Paddles** ① *T268-720 4322, www.antiguapaddles.com*, and **Antigua Nature Tours** ① *T268-720 1761, www.antiguanaturetours.com*, who offer excellent tours off this northeast shore. They begin with an exciting speedboat ride out to lush mangrove inlets of the North Sound Marine Park, where there is time for some kayaking, and then out to Great Bird Island for snorkelling on the reefs, hiking to the top and a relax on the beach with rum or fruit punch. Tours take 3½ hours and cost US$65, or US$55 for under 12s; no under sevens. They must be pre-booked and transfers to Seatons can be arranged. After Willikies the road is signposted to the all-inclusive resort, **Grand Pineapple Beach Antigua**, on the beach at **Long Bay**. If you go past the gate to the resort, the road ends at the beach where there is public access and a car park. With fine white sand and good swimming, there are vendors' selling cold drinks and beachwear and renting out umbrellas and sun loungers. Before you get there, take a right turn down a small road, which deteriorates to a bumpy track, to **Devil's Bridge** at Indian Town Point (look for signs for **The Verandah Resort & Spa**; another all-inclusive). This area on the Atlantic coast is part of the **Indian Town National Park** where rough waves have carved out the bridge and made blowholes, not easily visible at first, but quite impressive when the spray breaks through. It is said that African slaves from the nearby plantations threw themselves off the bridge in desperation, with locals saying 'the devil made them do it'. The limestone formation is often slippery because of the waves and it is advised to not walk across the bridge, but there's a good view of Long Bay and the headland.

ON THE ROAD

Jumby Bay Island

Located about 2 miles off the northern tip of the Parham Peninsula, and accessed by a 10-minute boat ride from a jetty near the airport, Long Island is also known as Jumby Bay Island after the bay on its western side and is the fifth largest island of Antigua and Barbuda. It is a 300-acre private island managed by the **Jumby Bay Island Company** (www.jumbybayisland.com) and is occupied by the all-inclusive **Jumby Bay, A Rosewood Resort** (www.rosewoodhotels.com), with 40 rooms and a collection of villas for those who like to be pampered, as well as an upmarket development of private super-luxurious homes.

At **Pasture Bay**, on the north side of the island, the hawksbill turtle lays its eggs during nesting season, June-October. The **Environmental Awareness Group (EAG)** (office upstairs at the Museum of Antigua and Barbuda in St John's, T268-462 6236, www.eagantigua.org, Monday-Friday 0900-1600), monitors the nesting activity through their **Jumby Bay Hawksbill Project** (www.jbhp.org; also see Facebook). When the project started in 1987, there were about 30 females nesting per season on the beach at Pasture Bay but today, thanks to their efforts, more than 70 visit and between them lay over 250 nests. People are advised not to seek (or disturb) the nesting turtles on their own; the project conducts supervised turtle-watching trips led by trained volunteer conservation guides. Guests at the resort can organize this at reception, while small numbers of visitors from the mainland can go across on Friday evenings from early July to late September from 1930 with 2½ hours of beach patrol; costs are US$30, US$28 for under 12s but no young children are permitted. Spaces are limited so contact them well in advance. Boats depart from Shell Beach Marina off Burma Road near the airport.

Nonsuch Bay and Half Moon Bay

Retracing the route back via Willikies you can head south towards Falmouth Harbour via Nonsuch Bay, where the secluded **Nonsuch Bay Resort** (T268-562 8000, www.nonsuchbayresort.com; also see page 55) offers day passes (1000-1800, US$150, under 12s US$80), which includes a boat trip across to Green Island for snorkelling, lunch, use of the pools, beach facilities and changing rooms, and afternoon tea, plus watersports for additional costs. There's an excellent choice including stand-up paddle boarding, kayaks for exploring the mangroves, dinghy sailing (which is great for children), hobie cats and kitesurfing, and there's instruction for most activities. Also overlooking Nonsuch Bay, **Harmony Hall** (see page 61) is an excellent place for lunch and a visit to the art gallery and is located in an old plantation house and sugar mill, Brown's Bay Mill, which dates to 1843. The **Harmony Hall Yacht Club** is also here.

Further south and a five-minute drive west of Freetown village, at **Half Moon Bay**, there is plenty of room on a lovely long, curved beach. The waves can be rough in the centre of the bay, but the water is calm, turquoise and clear at the north end where there are also trees and you can snorkel. One of the most beautiful bays on the island, if not the most beautiful, the sand has a hint of pink in it from crushed particles of coral and shells, and it has rock pools, beach loungers and surf. The hotel on the south side of the bay was built in the 1950s but has long been abandoned and is hurricane-damaged, but is interesting to explore. However, in 2016 the 108-acre oceanfront property was bought by a resort company so may well be developed soon. For now a snack bar serves cold drinks and ice cream, but has irregular opening hours, while vendors ply their wares in the car park.

Barbuda

laid-back island with bone-white and pink beaches and frigate birds

Lying 27 miles to the north of Antigua, and one of the two island dependencies, Barbuda covers 68 square miles of mostly flat coral limestone and lagoons, where the near-deserted beaches are an outstanding feature, and the Frigate Bird Sanctuary offers close-up encounters with these unusual birds. With a population of only around 1800, it's a quiet place with few paved roads and one main village, where life is slow and simple and the people friendly. Barbuda's charm lies in this easy-going way of life and its isolated beauty, and there are some wonderful barefoot luxury places to stay, as well as a couple of cheaper simple guesthouses. It's also close enough to Antigua to visit for the day.

Most residents live in the only village on the island, **Codrington**, which stands on the edge of the large lagoon of the same name and has an estimated population of around 1800. It is named after the Codrington family who leased Barbuda for 185 years from 1685 until 1870, and used it to supply their sugar estates on Antigua with food and slaves. They built a castle which dominated the town, but it was badly damaged by an earthquake in 1843 and little now remains.

After emancipation, all property belonged to the Codringtons and the freed slaves were trapped with no jobs, land or laws. After many years and court cases, Antiguan law was applied to the island, but while Barbudans may own their own houses today, all other land is generally held by the government.

The village is strung along the eastern side of Codrington Lagoon, which takes up much of the west of the island; its access to the sea is via Cuffy Creek at the northern tip. The water is shallow, and much of the shore of the northern half is marshland. It's an easy

Essential Barbuda

Finding your feet

The airport is a short walk to the centre of Codrington. Barbuda's ferry dock is called River Wharf Landing and is on the south side of the island; taxis meet the ferry and it's a 15-minute drive to Codrington. See Transport page 70.

Getting around

The island is very small so is easily explored on foot, or there are taxis, with drivers doubling up as informative guides. Car hire is available but sometimes difficult; the cost of spare parts and supply of fuel make it an expensive business for Barbudans to maintain.

Tip...

Barbuda has one bank, the Antigua Commercial Bank near the airport. It has an ATM, but is not to be relied on; bring cash from Antigua as few places in Barbuda have card machines so payments in guesthouses, bars, shops or for taxis are in East Caribbean dollars cash.

and pleasant place to wander around, and if you're lucky you'll enjoy some time chatting to the Codrington residents. Codrington has a tiny airport, a bank, fuel station, **Digicel** phone shop, bakery, small grocery shops and vendors selling fruit and vegetables, street food and coconut water, and a few rum shops. Cattle, horses and donkeys often wander about in the village and sheep and goats can be seen trotting off to their pens at sunset. There are occasional small horse races and on Sundays, starting about 1400 at the grassy low-key racetrack on the edge of the village.

Frigate Bird Sanctuary

Water taxis are organized from the jetty in Codrington any time of day but mornings are best for bird activity and it's not permitted to go after 1800, US$50 per boat of 4 people, and US$12 per additional person. Alternatively, you can visit as part of the Barbuda Express day trip, or one of the hotels on the island can organize an trip.

A 15-minute boat ride goes across to the impressive Frigate Bird Sanctuary in the mangroves towards the north end of the **Codrington Lagoon**, where thousands of birds mate and breed roughly between September and January. The sanctuary is well worth a visit to see these extraordinary birds (see box, opposite) and the colony is a contentious place indeed, where birds argue over landing rights, perch ownership and who owns each twig.

It is believed to be the largest breeding colony in the world, larger even than that of the Galápagos, and locals will tell you that there are some 2500-5000 birds. Visitors are taken to only one or two spots to view the birds, and ropes keep the boats from getting too close. The rest of the birds are left alone but you get near enough for photos of the male birds puffing out their red chests and flapping their wings. The lagoon is also home to other birds including brown pelicans, warblers, snipes, ibis, herons and kingfishers, and brown boobies nest alongside the frigates.

Barbuda

Where to stay
Barbuda Belle **3**
Barbuda Cottages **6**
Bus Stop Guest House **5**
Coco Point Lodge **2**
Lighthouse Bay Resort **1**
North Beach **4**
Palm Tree Guesthouse **7**

Restaurants
ArtCafé **1**
It's a Bit Fishy **1**
Outback **2**
Uncle Roddy's Beach Bar & Grill **3**

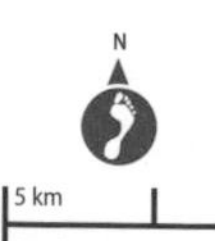

Around the island

Much of the island is covered in impenetrable bush with only one main paved road (in various states of disrepair) going from the River Wharf Landing in the south (an area of the island generally referred to as River), to Two Foot Bay in the northeast. But there are dirt roads and tracks fanning out to most of the beaches. Not far from River Wharf Landing are the ruins of **Martello Tower and Fort**, a popular spot for island weddings. This 32-ft-tall tower and fort were built by the British in the early